THE PENGUIN SPORTS LIBRARY

General Editor: Dick Schaap

HOW LIFE IMITATES THE WORLD SERIES

Thomas Boswell, a reporter for the *Washington Post* and contributing editor of *Inside Sports*, won the American Society of Newspaper Editors' prize for the best sports journalism of 1981. In a dozen years at his hometown *Post* Mr. Boswell, an Amherst College graduate, has written about boomeranging, Wimbledon, midnight golf, and The Masters. Above all, however, he writes about baseball.

HOW LIFE IMITATES THE WORLD SERIES

THOMAS BOSWELL

PENGUIN
BOOKS

*To George Solomon
and Donald Graham*

Penguin Books Ltd, Harmondsworth,
Middlesex, England
Penguin Books, 40 West 23rd Street,
New York, New York 10010, U.S.A.
Penguin Books Australia Ltd, Ringwood,
Victoria, Australia
Penguin Books Canada Limited, 2801 John Street,
Markham, Ontario, Canada L3R 1B4
Penguin Books (N.Z.) Ltd, 182–190 Wairau Road,
Auckland 10, New Zealand

First published in the United States of America by
Doubleday & Company, Inc., 1982
Published in Penguin Books by arrangement with
Doubleday & Company, Inc., 1983
Reprinted 1983 (twice), 1984, 1985

LIBRARY OF CONGRESS CATALOGING IN PUBLICATION DATA
Boswell, Thomas, 1948–
How life imitates the World Series.
(Penguin sports library)
Originally published: Garden City, N.Y.: Doubleday, 1982.
1. Baseball—United States—Addresses, essays,
lectures. I. Title. II. Series.
GV863.A1B67   1983   796.357'0973   82-16596
ISBN 0 14 00.6469 9

Printed in the United States of America by
R. R. Donnelley & Sons Company, Harrisonburg, Virginia
Set in Electra

THE PENGUIN SPORTS LIBRARY

The purpose of this series of sports books is simple: It is to make available in paperback, at a reasonable price, some of the finest books that have been written about sports, books that otherwise might not be in print. There is only one basic requirement for a book to be considered for this series: It has to be good. It has to be pleasurable reading. It can be fiction or nonfiction. It can be a play. It can be angry or funny or, better yet, a blend of both. The author can be famous or obscure. He can be an athlete or an academic. He can write about the beauty of boxing or the brutality of chess. He can be a cynic or a cheerleader. He can be anything except dull.

A secondary requirement for a book to be selected for this series is that I must read it. This is my pleasure. The wonderful thing about reading and rereading the truly outstanding books about sports is that they are about so many things besides sports.

—Dick Schaap
New York City

CONTENTS

MAY

JUNE

JULY

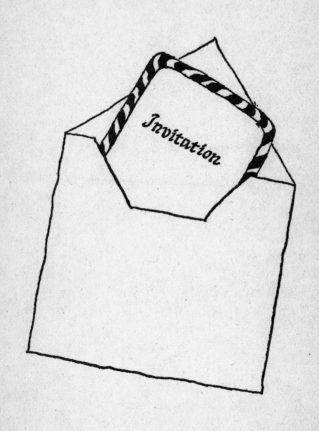

"This Ain't a Football Game. We Do This Every Day."

Conversation is the blood of baseball. It flows through the game, an invigorating system of anecdotes. Ballplayers are tale tellers who have polished their malarky and winnowed their wisdom for years. The Homeric knack has nothing to do with hitting the long ball.

Ride the bush-league buses with the Reading Phillies or the Spokane Brewers or the Chattanooga Lookouts, and suddenly it is easy to understand why a major league dugout is a place of such addictive conversational pleasures. In the world of the minor leaguer, which is split between short hours of athletic adventure and long hours of idleness, talk becomes a staple of sanity; the man who does not have a way with a yarn, a joke, a tale of pathos, or an epigram drawn from his own experience is condemned to be an outsider.

This rich verbal tradition—the way the game has taken on the ambiance of the frontier campfire or the farmer's cracker-barrel stove and moved it into the dugout—is what marks baseball so distinctively, not only among our games, but among all our endeavors. Baseball remains, in the best sense, archaic.

This passion for language and the telling detail is what makes baseball the writer's game.

Baseball constitutes a small, but fundamental, province of the American mind, a backwater of our spirit to which we hie when we want a sense of traditional appetites. In our daily cacophony, the national "pastime" is one of those notes we periodically strike in hopes of hearing a hint of middle C.

A narrative voice with conviction is often hard to find. But not in baseball. The minors teach two lost American arts: how to chew tobacco and how to tell a story. During twenty long ain't-never-gonna-get-to-the-promised-land seasons from Winston-Salem to Knoxville to Fox Cities, Earl Weaver learned how to do both, though the Red Man chaw cost him many a tooth before he ever reached the majors.

"I learned my biggest lesson in managing the first day in Class D," says Weaver, fifty-one, sitting in the Baltimore Oriole dugout, a cigarette cupped inside his hand like a schoolboy not wanting to get caught. "You've got a hundred more young kids than you have a place for on your club. Every one of 'em has had a goin' away party. They been given the shaving kit and the fifty dollars. They kissed everybody and said, 'See you in the majors in two years.' You see these poor kids that shouldn't even be there in the first place. You write on the report card '4-4-4 and out.' That's the lowest rating in everything. Then you call 'em in and say, 'It's the consensus among us that we're going to let you go back home.'

"Some of 'em cry. Some get mad. But none of 'em will leave until you answer 'em one question: 'Skipper, what do *you* think?' And you gotta look every one of those kids in the eye and kick their dreams in the ass and say, 'Kid, there's no way you can make my ball club.'

"If you say it mean enough, maybe they do themselves a favor and don't waste years learning what you can see in a day. They don't have what it takes to make the majors. Just like I never had it."

Weaver, who has quietly been staring at his dangling feet, feet attached to legs too short to allow his cleats to reach the dugout floor, glances up toward the field and sucks on his Raleigh. "I smoke these fuckin' Raleighs," he murmurs, "'cause with fifty thousand coupons they give you a brass coffin." Suddenly, the Oriole manager notices that the umpires and his rival manager are standing at home plate—waiting for him, looking into his dugout and staring at him. It's only five minutes before game time; the minutes have slipped away.

"'Scuse me," Weaver says, popping off his perch. "Be right back and finish the story."

The lineup cards exchanged, the ground rules synopsized, Weaver hops back on his bench, legs swinging. Nothing is out of the ordinary. His players are stretching, collecting gloves and shin guards, preparing to take the field for the National Anthem. Weaver ignores them. He is telling a story.

"So the first day you learn the lesson. As long as you manage, you're always going to be a rotten bastard. Or, in my case, a little bastard.

"That's the rule. To keep your job, you fire others or bench 'em or trade 'em. You're the one who tells them all the worst news in their life. You have to do the thinking for twenty-five guys, and you can't be too close to any of them."

The anthem is playing. Weaver stubs out his cigarette, unbuttons the top button of his uniform shirt and stuffs the Raleighs into their usual hiding place. "The horseshit cameras are always trying to catch me smokin' during the anthem," he growls.

When the music stops, the flustered reporter beside Weaver tries to apologize for overstaying his welcome, for interloping like a civilian in a war zone.

Weaver is genuinely surprised. "This ain't a football game," he says. "We do this every day."

That is baseball's greatest blessing and the source of its richness: you play it every day. Consequently, baseball has no "game face"—no mood of real or feigned mortal crisis that must be put on like a protective psychological mask before leaping into the fray. As Weaver's pitching coach Ray Miller puts it, "It's never fourth-and-one in baseball."

That sense of moderation—of both physical and emotional temperance in all the familiar acts of the game—is almost a philosophical precept. Given a choice between raw effort and controlled skill, the latter will usually win in baseball. As a result, the sport cultivates a certain balanced temperament, encourages a stable cast of mind. The sense of elemental sanity and order that we sometimes feel around baseball is not entirely a romantic wish; the game has, at its core, a distinct therapeutic quality.

Baseball has a name for the player who, in the eyes of his peers, is well attuned to the demands of his discipline; he is called "a gamer." The gamer does not drool, or pant, before the cry of "Play ball." Quite the opposite. He is the player, like George Brett or Pete Rose, who is neither too intense, nor too lax, neither lulled into carelessness in a dull August doubleheader nor wired too tight in an October play-off game. The gamer may scream and curse when his mates show the first hints of laziness, but he makes jokes and laughs naturally in the seventh game of the Series.

Above all, this Ideal which exists only in abstraction seems to have an internal tuning fork which gives him perfect emotional pitch. Strike that fork before each game, and the player vibrates with just the proper energy and spark, just the right relaxation and steadiness, which the game has always required. In other words, baseball's highest value—at least during those hours on the field— is the ability to achieve a blend of intensity and underlying seren- ity which, in daily life, we might call mental health.

Almost every player of enduring excellence has his own catch phrase for this quality—a sort of personal mantra.

"Enthusiasm and consistency," Rose calls it.

"Don't be sharp or flat. Just be natural," says Willie Stargell.

"Relaxation and concentration," echoes Jim Palmer.

The particular words, the dozens of ways to hint at the same goal, are not important. What matters is that this sense of bal- ance, of being in tune with the requirements of the game, runs just below the surface of the entire sport. It is baseball's refrain.

Perhaps the best proof that this feeling of equilibrium within baseball really exists is the sharp sense of deprivation when it's taken away. Ex-players invariably make the same distinction: "I don't miss playing the game. I miss the game." By which they mean the whole ethos of the sport. Like the lawyer disbarred or the priest defrocked, the jettisoned baseball lifer, once he is di- vorced from his discipline, his baseball code, often feels at sea.

The important point here is not that baseball is, in some sense, a separate, self-contained world with its private pass words and ar- duous initiation rites. What distinguishes baseball is the opposite quality—not the way it seems out-of-the-ordinary and remote, but the way it consistently invites us into its inner sanctums.

The game is so appealing because it is so profoundly normal and open and welcoming to us. Baseball is to our everyday experi- ence what poetry often is to common speech—a slightly elevated and concentrated form.

Walk into a major league locker room, and immediately you feel reassured. These folk are of normal size, speak in a normal tone of voice, and, both up to and after the first pitch, act like sensible men. Their game is rife with jabber; the constant inter- splicing of talk and action may be what most enriches the game.

When you walk into a ball park on a summer evening, several hours before game time, even before the earliest regular ticket gate is open, the first sound you will hear is chatter, punctuated by bat- ting-practice cracks of the bat. As you walk up the ramps and catwalks of Fenway Park, the voices from the field reach you before the first green slice of grass or Monster comes into view. An empty Yankee Stadium is an echo chamber; from the mezzanine press box, you can detect every word as the pinstripe scrubeenees take their early hitting, challenging each other to grape-soda bets.

It is impossible for any familiar face to walk through a locker-room door without some glancing comment, some deflected jibe or critique. The art of agitating has been raised to a near-science in baseball; no one is allowed to be above the needle, or, conversely, is too low to be worthy of a jab. Reporters, for instance, are called "green flies at the show," because, in the minors, buzzing green flies are a symbol of annoyance, while "the show" is the universal busher's term for the majors.

Some writers are ridiculed, some are liked, some are respected and a few are feared; these categories seldom overlap. However, all scriveners have one thing in common—they are part of the general agitating. Word of foibles or embarrassments spreads fast.

For example, several years ago, Jim Rice offered to stuff me in a trash can if I persisted in asking him who, what, where, and why concerning a collision in which he had flattened an umpire at home plate that night. Not wishing a long suspension, Rice thought silence the better part of valor. Not wishing to become mistaken for rubbish, so did I.

The next day, in another team's clubhouse, the first words I heard were, "Watch out, Boz, there's a trash can right behind you."

"I told Rice the same thing you would have," I told the agitator. "'Which trash can would you like me to get into, sir?'"

No tale of woe or mishap is allowed to remain unexamined. For a month after Don Sutton and Steve Garvey had a clubhouse fist-fight, then patched up on national TV, I was greeted around various batting cages with the predictable opening line, "Look out, here comes the team wrecker."

It made a dull and pitiful story to tell players that my original piece, which supposedly precipitated the brawl, was tepid stuff that another paper had mangled and misrepresented until it sounded like fighting words. Who wants to hear a writer whine that he was misquoted?

The last straw, however, came in the White House. Rose had

come to the Oval Office so President Carter could congratulate him on his 44-game hitting streak and make a few vote-getting softball jokes. After a hokey press conference, Rose, whose Reds were locked in a pennant race with Los Angeles, spotted me and couldn't resist. "Whatever you're doing to the Dodgers," he said, "keep it up."

The semiconscious purpose of this endemic teasing, prodding, and testing is to break ice, to make that lifeblood of chatter flow more easily. Because Rose had established a tone of needling, it was easy to ask him a favor. He was going to play in L.A. that week. Could he give Sutton and Garvey a hard time for me, tell them it was all right to punch each other, but stop trying to make it look like it was my fault? Rose, apparently, transported the three-thousand-mile needle. The next time I saw Sutton and Garvey each immediately apologized separately for causing me the tangential aggravation of being associated with their squabbles.

The point of interest here is that very little in baseball stays quiet or hidden for very long. The sport seems to have a passion for analysis, swapping of tales, trading of gossip. Everything contributes to it, a sort of verbal cross-pollinization. Before every game, both teams mingle around the batting cage, creating a bizarre atmosphere where one-liners, insults, nicknames, rumors about who's going to be traded or fired, practically fill the air. In truth, baseball may have spawned more lore in the dugout and by the cage than it has on the field.

In other major sports, reporters must acquire the habit of generating stories, whether or not they exist. Pickings are often slim. In baseball, stories seem to be left on the doorstep each night. Among sportswriters, few would disagree that baseball is either the easiest or the hardest journalistic job—depending on whether you consider it a blessing or a curse to be deluged with a flow of fresh material. Other sports must be explored; baseball merely asks that it be absorbed and sifted.

Perhaps the proper way to cover baseball is to mirror the mood of the sport: meander, loaf, strike up conversations at random, pursue tangents. Investigating the latest sore arm or change in the pitching rotation may capture the facts of the matter, but it can also lose the essence of the game. The ideal way to appreciate, and chronicle, baseball may be to treat it as though you were an ardent, but fledgling, connoisseur. This is possible because, at every level, baseball is studied in greater subtlety than any other pro sport. Over the past century, this garrulous game has explicated itself with greater attention to nuance than any other sport. It's tough to stay baseball-dumb in a ball park; any coterie of good fans constitutes a sort of seminar on the "inside" game. It is a tradition that the game's many fecund pauses be used as an opportunity to inflict insights and prejudices on all adjacent fans. Baseball provides far more time for disputation *during* the game than any sport. What other game could brag that it offers *dis*continuous action?

Just as important, baseball's strategy is by far the most exposed and self-evident of all our games. Any savvy football or basketball coach can do a postgame dance of the veils and bamboozle the toughest interrogator; their games are intrinsically tangled and technical. The players' minds and the watchers' minds are on different planets. In baseball, by contrast, the absence of mystique is a virtue, since the lifelong fan is confident that he knows what each player *should* be thinking in any given situation. Consequently, everybody is accountable. The second guess is the first article in the baseball fan's Bill of Rights.

The athlete and his spectator are of one mind, though the player must often wish that he could escape such confident scrutiny. Because of this, one of baseball's pleasures is the clubhouse postmortem after each game. Every contest, at the technical level, is a bit like a brain-teasing detective puzzle. Who is at fault? Where does credit lie, and to precisely what degree? What threads of the game's plot are, perhaps, still hidden?

Like an amateur Sherlock Holmes, it is useful to set aside preconceptions; resist all broadcasting of aspersions. Observe, deduce, sniff, listen to tone of voice, pluck at loose strings to see what will unravel. Each player knows all: who blundered, who exposed a fundamental weakness of talent or character, who performed above expectation. And each can give a clue. The knack of "working a locker room," piecing together the puzzle of how the game was won or lost, is just intuition.

Who has reason to testify against the accused? Who can offer a proper defense? Who can file a brief of praise? Major leaguers, it is a pleasant shock to learn, are extremely thick-skinned about valid criticism. No castigation in print is likely to match the severity of their own. Because players are so surprisingly willing to analyze themselves and each other, a good ball game often resembles a fine chess match that is begging for annotation. Here an exclamation mark. There a question mark. Sometimes both apply to the same play or decision.

Perhaps the trick to forming a so-called "expert opinion" is to avoid the trap of believing that you are one. For instance, the opinions that appear under my name, no matter how subjective they sound, are almost never my own. They are an amalgam, a blending and counterpointing of the critiques of several players from both teams. All that most ballplayers ask is a fair trial—so long as it is a trial by their peers. It's a rare player who can resist giving a candid opinion when it specifically concerns "the game." Once outfielder Carlos Lopez disabled two Baltimore mates in a week in collisions while chasing flies. Fellow Oriole outfielder Ken Singleton, asked for a general evaluation of Lopez as a center fielder, said simply, "He'll never take me alive."

From such morsels are cautious judgments formed.

When dealing with stone hands or hanging curveballs, why not be as tart and prickly as the crackling jargon of the dugout? Even players gag on a treacly game story.

However, as soon as we move from appraising the athlete to considering the person inside the uniform, a firm line must be drawn. There is no open season on a man's personality; he does not sign it away with his contract, no matter how rich it may be.

This might seem obvious. But it isn't. Especially in baseball. Among athletes, baseball players may be uniquely vulnerable to hard use by their press. Certainly, there's no sport where the adversary relationship between scribe and jock is as testy as in baseball, because there is no sport where they have half as much constant elbow-to-elbow contact. That unrelenting eight-month familiarity—from hotel lobbies to coffee shops to locker rooms to batting cage to dugout to late-night taxis shared—is the source of baseball's rich lore and literature. To a writer, this is Eden where fruit comes unbidden to hand. But there is one inevitable snake in the garden: Too much familiarity breeds either too much affection or too much contempt. Or both.

One of the first rules of journalism is to get close to the subject;

listen to the quarry breathing. In baseball, the precept often needs to be reversed: Keep your distance.

The worst thing a ballplayer can be to a writer is an enemy. The second worst thing is a friend. It shouldn't be necessary to be either.

It is a psychological perversity in human nature that people are more likely to speak honestly, and even movingly, to strangers or to people they half-know but respect, than they are to most friends.

Why do you think psychiatrists sit behind you, scribble in their notepads, speak in prodding monosyllabic questions, and make particularly sure that you don't get to know them too well? They're just reporters who never file a story. The writer's principle is the same: be empathetic, be decent, but don't be phony and pretend you're a friend. The thin glass partition of professional formality, even the conspicuous on-the-record notebook that seems like a barrier to communication, is really a fine ally. We find it easier to be direct with the doctor, the minister, the lawyer precisely because they assure us that they will remain professional and play by the rules.

There are few words in the English language more seductive than, "I would like to hear your story."

There is one catch to this simple approach. What happens when someone, led on by that greatest of all aphrodisiacs—his own voice—goes a bit too far and says suddenly, "You're not going to print *that*, are you?"

The correct journalistic answer is, "You said it. That means I can write it."

My answer is usually, "Well, let's talk about it. Is there some more palatable way to say the same thing?"

But, what happens when the best interests of the story conflict with a twinge of private conscience? On "Lou Grant" that would be worth sixty minutes of crisis. In my case, I just say, "What the heck," and leave it out of the story every time. After all, it's not going to say, "Here lies Thomas Journalist" on my tomb.

Besides, most of what people want to keep under wraps is trivial: petty jealousies, professional feuds, etc. By contrast, most of the things they have thought about most seriously all their lives, they are perfectly willing to uncover.

Ask Jerry Coleman why, at the age of fifty-five, he made the almost-certain-disaster decision to become the rookie manager of the San Diego Padres after twenty years out of baseball uniform.

"I was sitting on an airplane," begins Coleman, sitting in his longjohns, stocking feet up on his office desk well after midnight following a Padre defeat. "A man said excitedly to his wife, 'Come here, dear. You've got to look at this view.'

"It dawned on me that I was fifty-five years old and I didn't look out windows anymore. Nothing new is happening to me. I'm going past things without noticing them. My idea of a perfect 'off day' is never to get dressed.

"I told myself, 'You can't be this jaded,'" said Coleman who played in six World Series as a Yankee (MVP in one), flew 120 combat missions as a Marine pilot in World War II and Korea, earned two Distinguished Flying Crosses, then, after his baseball retirement, had dual successful careers as a shirt company executive and a play-by-play broadcaster.

"So, when the Padres offered me the managing job, I took it, even though I hadn't considered managing in twenty-five years. Will I be a success? Well, they say one quality of greatness is singularity of vision—tunnel vision. Diversified thought tends to dissipate itself. So, I guess I'm in trouble . . . But I'm looking out windows again."

Ask Rabbit Miller, the Oriole pitching coach, why he decided to quit playing and start teaching when he was a twenty-eight-year-old AAA reliever on the brink of making the majors after ten years of struggle in the bushes.

"On New Year's Day, 1974, I was away from my wife and son playing winter ball in Venezuela—chasing that big league dream, just like I had ever since I left high school," recalls Miller. "That day, one of my best friends, another pitcher named Mark Weems, drowned. For three days, Don Hood and Bobby Bailor and I searched the beach for the body, so we could send it back to Mark's family to be buried.

"On the fourth day, two of us found what was left of Weems' body washed up in a cove. I'd been thinking during those days about everything in my life. I stayed alone with the body all that night until the authorities came back the next morning.

"I said to myself, 'This isn't a dream world you're living in. It's a lot more real than you think.' Maybe I just grew up. That's when I decided to stop pitching, stop spending the year-round chasing the majors, and start coaching.

"Ever since then, I've had nothing but good luck. Or maybe it just seems that way."

Most of what we want to know isn't controversial or scandalous. It was once said, by a cynical critic, that the limits of Ring Lardner's vision were defined by the boundaries of Frank Chance's diamond.

In baseball, as in any good subject, the question is not one of boundaries. After all, a baseball field is not really a diamond. Fair territory is a 90-degree arc, defined by the foul lines, which extend, theoretically, to infinity. The limits of the baseball world are not intrinsic to the game. All man's occupations extend to the horizon, if we could but see that far. Baseball's fair territory may not be the whole compass, but it is a slice of our reality; the limits of our vision are our own and not the fault of the game. Even within the small realm of baseball, we might catch glimpses of the horizon, if we could.

For those who like their truth with capital letters, baseball, as a steady diet, probably will not suffice. The game is simply one of our many human kaleidoscopes. Shake it lightly each day and the colors, configurations, and symbols seem totally changed. The picture, like our sense of the game and the people in it, is never the same two days running. Each time we return to the game and its folk we see a different scene, a different mood, a different trait of character or twist of personality. What does baseball have to offer? Just a bit of everything, a vast serendipity.

Now, let us follow the months and moods of the baseball season—March to October—as they take us to both familiar and unfamiliar places and people.

In Spokane, we will find 300-pound Frank Howard, the Gentle Giant, telling his bush-league babies, "How can you wheel that lumber tomorrow if you don't pound that Budweiser tonight?"

We will meet a Fenway Park bleacher usher who says, "We're a select group chosen to break heads. Last week I wrestled a guy down and hit him in the mouth with the best punch I ever nailed a fan . . . don't get me wrong, he was wearing a Yankee hat."

And we will go to a 30,000-seat modern ball park in Matanzas,

Cuba, where there are no ushers and no gates, where fans carrying machetes and lost cows wander into the stands.

To be sure, we will see plenty of heroes and history . . . World Series home runs by Reggie Jackson and pennant races as emaciating as death marches. But we will also go with Graig Nettles as he visits the mountainous, bleak third-world village of an unknown minor leaguer named Dave Concepcion. There, the pair who will both one day be candidates for the Hall of Fame, share the best meal that Ocumare, Venezuela, has to offer: barracuda head soup.

From spry ninety-year-old shortstops in St. Petersburg right through The Greatest Game Ever Played, we will meander through all of baseball's realm.

The Greatest Game Ever Played

> I was trying to will the ball to stay up there and never come down.
>
> > Carlton Fisk on watching the Yastrzemski pop-up that ended the Red Sox-Yankee play-off

A baseball game, at its best, can be like an elaborate and breathlessly balanced house of cards. Tension and a sense of crisis build with each inning. Each deed of the game, each player, finds his supporting role. In 1978 that house of cards was built not for one afternoon, but for an entire six-month season. By closing day each player seemed to carry with him a nimbus of symbols, an entire personal history like some Athenian warrior whose exploits against Sparta were memorized by an entire community.

In fact, one game—the play-off game between the Yankees and the Red Sox that decided the Eastern Division of the American League—served as an almost perfect microcosm of seventy-five years of baseball warfare between the Apple and the Hub—a distillation of the game's richest and longest rivalry.

In the history of baseball, only one other moment—Bobby Thompson's home run to end the '51 play-off between the New York Giants and the Brooklyn Dodgers—has provided such a monumental house of cards as the bottom of the ninth inning of this Yankee victory.

When that impossible distinction "best game ever" is being thrashed out in heaven, these games must be mentioned first. Perhaps they should each have a crown—best in the annals of their respective leagues.

The '51 play-off, marvelous for its fireworks and confetti, was the epitome of baseball's age of innocence, a game that any child could grasp.

The '78 play-off, however, pitted teams of darker and more complex personality in a far subtler game—a contest for the student of inside baseball. Is there any other kind?

The '51 classic ended in raw pandemonium; the '78 masterpiece in utter profound silence. Certainly, it is possible to prefer the latter in such a matter of taste.

It must not be held against this masterpiece that it merely ended a divisional race, that the Yanks still had to upend two more pretenders before they could keep their World Championship for a second consecutive year. New York needed just four games to eliminate Kansas City in the American League playoffs and only six to lick Los Angeles in the World Series. Neither joust reached a moment of primitive emotion.

To beat the Bosox, the Yankees bled for six months, only to find themselves tied after the 162nd and last game of the regular season. Their final margin of triumph—5–4 in this one-day sudden-death showdown—was thin as smoke, a distinction almost without a difference between the two most powerful teams in the sport.

Even now, that concluding moment of delicious indeterminance remains as fresh as the crack of the first line drive of spring. Baseball returns. But the Yankee-Red Sox play-off of 1978 lasts.

The sun is warm in Winter Haven now, the Florida orange trees nod their full branches over the outfield fences of the Red Sox spring training retreat.

But for Carlton Fisk, and many another Sox and Yank, the air still seems crisp, the sky a dazzling autumn azure and one solitary pop-up hangs high over Fenway Park.

The final split-seconds of that play-off afternoon are one of baseball's indelible frozen paintings. Let Fisk speak about the moment when the air burst from a balloon that had been blown ever larger for 163 games.

"I knew the season would be over as soon as Yastrzemski's pop-up came down," said the tall, patrician catcher with his hair parted in the middle like Henry Mencken. "It seemed like the ball stayed up forever, like everything was cranked down into slow motion. I was trying to will the ball to stay up there and never come down . . . what a dumb thing to have run through your mind. Even the crowd roar sounded like a movie projector at the wrong speed when everything gets gravelly and warped.

"After the last out, I looked around and the crowd was

stunned. Nobody moved. They looked at each other like, 'You mean it's over now? . . . It can't be over yet . . . oh, nuts . . .'

"It had only been going on for half a year, but it seemed like a crime for it to end."

The buildup to that final crescendo actually began more than twenty-four hours before. The great play-off of '78 was, in reality, two days of absolutely contrasting atmosphere and mood.

Boston's Fenway Park is normally best on the worst days, in raw, misty spring and foggy fall. The streets around the Fens are crowded, narrow, and damp. Taxis blow their horns at the herds of Soxers in Lansdowne Street. That's the way it was on the first day of October—the last day of the regular season. A healing rain caressed that ancient, indescribably delicious ballyard—a rain of balm and absolution. In that soft October drizzle the Sox of Boston were washed clean. Just as New England was ready to give up hope, the prayers of Red Sox fans were answered. On that final Sunday, Boston won and the New Yorkers, playing three hundred miles away in Yankee Stadium, lost.

The most spectacular and sustained pennant race in American League history had reached the only climax worthy of it—the two best teams in baseball each had 99 victories. One of them would have to win 100.

Just two weeks before, the Red Sox had finished one of the most ignominious collapses in history—losing 17½ games in the standings to the inexorable Yankees, blowing all of a 14-game lead, and falling 3½ games behind with only 14 to play.

If Cotton Mather had been alive, he would have been a Bosox fan. And he would have been mad.

In other towns, the incipient collapse of a beloved team might bring forth prayers and novenas, as Brooklyn once lit candles for the Dodgers. In fickle Fenway, however, the faithful reacted as though the Sox had deliberately knelt in the hallowed Fens and licked the Yankees' boots.

The Red Sox have long memories. It is their curse. They are an imaginative team—more's the pity—susceptible to hauntings and collective nervous breakdowns. They prove that those who *cannot* forget the past are also condemned to repeat it. The evil that the Bosox do lives after them. The good is oft interred with their moans. Somewhere it must be written that the Carmine Hose shall suffer. When the Sox are winning, every player is a minor deity. When the angels fall, they are consigned to the nether regions.

So, that final-day victory, Boston's eighth in a row and twelfth in 14 games over the last two weeks, was like an emotional reprieve from the gallows. The entire final week of the season was summarized in that final chilling Sunday. Each day Boston would throw an early lead on the scoreboard, hoping to shake the New Yorkers' faith in their tiny 1-game lead. And each day the Yankee dreadnought would send its message back via the radio waves with an answering victory. A new punishment had been found to fit the Sox felony of squandering a huge lead—torture by victory. A sense of fatality, or inexorable and well-deserved punishment, seemed to hang over the Sox. The Prayer to St. Jude, patron saint of lost causes, was tacked to their bulletin board.

Finally, the ghost was all but given up. Brave talk ceased. Predictions of a play-off were swallowed. During that Sunday morning batting practice, the Sox were grim. Then the spirit of mischief seemed to enter Fenway. Toronto's flaky outfielder Sam Ewing snuck through the open door in the scoreboard and posted a fictitious "8" next to the name of the Yankees' opponent—Cleveland. The early-arriving crowd went into a tizzy that did not stop for three hours. Bizarre echoing eruptions rumbled through the stands whenever word of the Yankee demise arrived by radio. All afternoon, Sox relief pitcher Bob ("Big Foot") Stanley kept a transistor radio to his ear in the bull pen, leaping to his feet to lead hundreds of fans in ovations for Cleveland's runs. Slowly, a ripple, and finally a roar would erupt from 32,000 people as, one-by-one, the blessed message was passed like a fire bucket. Before the game even ended—with Boston ahead, 5–0, and New York behind, 9–2—the scoreboard exulted: "Next Red Sox Home Game Tomorrow."

This was the afternoon that made '78 unique in baseball's century.

Two other teams had suffered breakdowns comparable to Boston. The New York Giants of 1914 got the rubber bone for blowing a 15-game, Fourth of July lead to the Miracle Braves of Boston, and eventually losing by a craven 10½ games. And the '51 Dodgers had a 13-game lead on August 11, only to be tied on the last day of the season, then beaten. But no team had ever looked into the abyss of absolute self-betrayal and recovered from it, come back to finish the season—despite injuries—like a furious hurricane.

At their nadir, the Sox had lost 6 straight September meetings with the Yankees by a total score of 46–9. They were outhit, 84–29. "It was so lopsided," said Boston pitcher Mike Torrez, "that you wouldn't have believed it if it had happened to the original Mets."

The real victims of the Boston collapse were, in part, the Yankees. The Horrid Hose were so disgraceful that they drained the glory from the Yanks' great comeback. "Never sell the Yankees short," said Boston coach Johnny Pesky, who has hated pinstripes for forty years. "They played great the last three months [52–22]. They'll never play that well again as long as they have assholes."

While other teams are too tight to breathe in a crisis, the Yankees spit their tobacco and smooth the dirt with their spikes. The Yanks, with their almost unsinkable raw talent, their polished passion for the game once the contest begins, and their partial immunity to the pandemonium that swathes them, have gradually come to resemble a sort of Leviathan with hiccups.

In midseason the champions were hemorrhaging in Boston. There are other New England sharks than the mythical Jaws of Amity. The pearly white teeth snapping around them on those moon-bathed nights at Fenway were the healthy and rapacious Sox. "If Boston keeps playing like this," said New York's Reggie Jackson, "even Affirmed couldn't catch them. We'll need motorcycles . . ."

Every day and every night in those final hours of troubled manager Billy Martin the scene around the Yankees was the same. The crowds in the hotel lobbies, at the ticket windows and outside the players' entrances were huge, pummeling the players with kisses and curses.

Meanwhile, the Sox read their press clippings. Everyone from Ted Williams to the cop in Yawkey Way said these Sox were the best edition since '01. What blighter would point out that the Fenway Chronicles show an almost inexorable baseball law: A Red Sox ship with a single leak will always find a way to sink. For documentation, see the Harvard Library. Doctoral theses are on file there.

In other seasons, the Sox self-immolation was a final act consonant with the team's public image for generations—a green wall at their backs, green bucks in their wallets, green apples in their throats. Red Sox fans had come to view their heroes with deep skepticism, searching for the tragic flaw. No team is worshipped with such a perverse sense of fatality. "Human, all too human," that's the Red Sox logo.

Ever since the day sixty years before when dastardly Harry Frazee sold Babe Ruth to the Yankees, fortune had forsaken the Sox. The axis of baseball power swung south with Ruth. Since Boston last raised a Series banner in 1918, the Yankees have been champions 22 times.

This grim heritage, however, was an unfair burden to the '78 Sox who were the antithesis of their predecessors. If the Sox had a critical flaw, an Achilles' heel, it was their excess of courage, their unquestioning obedience to the god of guts. This, they swore to a man, was the year for that eternally receding World Series Triumph. Let the '80s be damned.

The Sox scapegoat was easy to find—doughty little Manager Don Zimmer, the man with the metal plate in his head whom Bill Lee contemptuously called "the gerbil." Zimmer was publicly seen as a hard guy who was given a high-strung, high-octane Indy race car and kept the pedal to the metal as though he were driving an old dirt-track stocker. Naturally, the engine blew and the Sox coasted to a dead stop.

However, the Yankees also had catastrophic pitching problems, constant injuries for the first 100 games and a manager who had to be fired for his own health's sake.

Why were the Yankees so good at cutting their losses, while the Red Sox were so poor at minimizing theirs? Why did the Yankees have the restraint to let their injured heal in June, when the Sox were pummeling them, while the Sox exacerbated their miseries by going full throttle?

It's all tied up with history and that old Yankee fear. It's axiomatic in the Northeast that no Red Sox lead is safe. And it is cradle lore that no Boston team ever has faced up to a Yankee challenge in September. Therefore, Zimmer had little choice but to push his delicately balanced power plant until the black smoke poured from the exhaust. Mythology forced his hand. Only a 20-game lead would suffice.

The Sox pushed that lead to 14, but then the black flag waved the Sox into the pits, while the Yanks kept circling the track.

The hordes of invading Yankee fans even took to taunting the Sox in their own lair. In the tunnel under the Fenway stands, Yankee fans set up a cheer each night as they passed the doors of the Boston locker room. "Three, three, three . . . two, two, two . . . one, one, one . . . ZERO, ZERO, ZERO," they counted down the dwindling Boston margin each night as the Yankees swept the famous 4-game series that will live in lore as The Boston Massacre.

As soon as the massacred Bostonians, the despair of eight states, threw in the towel, gave up the ghost, and tossed in the sponge, they pinned the Yankees' ears back in their seventh-and-last September meeting. That, of course, is the visceral clubhouse definition of choking. If you can't tie your shoelaces under pressure but play like a world-beater as soon as it's too late, that's worse in the dugout world than being a no-talent klutz. That is called taking the apple.

Even if Boston's sweet fruit of victory had a bitter pit of self-knowledge at its center, the hard swallow was medicinal. One day the Sox were pathetically cornering reporters, asking, "Tell me, what's wrong with us?" Soon, it seemed, they would be asking that sorrowful question of lampposts and parked cars. But a small thing like one victory over New York, even one that seemed meaningless, broke the grip of the curse.

So, when the Yankees arrived at Fenway on Play-off Day, they no longer came either as June victims or September conquerors. They came as October equals—very worried equals.

The house of cards was finally built. And it was monstrous. Which way it would fall no player claimed to know.

At baseball's showcase World Series games, the batting cage is as congenial as a Kiwanians convention. Teams arrive for fame and fun; no grudges fester. Before the play-off, the Yankees and Red Sox circled each other like lions and leopards around the same African watering hole. Their only words were taunting barbs disguised as light humor.

Some celestial handicapper must have written out the lineup cards. They were too symbolic to have been penned by mortals named Don Zimmer and Bob Lemon, the Yankees' caretaker manager.

Each team spotted the other a Golden Glover as both Dwight Evans and New York's Willie Randolph were sidelined. But far better for symmetry were the starting pitchers: Torrez against Ron Guidry, the man called "Lou'siana Lightnin'."

Just a year before, Torrez had been the Yankees' World Series pitching hero, winning 2 games. Then the Sox signed him at free agent auction for $2.7 million—their loud pronouncement that they would match the Yankee pocketbook. Just four days before, Torrez had emerged from the emotional low point of his career. If one player's failure epitomized the charge of gutlessness made against all the Sox, it was Torrez. For forty days down the stretch when he was desperately needed, he had not won a single game, while losing 6.

The Sox feelings about the great Guidry were simply summed up. "We have the home field. We have the momentum. They . . ." said shortstop Rick Burleson, pausing, "have Guidry."

Guidry's feelings were even more elemental. Asked if a mere 1-game play-off were fair, the left-handed executioner answered, "One's enough. I can only pitch one."

Discovering Guidry in the Yankee locker room is like stumbling over a dog in a cathouse. His story is the hidden moral kernel in the vain bluster of the Yankee saga. Imagine, if it can be done, a player amid these New Yorkers who has the innate confidence of an only child, the proud self-containment of a Lou'siana Cajun, and the strong silences of a small-town boy raised on hawk hunting and walking the railroad tracks.

No star player is so invisible on his own team, whether loping across the outfield or lounging in the dugout. But for this play-off, no player approached Guidry for being conspicuous. The reason was cogent—Guidry entered the game with the best record of any 20-game winner in the history of baseball: 24–3.

Every game needs a call to arms, but this one started with trumpet blasts.

A brilliant fall light—a painter's vivid stark light—bathed Fenway as Torrez began the day by throwing his first four pitches to

Mickey Rivers low, high inside, and outside. The Yankee speedster waited only one pitch to steal second base.

"So that's it," the throng seemed to say by its sigh. It was going to be just like last time, when New York jumped to leads of 12–0, 13–0, 7–0, and 6–0 in four Fenway days. When the long history of the Sox sorrows is written, those horrific first innings in September would rank infernally high. Each game came complete with the same chilling footnote: "Ibid . . . for full details, see previous night's game."

Would it be so again? Always, it was Rivers beginning the psychic unraveling, stealing second as though it had been left to him in old Tom Yawkey's will. That sad lopsided spectacle seemed underway again when Torrez made an egregious error—throwing Reggie Jackson a fastball strike on an 0-2 pitch with 2 outs. The ball climbed to the level of the left-field light towers, climbed until it seemed to look in the faces of the teenagers, who had scrambled atop the Gilby's Gin sign beyond the wall. The Yankees would lead, 2–0, Guidry would breeze. The great day would be a dud. But the groaning crowd had forgotten the Fenway winds.

Whenever the Sox and Yanks meet in Boston, the first order of business is to inspect the flags. The Yankees, a predominantly left-handed hitting team, desperately want an inward breeze to enlarge the confines of the cozy Fens. The Sox, designed along Brobdignagian lines, with seven home-run hitters, would settle for dead calm. Only when the flag points toward the plate do they droop. When the Yanks arrived in early September, for four straight days the Sox grumbled as the wind blew, sometimes thirty miles an hour, straight in from left. Betrayed again, even by Fenway Park.

So, when Jackson's blast was suddenly stymied by the wind and fell almost straight down, nearly scraping the wall as it fell into Carl Yastrzemski's glove, a marvelous sense of irony swept over the Boston dugout. The Yankees had been robbed by the same fates that had bedeviled Boston.

"That was no wind," said Lee later. "That was Mr. Yawkey's breath."

It is a unique quality of baseball that the season ticket holders who see all of a club's crucial games believe they can also read the minds of the players. Each team's season is like a traditional nineteenth-century novel, a heaping up of detail and incident about one large family. After 162 chapters of that tome, chapter 163 is riddled with the memories, implications, and foreshadowings of the thousands of previous pages. Any play that rises above the trivial sends a wave of emotion into that ocean-size novel of what has gone before. Since everyone is reading the same vast book, the sense of a collective baseball consciousness can become enormous. With each at bat, each pitch, there is an almost audible shuffling of mental pages as the pitcher, hitter, and catcher all sort through the mass of past information they have on one another.

Just this sort of extended personal history existed between the Yankee star Guidry and the Boston captain Yastrzemski to begin the second inning. In a word, Yaz was harmless against Guidry when the left-hander was at, or even near, his best. So, when Yastrzemski rocked back on his heels on the second pitch of the second inning to thrash at a fastball in his wheelhouse (up-and-in), it should have been a feeble mistake. Instead, it was a home run—a hooking liner that curled around the right-field foul pole by less than a bat length. Yaz had turned the Lightnin' around.

Suddenly, the afternoon bristled with potential.

Guidry was at his weakest. Torrez, who was to strike out Yankee captain Thurman Munson three times with nibbling, teasing sliders, was at his best. In other words, they were even.

"When these teams play," Fisk had said two weeks before, "it is like a gigantic will controls the whole game. And it's either all behind one team, or all behind the other."

But this day the forces of the game could not make up their minds. It was a beautiful ambivalence.

The crowd seemed to be in the grip of angina, the cheers caught in their nervous throats. The Keep Your Sox On faithful sat silent in their fireman caps decorated with the nicknames of their undependable deities: Boomer and Butch, Soup and Scooter, Rooster and Pudge, Eck and Looie, Big Foot and Spaceman, Dewey and Yaz. By the end of the fifth, the day's work more than half done, the ball park was so silent that those in the rooftop seats could hear Blair pleading to his Yankees, "Let's go, man. Let's go."

For this single afternoon to achieve permanence, it had to be a miniature of the entire season, a duplication of the same emotional roller coaster. So, in the sixth, the Sox scored again, Burleson lining a double over third and Jim Rice clipping an RBI single to center. As Rice's hit, his 406th total base of the season, bit into the turf, it seemed that the game, the year, and a Most Valuable Player duel between Rice and Guidry had all been decided on a single pitch.

More folly. Any historian knows that a 2–0 lead after the sixth is the quintessential Red Sox lead—just enough to merit euphoria; just enough to squander. After all, in the seventh game of the 1975 World Series Boston could taste its incipient upset over Cincinnati, leading 3–0. And that turned to dust.

Every seesaw needs a fulcrum, and Lou Piniella quickly provided one for this game.

A ground out and an intentional walk put men on first and second, 2 outs, and Fred Lynn at bat. When fragile Freddy yanked a Guidry slider into the right-field corner, every dugout mind had the same thought: "Two runs." Piniella, however, materialized directly in the path of the ball. He was so far out of normal Lynn position that he ought to have had a puff of magical smoke curling up behind him.

"It was a ridiculous place for him to be . . . about twenty yards from where he normally plays me," said Lynn.

"I talked to Munson between innings," said Piniella afterward. "We agreed that Guidry's slider was more the speed of a curveball and that somebody could pull him." Even so, Piniella was stationed in a sort of private twilight zone.

"It was a hundred-to-one shot any way you look at it," said Lynn. "He plays hunches out there. The man's just a gambler."

At bat, Piniella says, "I've guessed on every pitch that was ever thrown to me . . . don't do too bad, do I?"

To those in the stands, the play looked routine, like so many in baseball: a blistering line drive directly at an outfielder standing a few feet in front of the fence. It was the hallmark of this game that its central plays reflected the true daily life of the inner sport. They were not flamboyant and egalitarian, but exclusive and subtle. Baseball's well-kept secret is that it has never been solely a democratic national pastime, but an elitist passion as well.

The Babe and the Iron Horse will never understand what happened next. Big Ed Barrow and Colonel Jacob Ruppert will take a lot of kidding in baseball heaven when tales are told of the tiny home-run hero of the Play-off. Since the roaring '20s, the diamond nine from New York that wore gray pinstripes has meant heartless hegemony, monolithic muscle. Bucky Dent, though he bats last in the Yank order, nonetheless is a symbol of power himself—the power of cash. For two seasons George Steinbrenner was obsessed with getting Dent away from the Chicago White Sox. Finally, a trade was made.

When Dent dragged his bat to home plate with 2 out and 2 men on base in the Yankee seventh, then fouled the second pitch off his foot, hopping out of the batter's box in pain, he looked as ineffectual and inconspicuous as a CIA agent with a bomb in his briefcase. Normally, the worrywart Fisk uses such delays to visit his pitcher with admonitions, or to demand warm-up pitches. "Fisk is out at the mound so much," needles Lynn, "that I've threatened to change the number of Carlton's position from '2' to '1½.'"

But for Dent, what's the worry?

As Dent was administered a pain-killing spray, on-deck hitter Rivers, who had forgotten his sunglasses and butchered a flyball earlier, suddenly became uncharacteristically observant. He saw a crack in Dent's bat and fetched him another one of the same style. Of such minutiae is history made. That and fastballs down the middle.

"After Dent hit it," said Fisk, "I let out a sigh of relief. I thought, 'We got away with that mistake pitch.' I almost screamed at Mike.

"Then I saw Yaz looking up and I said, 'Oh, God.'"

Several innings before, the wind had reversed and was blowing toward the left-field corner. Yastrzemski watched that boosting wind loft the ball barely over the wall, fair by thirty feet. As the 3-run homer nestled in the net, Yastrzemski's knees buckled as though he had been hammered over the head with a bat.

The Yankees erupted from the dugout like souls released from Hades. What followed seemed as inexorable as a shark eating the leg after it tastes the foot.

Quicker than you could say, "Rivers walks and steals second again," Torrez was leaving the game. Though he had fanned the next hitter—Munson—three times, Zimmer waved in Stanley.

Naturally, Munson doubled to the wall for the inning's fourth run.

When Reggie Jackson, the Hester Prynne of sluggers who walks through the baseball world with a scarlet dollar sign on his chest, knocked a home run into the center-field bleachers in the eighth, it seemed like mere hot doggery. And when Jackson slapped hands with Steinbrenner in the box seats before greeting any of his mates to celebrate the 5–2 lead, it was just another of Reggie's compulsive theatrical gestures.

Little did the crowd suspect what all the players knew—that the war had not ceased.

Beyond the Fenway fences, the trees of New England were tinged with reds and oranges. They might as well have been tears.

This game, like the entire season, was about to be salvaged by the sort of Red Sox rally against fate that had no historical precedent.

If Torrez and Guidry went down as the pitchers of record—the official loser and winner, then Stanley and that ornery Goose Gossage were the pitchers of memory.

In the eighth, Jerry Remy grounded a double over the first-base bag off Gossage and scored on Yastrzemski's crisp single to center. Yaz followed Remy home when Fisk and Lynn cracked singles, using their quick strokes to combat Gossage's numbing speed.

The bear trap was set for the Yanks—men on first and second with only 1 out, and the lead down to 5–4.

The great book of the season had, however, been turned to the wrong page to suit Boston.

Gossage mowed down Butch Hobson and George Scott—low-average sluggers with long, looping swings. Neither could get untangled quickly enough to handle his rising fastballs.

Never mind. The stage has been set for the bottom of the ninth with Gossage protecting his 5–4 lead.

From the press box, baseball is geometry and statistics. From the box seats, it is velocity, volume, and virtuousity. From above, Gossage is a relief pitcher. From ground level, eye-to-eye in his own world, he is a dragon.

Nevertheless, the brave Bosox started beating on Gossage's ninth-inning door. The feisty Burleson drew a 1-out walk.

Winning is an ancient Yankee story, a heritage of talent, mixed with an audacious self-confidence and an unnerving good fortune. Losing is an old sadness for the Sox, a lineage of self-doubt and misfortune. All those threads of history and baseball myths were about to come together in one play.

The 5-foot-6 Remy slashed a liner to right when the Goose's 0-2 fastball laid an egg. The assembled parishioners sang "Hallelujah," then groaned their eternal "Amen" as they saw the ball fly directly toward Piniella. Little did they, or Burleson on first, know that only one person in the park had no idea where Remy's liner was—Piniella.

"I never saw it," he said. "I just thought, 'Don't panic. Don't wave your damn arms and let the runner know you've lost it.' "

So Piniella the Gambler stood frozen, trusting, as he has so often, to luck. While Piniella waited for the streaking ball to hit at his feet or in his face, Burleson waited between bases, assuming Piniella had an easy play.

These Yankees, who seem to abolish chance with their poise, let luck fall about their shoulders like a seignoral cloak. "I never saw it until the ball hit about eight feet in front of me," said Piniella later, drenched with champagne. "It was just pure luck that I could get my glove on the ball and catch it before it went past me. If it had gone to the wall, those two scooters would still be running around the bases."

Had Burleson, after stopping in his tracks, tried to go first-to-third, he would have been a dead Rooster. Piniella's throw was a one-hop strike to the bag. Had Piniella not had the presence of mind to fake a catch, Burleson would have reached third easily. From there, he could have scored to tie the game on Rice's subsequent fly to Piniella. From second, he could only tag and go to third.

If Dent's homer has been discussed throughout America, then Piniella's two gambles—his out-of-position catch on Lynn and his blinded grab on Remy—are still being dissected in every major league dugout. "It's the play I'll always remember," said Graig Nettles.

Steinbrenner will never forget either. "I have a tape cassette of the whole game in my office," said the owner. "I don't know how many times I've watched that game. And I always stop at the Piniella play and run it over and over. What if Jackson had been out there? He's left-handed, so the glove's on his other hand, the ball gets by him, Remy has an inside-the-park homer, and we lose.

"It's annoyed me that our play-off game seems to have been overshadowed by us beating the Dodgers in the Series for the second year in a row," said Steinbrenner. "Don't people understand? Somebody wins the Series every year. There's only one game like that in a lifetime. I'd call it the greatest game in the history of American sports, because baseball is the best and oldest game, and that's sure as hell the best baseball game I ever saw."

If any game ever brought seventy-five years of animosity to a climax, this was it.

"When they had two on in the ninth with Rice and Yaz coming up," said New York's Roy White, "I was just holding my breath. You wanted to close your eyes and not see 'em swing. The wind was blowing out and I could feel that Green Monster creeping in closer."

"All I could think of was Bobby Thompson and that '51 play-off," said Nettles. "I figured if anybody was going to beat us, those were the guys."

This play-off lacked only one thing: a time machine. When Captain Carl, Boston cleanup man, stood at the plate facing Gossage with the tying run dancing off third and the winning run on first, that moment should have been frozen. The 32,925 standing fans, the poised runners, Yaz's high-held bat, Gossage's baleful glare: For once baseball had achieved a moment of genuine dramatic art—a situation that needed no resolution to be perfect. A game, a season, and an entire athletic heritage for two cities had been brought to razor's edge.

"I was in the on-deck circle, just like I was when Yaz flew out to end the '75 Series," said Fisk. "You know, they should have stopped the game right then and said, 'Okay, that's it. The season is over. You're both world champions. We can't decide between you, and neither of you should have to lose.'"

Sports' moments of epiphany are written on water. The spell of timelessness must be shattered, the house of cards collapse. Yaz cannot stand poised forever, waiting for the Goose. Art may aspire to fairness, but games cannot aim that high. They must settle for a final score.

"I was thinking, 'Pop him up,' " said Nettles. "Then, Yaz did pop it up and I said, 'Jeez, but not to me.' "

When the white speck had fallen into Nettles' glove, the Fenway fans stood in their places. For long minutes no one moved, as the baseball congregation drank in the cathartic sweetness of the silence. Proud police horses pranced on the infield, waiting to hold back a crowd that never charged. "They should have given both teams a standing ovation," said Nettles. But he was wrong. This was better.

Finally, the whir of a public address recording began. Gently, softly, the music of an old-fashioned melancholy carousel drifted through Fenway Park. The sun was going down, so we all went home, bearing with us canvases for a lifetime.

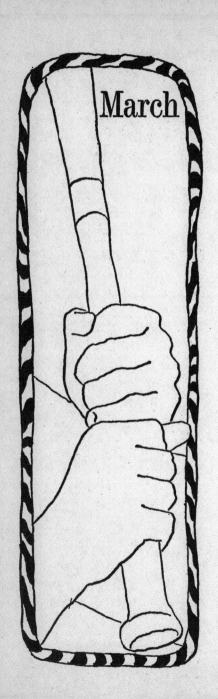

March

A Country for Old Pitchers

Ponce de Léon named the island well, sailing into San Juan harbor in 1508—"*Que puerto rico*." Literally, what a delightful port. For baseball players, too, it is the most delightful of winter harbors. This city and its three local teams—Caguas, Bayamon, and Santurce—are the Ritz of winter baseball.

For major leaguers, playing "beisbol" in San Juan is the epitome of a working vacation. There are many other professional winter teams—nine in Mexico, eight in Venezuela, four in the Dominican Republic, and three others on this island in Ponce, Mayaguez, and Arecibo. But San Juan, the players vow, is second only to playing baseball in paradise.

Mexico has awful bus rides. The Dominican Republic is hardly cosmopolitan. Venezuela has a bit of both drawbacks, plus a reputation for violence. But here, the big leaguers find the sun bursting through their high-rise apartment windows along Condado Beach and look out to see the pure green Atlantic crashing on the barrier reef a mile out to sea. Tropical birds fly past their twentieth-story balconies.

A mile of luxury hotels stretches from the ancient ruins of Castillo del Morro to the coral reef of Isla Verde. Now, in the depths of Puerto Rico's winter, the temperature is 85° F. every day, 70° F. every night. Here the manager of league champion Caguas, Doc Edwards, wears a silk blackjack dealer's shirt to the ball park. "*Que passa* (What's happening), Dude," says the hip blond skipper. "Ain't no place else to play this game."

Winter ball in Puerto Rico has many faces, many moods. It is as exotic as the Ponce manager bringing a teenage religious mystic from New York to sit on his team's bench during the play-offs—just for luck. It is as volatile as the Santurce ground crew charging, en masse, into the box seats to pummel fans who had heckled them for removing the tarpaulin too slowly. It is as fanatical as the Santurce and the Caguas fans dividing the stadium in half, so that on every play one side of the stands rises and roars gesturing to the other half of the crowd, which sits mute. However, for the players it is above all a chance to make $1,500 to $2,500 a month, escape the chill factors of the Stateside world, and work on their games. Why aren't more Pete Roses and Catfish Hunters here? Because rules forbid it. Without restrictions, the Condado strip casinos would be so full of ballplayers in white James Bond dinner jackets that no one would be able to move.

A limit of eight "imports" from the mainland is placed on each team. The fans here would not stand for a *gringo* team. As it is, they yell, "Yankee, go home," at Edwards when he pulls a Puerto Rican pitcher. Those eight imports must fall into three categories: 1) minor leaguers with enough promise to be recommended by their clubs, 2) young major leaguers with no more than three full years' experience, 3) marginal or injured big leaguers with less than 186 at bats or 60 innings pitched. Any Puerto Rican, major leaguer or not, can play.

"This is a tremendous proving ground for the top minor league prospects, a chance to gain experience at a level somewhere above AAA but below the majors," said Santurce Manager Jack McKeon, who went on to be general manager of the San Diego Padres. "For a young major league player the conditions are ideal here to learn to field a new position or work on an off-speed pitch or learn to steal a base," said McKeon. "It's no pressure cooker. Here you have room and time."

And much, much more. For John Wockenfuss, a journeyman catcher for the Detroit Tigers, winter ball means a coral reef off secluded Isla Verde beach where he can skin dive all day with his spear gun among the tropical fish. "The grouper are this big. I just shot a thirty-pounder," Wockenfuss said while holding his arms far apart, grinning through his bushy off-season beard. "Sometimes the fish are so huge you think a shark has gotten through the barrier reef."

For Sixto Lezcano, the brilliant young St. Louis outfielder, this 60-game season from late October to early February is a chance to come home to the fern- and orchid-filled rain forests of the mountainous, undeveloped interior where he grew up. "I walk and walk into the mountains and breathe the air. It's like when you were ten or twelve," said Lezcano who, like his idol, Roberto Clemente, is a winter ball-batting champion—.361. As for so many other big leaguers, Puerto Rico means a partial escape from Lezcano's fish-bowl life in the United States. "I hitchhike from town to town to the games," Lezcano says. "Nobody knows who you are. You feel like another human being. You see, 'Tato' Lezcano is nobody."

But for others—like Orlando Isales, eighteen, and Ruben Gomez, fifty—winter ball is a chance to be a somebody, either for the first or the last time.

At Hiram Bithorn Stadium here, the children from the housing projects sit on the fence beyond center field to watch their former playmate—the teenage Isales—hit home runs and drop flyballs for Santurce. Isales sneaked into this pretty 18,000-seat stadium that looks, from a distance, like a marble Chavez Ravine, many times since it opened in 1961. He had come, of course, to see Clemente. Now, he plays Clemente's old position—right field for Santurce. It sounded like a fantasy until manager McKeon broke the spell by saying, "I've tried to hide Isales' glove everywhere, but they always find it. He does the least damage in right field."

If winter ball is primarily a proving ground for the likes of Isales, and a place for Lezcano to polish his skills, it is also a preserve for aged Latin baseball legends. Gomez—he is called "*El Divino Loco*," the crazy God—has found the Fountain of Youth here. The ex-Giant pitcher of Polo Grounds days is now in his thirtieth season hurling for Bayamon, the team located just down the road from the Hacienda of Ponce de León. Gomez may be the spirit of baseball in Puerto Rico. He gets up at sunrise every day—he is too full of life, he says, to sleep much and thus he keeps his weight down—and goes to the pier to fish. In the morning he plays golf; in the afternoon he builds cars from the frame up, selling some, renting others, but always keeping the fastest for himself. Toward sundown he heads for the ball park, negotiating the deserted beachside highway at 120 miles per hour.

"I have never cared about my safety," says Gomez proudly, perhaps forgetting that day twenty-some years before when the sight of Joe Adcock approaching the mound with an upraised bat induced him to flee through the center-field gate of the Polo Grounds.

If the police stop him, Gomez simply blurts, "I am hurrying to my wife." Only once did a *policia* dare to tell the island's venerable celebrity, "Señor Gomez, all Puerto Rico knows that your wife died seven years ago."

"In that case," said Gomez, switching to his change-up, "I'm going to the cemetery."

These days, the old junkballer only pitches once through the batting order. That is his only concession to a half-century. This is the country for old pitchers.

The silken tradewinds bathe this island in an air that Christopher Columbus called "very soft as of April in Seville." To Mike Cuellar, these lush, humid breezes are more medicinal than linament for reviving his aging soup bone. This is the last chance for Cuellar. He was released outright by the Baltimore Orioles, the team he won 125 games for in six seasons from 1969 to 1974. So Cuellar has come home to pitch winter ball for the Caguas Crillos and try to turn back the clock. The Cuellar one meets here—calmly pitching his team into the island championship series—is an entirely different man from the reclusive, enigmatic left-hander that other ballplayers in the States call "Crazy Horse."

Like many a Latin player, Cuellar can be himself only in this Caribbean setting. What North Americans see seven months of the year is the defensive shell, the almost religious ritual of self-protection of a man who has been exiled by his profession. The Cuellar of the major leagues is a clubhouse legend—the epitome of the unfathomable Latin Ballplayer. When he pitches or must fly in an airplane, Cuellar wears his lucky blue clothes and special medallions. He will not sign his name on the day he pitches. He must eat his pregame meal with his catcher. During games, he smokes nine cigarettes, one every inning, and always while sitting in the same seat. To start each inning, he must pick up the ball dead out of the grass, even if he must dodge a teammate's toss and wait for the ball to stop rolling. After outs, he will accept the ball only from his shortstop. And, of course, his sequence of twitches and hitches before each pitch is unvarying. If the hitter steps out, Cuellar recycles all his gestures.

It is a beautiful paradox that out of this orderly, priestly rite comes perhaps the most confusing and unpredictable concoction in baseball. Obviously, Cuellar's four 20-win seasons and his Cy Young Award (1969) can be attributed not to a feeble, superstitious mind but to a very observant and crafty one. Nevertheless, to North Americans Cuellar was a closed book, as were so many great Latin players from Clemente to Juan Marichal.

"He had a phobia about sportswriters," says Elrod Hendricks, Cuellar's friend and catcher for eight years. "They either ignore him for months or quote him in pigeon English. It drives him crazy." Yet it is not just the press that Cuellar can tune out, like a man switching off a hearing aid. It is the entire Yankee world that he often ignores. "Mike often goes into seclusion," says Hendricks, who is from the Virgin Islands. "He is a hard person to talk to about personal things. I know he hasn't seen his parents since he left Cuba, but we roomed together for eight years and he never once said Castro's name.

"He likes to take himself away from the rest of the world. He goes to every movie. He'll confide only the smallest things to a chosen few when he's in the States."

But here in Puerto Rico, his adopted home, all that changes. "Sure, we can talk now," says Cuellar to a U.S. sportswriter a half-hour before he is scheduled to pitch. "It doesn't matter." On his own turf, Cuellar signs autographs on game day, wears brown clothes to the ball park, and will catch anything anyone throws to him. His gestures on the mound stay the same, but he laughs, "It's just part of me now. I never think of it." In Baltimore, Cuellar seemed invisible, sitting in the trainer's room or the whirlpool, staying out of the team's needling and card games. But in the Caguas locker room, Cuellar is a bit the father, a bit the jester, and a hero to boot. "He's one super person," grins Sixto Lezcano. "He helps all us kids."

"I like to work with the young pitchers, the way Ruben Gomez helped me. That is," says Cuellar, "if they will pay attention. Some of them already think they know everything," he says, a pained comic expression creasing his leathery face. "That's funny. I don't know anything yet after all these years. I have to learn every day."

Hendricks claims that he has caught only two pitchers who "remembered darn near every pitch they'd thrown in ten years— Jim Palmer and Cuellar." Palmer's book on hitters is an example of severe Anglo-Saxon logic—fastball on the fists, curve low and away. Cuellar's book borders on pagan illogic and intuition. "I know what the hitters are thinking about," says Cuellar, a sentence that would give Ted Williams nightmares. "I try to make the mind confusing." Take, for instance, Al Kaline, he of the 3,000 hits.

"Fastball hitter," says Cuellar. "Every pitcher knows no fastball can get past him." So what does Cuellar throw him? "Fastballs," said Cuellar, an impish expression playing around his moustache. "He wouldn't expect it because I'm not a power pitcher. Yes, I was always lucky with him with fastball."

Ah yes, luck. Cuellar claims it is one of the two absolute essentials of pitching. The other is that, "The first pitch, whatever it is, must be a strike."

"Mike always thinks two pitches ahead," says Hendricks. "When they make an out on one of his 'set-up' pitches, he looks like they've spoiled his fun."

So much for the myth that Latin players are more colorful than competitive. "Fans down here go to war over their ball clubs," said veteran catcher Elrod Hendricks who has played winter ball for seventeen years. "They take defeat much harder than the players." As revered Bayamon pitcher Gomez discovered years ago the night he returned to his beloved, hand-built Eldorado in the Mayaguez parking lot and found all its windows smashed. Gomez opened his trunk, took out an old bat, and retaliated against every windshield in the lot. Rather than being arrested, he was given a police escort as far as Arecibo (halfway around the island) at which point the pursuing Mayaguez fans finally turned back.

Ironically, Puerto Rico's charms include a reputation as the least-dangerous of all the winter leagues. "Usually, your experiences here are memorable, rather than fatal," says veteran major leaguer Roric Harrison. "You don't play here for money. It's a break-even deal at best, even if you stay away from the roulette wheel. You play for the experience." But in winter ball, experience is a word that needs a broad definition. In most players' cases, the memory does not dwell the longest on a game won or lost, but on something that happened along the way—something exotic, perhaps like Julio Gotay.

"Frank Robinson was the Santurce manager and Gotay was playing second," says Harrison. "Willie Montanez and Felix Millan got together for us [Caguas] and made a cross out of two tongue depressors and a shoelace. They left it out at second base.

Well, when Gotay saw it, he wouldn't go near his position. He stood on second base and wouldn't move, yelling 'Don't touch.'

"Robinson went out and cussed him for being a backward, superstitious fool. And Hendricks picked up the cross and stuffed it in his hip pocket. "On the next pitch, the hitter whipped the bat back on a checked swing and hit Hendricks [the catcher] in the head and knocked him cold. Both teams gathered around Elie, except Gotay. He's back standing on second base shouting, 'I told you. I told you. No touch. Evil.' "

The experience Harrison will remember longest, however, is the night many years ago when he and Graig Nettles first had dinner at Dave Concepcion's house in Ocumare, Venezuela. For Nettles and Harrison, that night was the epitome of the culture shock that hits Americans who play winter ball in Latin America.

Concepcion, the shortstop of the twice world champion Cincinnati Reds, was then a skinny AA teenager who asked to have the honor of inviting his two American winter league teammates to his home. A ninety-minute ride from Caracas brought Nettles and Harrison to mountainous Ocumare and a small one-room house divided into sections by cloth hanging from the ceiling. The room was full of smiling people and barking dogs.

"Dinner was barracuda head soup," said Harrison. "That was their top-of-the-line meal. It was a pot of water with a barracuda head floating in it with the eye looking at us, a piece of potato on one side, and the vegetable on the other. One of the dogs just sat there and looked at us. He knew two *gringos* weren't going to eat any barracuda head."

Nettles and Harrison worked on the broth, but avoided the *pièce de résistance*.

"We said we were really honored," said Harrison, "and that now we'd go out and get the beer, if they'd keep the soup warm. So we came back with a case of Polar beer and we all drank and ate bread, and eventually Nettles slipped the barracuda head to the dog, just like the mutt knew we would.

"That was one of the best experiences of that part of my life. Meeting those wonderful people who had nothing and gave us everything.

"That taught me that if you're going to play winter baseball," said Harrison, "you better come with your mind open, a sense of humor, and leave all your American standards behind. You're coming to a world that is at a different place in history. It's like going back in time to something like the American Wild West. You are going to see excesses of violence and of generosity and extremes of wealth and poverty with not much in between. The things that happen to you down here . . . well, if you don't hang loose, you're lost."

The adjustment for American players and managers coming to winter leagues in Puerto Rico, Venezuela, Mexico, and the Dominican Republic are far greater than that for the average vacationer. Tourists here in San Juan, for instance, explore the alabaster coastline of expensive hotels, casinos, bars, and beaches. Or they visit the ruins of Old San Juan or drive into the mountainous rain forest. But the ballplayers see the real *"beisbol fanaticos"*—the struggling people of the urban projects, and the *jibaros* living in their scabrous hillside shanties. In short, a genuine cross section of a Puerto Rican population 70 percent of which gets U.S. federal food stamps.

Hiram Bithorn Stadium here is no bilingual, polite vacation world. It is not listed in official Puerto Rican guide books. Its atmosphere is reminiscent of a rough-and-ready "Gunsmoke" saloon. Fistfights are part of the entertainment. Automobile horns caterwaul in the parking lot. Cars are abandoned astride curbs. Thousands of people scurry across the plaza of cobblestones and palm trees, past the bronze statue of Bithorn, Puerto Rico's first big leaguer. The sign in center field reads, "India beer—*buena, buena, buena,*" and teams like Caguas and Santurce wear advertisements for rum on the backs of their double-knit jerseys.

Money is not freely spent. Parking is twenty-five cents. There are no programs. If you can't tell the players without one, you shouldn't be here. There is no seventh-inning stretch. Puerto Ricans stretch when they feel like it. Since the stands are divided in half along intractable partisan lines, the feeling of a family party exists on both sides of the dividing line. A person squeezing into the middle of a crowded row will not allow any of his fellow rooters to stand up to make room. Instead, he pats the seated strangers on the shoulder or head as he passes as though he were bumping knees and feet with his oldest friends.

Every play, almost every pitch, is a full-scale celebration of noise and marvelous, expressive waving of hands. Tambourines, air horns, triangles, police whistles, and voices are strained to the limit, not only by children but by jubilant white-haired men as well. "Every single inning is like nothing you ever experienced in the States," said veteran big leaguer Kurt Bevacqua of Caguas. "I never knew baseball was this exciting a game until I came here." Or as Sixto Lezcano, who grew up here, said proudly, "Puerto Ricans are sentimental, lovable people. They get too excited for words. They just love anything. If the umpire gets hit with a foul ball, they laugh their heads off. Every little thing can be a cause for joy."

Yet Puerto Rican emotion is tame by Latin winter-ball standards. In fact, that sense of relative safety is why many American players are there rather than in countries like Venezuela, where crowds are often three times as big and salaries correspondingly higher. Harrison, who has toiled for six major league teams, admits he is a bit nostalgic for Venezuela and Mexico, where he has played. After all, in San Juan he has had only one sawed-off shotgun and one pistol pointed in his face, and in both cases the plainclothes policemen who held the weapons left after learning Harrison was a ballplayer. Only one of Harrison's Stateside Caguas teammates—Kevin Bell—has been mugged in front of his hotel.

Harrison, who has a bit of conquistador in him despite coming from a family of academics, genuinely misses the Venezuelan customs. The fans in the losing half of the stands light a bonfire of rubbish every night to signify their capitulation. Each team has an old hunchback as a bat boy to bring luck. And every team has its own guard with a tommy gun stationed in the dugout. But most of all Harrison misses his buddy, El Turko, the professional assassin. He is the Venezuelan equivalent of a double-agent who greeted him outside the clubhouse every night and led him on the rounds of nightclubs and bullfights.

"Sometimes, of course," said Harrison, "Turko has to go out of the country on government business."

El Turko, a rabid fan, was a constant comfort to the major leaguers in Caracas. When a leather-lung heckler threatened Oscar Zamora, the slender, middle-aged executioner asked the fan, "Do you know who I am?"

"Yes, señor."

"Then you know that if Oscar Zamora so much as gets a sore arm, I will kill you."

Such stories are the staple of winter-ball conversations. Virgin Islander Elrod Hendricks remembers his first Caribbean World Series game with a hundred soldiers with machine guns ringing the field. The Mexican fans at Hermosillo became an instant legend the day they dumped a bucket of urine on Maury Wills' head.

Yet the Americans here profess their love for Latin ways in the same breath that they slap their knees about the dangers and escapades that fascinate them. "The people are so darn good down here," says Santurce Manager Jack McKeon. "I have so much respect for this area. People will do anything for you."

Harrison admits, "Ballplayers get special treatment. Even the blackjack dealers help you win a few hands, then they give you a look that means, 'That's enough. Leave.'

"And the Latin fans idolize us. In Mexico my father and I were fishing at sunrise and our car got stuck on the beach and the tide was rising. The water was up to the hubcaps when a busload of peons going to a factory stopped. When they found out who I was, the whole bus emptied and they got down in the mud in their good clothes and pushed the car a quarter of a mile. And not one of them would let me give him a cent."

If many American ballplayers find the generosity and affection of their hosts particularly estimable, they snicker at the Latin athletes' addiction to macho games. "Latin players are comically obsessed with establishing a pecking order of toughness among themselves," said one player who was not anxious to get pecked. "The same guys will keep challenging each other day after day to 'slap fight' [boxing with open hands] in the locker room. It's so important in this culture for a man always to be the aggressor."

If machismo is essential here, efficiency often is not. "The biggest economic problem in Puerto Rico is jobs," said Harrison, noting the 30 percent unemployment. "And everyone knows there are more jobs available when something breaks than when it is kept in working order. It seems there is no such thing as preventive maintenance here."

The consequence is that a beautiful fifteen-year-old stadium like

Hiram Bithorn is already in shabby condition. Older stadiums in Ponce, Mayaguez, and Arecibo are considered a scandal by American players. But Americans do not visit this island in the Caribbean to play on manicured fields or dress in spotless lockers. They come for baseball experience, but stay long enough to pick up another sort of Latin seasoning.

"You are here as a sort of mercenary," said Harrison. "You're using their country and their league for your purposes—anything from getting over a sore arm to forgetting a divorce.

"But if you get out and blend in, you can give something back. There are people here to whom it is practically a highlight of their lives to have some contact with a major league player."

And in return? "Nettles and I still talk," said Harrison, "about Dave Concepcion's family and their barracuda head soup and our Polar beer."

The Season of Sweet Boredom

"In winter, I get cabin fever bad. I wish I had a tape recording of the sounds of batting practice . . ."
            Ray Miller,
            Baltimore Oriole pitching coach

The third-base box seats get the warm morning sun, so that's where us old men sit—feet propped on the seat back in front, napes of necks on the cool blue railings behind. Anyone who comes to spring training in February is, of course, an honorary old man. No one who is unwilling to smell, taste, see, touch, and feel as though for the first time or last belongs there.

Miami Stadium, this ancient corrugated-tin ball park for 10,000, is the spring home of the Baltimore Orioles and the perfect shrine in which to worship baseball's annual idyll to indolence. This is Nirvana for the dormant senses. The 80° air is blessed with odors so serene that you must sniff to identify the traces of fresh-mown grass, infield dust, and Florida humidity. In the Oriole dugout the scents of old gloves cured in oils, and new bats rubbed with pine tar, mix with the aroma of the hot black coffee in Manager Earl Weaver's cup. The soft, steady breeze makes you feel as baked and quiescent as the red clay of the pitcher's mound. If the winds could carry words, then these cloudless Miami skies would bear the legend: Released from all cares.

"It's so boring," says pitcher Jim Palmer. "Don't you just hate it?" Then he laughs. "Actually, this is my favorite time of the season. There's no such thing as 'Who's coming up in the bottom of the seventh.' "

That is the gist of February baseball: the motions, gestures, sights, and sounds of the graceful game without its distractions. "Every day is like those special afternoons in summer when you go to Yankee Stadium at two o'clock in the afternoon for an eight o'clock game," says Miller. "It's so big, so empty, and so silent that you can almost hear the sounds that aren't there."

This is the biggest ball park in Florida, and perhaps the best for watching the game with that artist's gift of second sight. As you step from the junkies and bums of Miami's deteriorating 10th Avenue through the untended gates of the stadium, you are struck by the smell of fresh paint and the sight of huge, old oil paintings. The cavernous, dimly lit underbelly of the stands is covered by several thousand square feet of Ash Can School sports murals—a turn-of-the-century barge fight, a suicide squeeze play in mid-pitch, buxom babes battling at the roller derby. In an art gallery they might not pass muster; in a ball park they are magnificent. The squeeze play is a perfect introduction to spring baseball: motion and facial expression captured for its own sake without any hint of a result.

Only one hundred people passed through this open portal today —construction workers on a break, idle teenagers, and genuine old men in the peculiar out-of-date caps and comfortable shoes that appear in the gentlemen's wardrobes once they no longer care about the appraising eyes of women. No two of these watchers sit within ten feet of each other. These groups of one exchange conversation in speeches of two words: "See that . . . Pretty good . . . Not bad . . . Strong arm . . ."

Ballplayers tend to draw circles around themselves. It is hard to step across that invisible boundary—all you have to do is prove to them that you care. Not even care about them, just care about their game. The cost of such proof? Nothing. The only admission today is the admission that you love baseball. The fact that you are here is quite enough.

"Hey, Jack, you bum," an Oriole coach yells to an elderly fan. "Who are you going to root for this year? Us or the Yanks [who train twenty miles away]?"

"Well, not the Yanks," growls the old man, pretending to be grouchy. "You guys got an outfielder who can catch the ball yet?"

Here we find the few people baseball players truly call their friends. In a September pennant race, under the world's fickle eyes, that camaraderie with a major leaguer has no price. The cost of such friendship in February is one quiet, knowing smile. The Orioles lean on the railings and talk to anybody who wants to chat. They are about as aloof as fishermen on a pier digging through a can of bait.

"We'd give an autograph to anybody who was here today," says Palmer. "But then, the people who are here today aren't the kind who would ask for an autograph. They're my idea of good baseball fans. Anybody who comes to watch you run wind sprints and play catch and cover first base on bunts is obviously here for the esthetics. They have a feeling for the game. They're always good people to talk to."

Like any holiday from life, these days of utter unconcern cannot last long. "I don't even hurt anywhere yet." Palmer laughs, the eternal, self-confessed hypochondriac. Soon the curveballs must snap once more, the fastballs hop. The smell then will be the whiff of success; the only flavor will be the taste of dust after striking out. The field of vision narrows as soon as the score is kept. The "regulars" report this week.

The drama which is common to all games will return to baseball soon enough. The unique peace that sometimes seems to lie—like the quiet benediction of a solitary Yankee Stadium—at the center of our most tranquil game will gradually recede. But for a few more days, a few more hours at least, spring training is allowed to languish in its season of sweet boredom.

Interstate Rte. 60 winds through swampy Yeehaw Junction and across desolate Lake Kissimmee from Vero Beach on the Atlantic to St. Petersburg on the Gulf of Mexico. That ribbon of blacktop —surrounded by a wilderness inhabited by alligators, pelicans, and snakes—cuts a line across Florida.

It is a line that connects the old and new in baseball's spring-training world. Spanking new Vero and lazy old St. Pete are the extremes of the grapefruit league in atmosphere, philosophy, and taste. Vero Beach is color-coordinated, youthful, profit-conscious Dodgertown—a 410-acre complex that dominates the life of its small town. Unhurried St. Petersburg with its wide boulevards and palm-filled parks is proud to be called Codgertown for its legions of senior citizens. Baseball is just part of a way of life devoted to moving slowly and smelling every flower.

The seats of Al Lang Field in St. Pete look out across the sailboat-speckled expanse of Tampa Bay. The fans at Lang joke that their average age is deceased, or it would be if not for the therapeutic climate of Sunshine City. The Grand Old Game, especially at half-throttle in March, appeals to fans who like to arrive hours early and chat through batting practice. What's the rush?

The old green-on-green ballyard where Ruth sweated is gone, replaced by a new concrete stadium to accommodate the Cardinals and Mets. Naturally, traditionalists—that's to say, everyone—are riled. Don't like the newfangled thing, they say. It'll give you sunstroke because so many seats have no shade. Or a foul ball will conk you from behind after it deflects off that fancy overhang behind home plate. Ought to string up that young architect.

Baseball just suits the St. Pete mood. George Foster can be measured against spring memories that go back to 1922. The game's action is orderly, not too sudden. The rules don't change. Before and after games, a parade of fans strolls along the three blocks of Beach Drive that separate Lang Field from the venerable Soreno Hotel. The fans help each other along with their canes and walkers, or just a friendly elbow.

"You know my husband, Stanley," said a little lady in a Cardinals cap. "He thinks he'll live to be ninety-five and die in his sleep. I'm the practical one. I told the children, 'I don't want you to keep me alive to be a drain on everyone.' "

The Soreno's ballroom is crowded each night for chamber-music concerts. Hundreds listen to Bach. In a TV room to the side, two watch "Kojak." In such a gentle, old-world atmosphere, it is no surprise that ushers stop guarding the ball-park gates in the second inning. Who would keep anyone—whether in a first or second childhood—outside the park over the matter of a $2.00 ticket?

Most of Florida's camps have some of the St. Petersburg flavor. In Winter Haven, home of the Red Sox, orange trees drape their fruit over the outfield fences. For every town like Miami (Orioles) or Bradenton (Pirates), where the park is old and in a decaying section of town, there are several like West Palm Beach (Braves), Tampa (Reds), and Ft. Lauderdale (Yanks) where the view is of light sparkling on water or palm trees beyond the fences. The scenes in all these parks are reassuringly familiar. This is the way spring training should look.

Only in Vero Beach does it seem like the season has already started. Every game in Vero is a sellout, and the traffic jam stretches back a dusty mile. Almost all Florida camps, even the prettiest, are depressingly close to major highways littered with gas stations, fast-food chains, and general asphalt blight. Dodgertown is set back in its own woods, surrounded by 27 holes of Dodger-owned golf courses.

The wealthiest teams—Reds, Yanks, Phillies—only have a spring-training "complex" with perhaps two auxiliary fields, a few batting cages and a main clubhouse. Dodgertown, which was completely rebuilt in the '70s, is a nexus of seven industrious profit centers spread over 410 acres, each trying to outearn the others. There is a Dodger restaurant, a Dodger citrus farm, a Dodger mobile-home park, and Dodger Pines Country Club. The streets running through this flourishing mini empire are named Campanella Drive, Koufax Boulevard, and the like. Nothing in all of Dodgertown is painted in any color except blue and white, and nothing has a name that is not a baseball spin-off.

"Every other spring-training camp is an expensive tax write-off to the club," said Charlie Blaney, manager of Dodgertown. "We're not a drag on L.A. money. We look on the spring-training part of Dodgertown as simply the research and development end of the baseball business."

Beautiful little 7,000-seat Holman Stadium, which almost looks like a blue miniature of L.A.'s Chavez Ravine, is what Blaney calls "the flagship of Dodgertown."

In 1974, Dodgertown opened a new 23,000-square-foot administration building with nearly every wall decked out in life-size Dodger action photos and memorabilia. The building includes (in part) a major league clubhouse, a minor league clubhouse, a small but self-sufficient hospital, dining room and kitchen, main lobby, canteen, recording studio, photo darkroom, Western Union office, interview rooms, staff social rooms, press room, trainers' rooms, equipment room, and two laundries. Does Dodgertown start to sound more like a retreat for IBM executives than a locker room for jocks? Well, that's just what the Dodgers thought, so they made it one. Why make money six weeks a year when it could be fifty-two?

"Of course, I'm the wrong person to ask about Dodgertown," said Manager Tommy Lasorda. "I think it's heaven on earth."

It is a long, long way from the leisure of St. Petersburg to the constant hyperactivity of Dodgertown. At Lang Field, fans stay after the game to watch the sun glint on the bay. At Holman Stadium, a crew of dozens of cleanup men have swept away every discarded program and fallen kernel of popcorn before the last pitch is an hour old.

Once, Dodgertown was just an abandoned World War II air base. More than six hundred Dodger rookies cavorted in the old, dilapidated barracks. Snakes basked on the steps. Horseshoes was the big night-life activity. The showers turned themselves on, usually, legend has it, when the venetian blinds were dropped. And a deluxe room in the leaky barracks was one that came with two buckets.

All that is gone. Progress has arrived. If a flower moves, paint it blue.

Koufax: Passing the Art Along

None of the greats of baseball retired as young as Sandy Koufax, and perhaps none retired so well.

No one else in the Hall of Fame disappeared from the game so quickly. For thirteen years, he wandered from the coast of California to the coast of Maine, disappearing from public view for years at a time.

"I wasn't looking for anything . . . just looking for time," Koufax said. "It was a mindless period to do what I wanted to do and go where I wanted to go. I decided to take a few years for myself . . . I wanted to see how long I could stretch it."

After he had been out of the major leagues one year longer than the dozen seasons he was in them, Koufax quietly reappeared in a corner of the Los Angeles Dodgers clubhouse as a low-profile pitching coach, one of three such coaches in the Dodger organization.

Mr. K., the man who many say was, at his peak, the most overwhelming pitcher in the history of baseball, sits on a pedaling machine in the Dodgers' weight-lifting room. Cap tilted back, he looks as delighted as a bat boy to join in the big league banter.

Koufax has come home.

He wears the old number—32—and, if anything, is a few pounds trimmer than his playing weight in 1966 when he shocked his entire profession by hanging up his spikes at age thirty. "That's right," he says, with a wry and enigmatic smile, "thirty."

Koufax's hair is a distinguished pepper-and-salt. He is tan and utterly at ease. Like Joe DiMaggio, he has, with age, gone from movie-star handsome to some higher plateau.

"Hey, Sandy," said Dodger Manager Tommy Lasorda, "you're gonna pitch for us coaches in the charity game against the media men today, right?"

"I guess I'll be there," said Koufax, just as he did before Walter Alston handed him the ball to start the World Series.

"I knew it," said Lasorda, glowing, his mousetrap all set.

"That's why all them newspaper guys are lined up outside with bats."

Koufax is too delighted to be the butt of such a ridiculous joke to offer any retort. Everybody hits Sandy Koufax these days—the scrubs in batting practice, the paunchy L.A. reporters.

When Koufax stepped off the mound after the '66 Series, he had won 27 games with a 1.73 ERA. He had been baseball's Player of the Year for four consecutive years. He was not at the peak of his game: He was somewhere above it.

So, he will be remembered forever that way. "He could step on the mound and win today," said veteran Don Sutton.

Retirement is baseball's cruelest joke. What player has truly survived it without a sense of erosion? Willie Mays does not wear his bald spot well, nor Hank Aaron his spare tire. Mickey Mantle is a pulpy Oklahoma good ol' boy.

"Ted Williams, Joe DiMaggio, and Sandy," said Dodger Steve Garvey. "They're the only ones that seem to grow bigger with the years."

Perhaps Koufax does it best because he tries least. Williams and DiMaggio are both fiercely aloof. Koufax seems to tread an easy middle ground between pal and deity.

"This man was my idol," said young pitcher Robert Castillo, patting Koufax's embarrassed shoulder. "I snuck into every game he pitched."

At that, Koufax goes from eyes-down displeasure to mischief. "Well," said Koufax to Castillo, "where's the money? You can pay me now."

There is hardly a word strong enough for the way other players feel about Koufax; it almost goes beyond affection to a sort of total protectiveness for a man so gentle he seems misplaced in a jock shop.

"I played with Sandy in '66," said pitcher Don Sutton proudly. "It's like he's never been away. He's absolutely unchanged. He's the greatest, most sincere and humble . . ." then Sutton stops, as if laying it on too thick might reflect badly on Koufax.

"He helped me as a rookie and he helps me now. If anybody ever deserved to be at the top of the ladder, it's him," said Sutton. "A lot of people look around to see how they can keep you from climbing up there with them. Sandy has always gone out of his way to pull everybody up there with him."

That desire to pull others up the ladder is part of Koufax's pleasure now. "Pitching is a branch of learning, no doubt of it," said the southpaw who struggled for six big league years as a 36–40 pitcher before suddenly learning control. "You're part of a chain that goes back for generations passing the art along."

For a man so reticent as to be a recluse by baseball's gregarious standards, Koufax is almost shockingly candid about the other reasons for his return.

"I need the money," he said. "I'm not destitute by any means, but I always knew I couldn't stay retired forever. I just wanted to stretch it as long as I could.

"It took me eight years (as a player) to get to twenty thousand dollars a season. Then I had only four more seasons, so you can figure that out. I did some TV announcing for NBC for five years [salary nearly $100,000 a year], but nothing since then.

"I'm like a lot of older people living on fixed incomes," said Koufax. "I needed a regular supplemental income just to keep up with inflation."

Koufax has investments and real estate holdings, as well as a sports-medicine clinic in Eugene, Oregon.

"Sooner or later, you're going to say, 'That's enough of that.' You need to find something to do, another purpose," said Koufax.

"Also, it's hard to be away from possibly the only thing you ever did really well," he said, with an expression that looks more like hard insight than false modesty.

"Baseball is a way of life. It's pleasant to be in a large group with one pursuit—everyone working for the benefit of all. Other people find the same feeling in other ways. It's hardly unique to sports. It's like an orchestra making music together.

"Sometimes, on the right team, baseball can bring out a lot of the best in people. On the wrong team, I expect it can bring out a good deal of the worst."

Koufax, thanks to baseball, has always been able to lead a simple, untarnished, almost philosophical life.

"The game has a cleanness," he said. "If you do a good job, the numbers [statistics] say so. You don't have to ask anyone or play politics. You don't have to wait for the reviews."

That pursuit of pure pitching performance remains an essentially untransmittable lesson. Like a Talmudic scholar, Koufax can pass on the letter but not the essential mystery of his pitching teachings.

"Success and confidence," he said. "Who can say which one comes first? It took me six years to get them, and I still don't know which led to the other or how they sort of fed on each other. It's like relaxation and concentration . . . they go together, but it's hard to learn.

"Pitching is a static situation. You initiate the action. That means you can develop a special depth of concentration."

None of that is altered by the years. "I feel perfectly at home," said Koufax, "because the game doesn't change. There's no proficiency without dedication.

"It's surprising that baseball hasn't had to update anything since Ty Cobb. On a ground ball in the hole, a fast man's still out by a step and a slow man by two steps."

That seems to please Koufax. He mulls it.

It is that silence and self-containment that have always set Koufax apart, made his psyche a parlor game for baseball psychiatrists. No man ever refused to pitch a Series game on Yom Kippur before Koufax. No man, for that matter, ever retired at his earnings and performance peak.

"My retirement was entirely a medical decision," Koufax says now, just as he said then.

That, of course, explains nothing. Hundreds of pitchers have had arm problems that turned arthritic, that threatened to become chronic and cause lifelong discomfort or minor deformity.

It is difficult to find a fan or athlete who truly has a feeling for how Koufax could walk away after a 27–9 season. Obviously, he still had a brilliant, if painful, pitching future ahead of him.

"I didn't believe it when I heard it," said Sutton, then a rookie. "I called Sandy that day. He said, 'There are some things in life I might be jeopardizing, if I keep pitching with this elbow . . . you know, I might want to swing a golf club sometime during the rest of my life.' "

That brings us to the edge of Koufax, which may be as far as he will ever allow anyone to go. How is the great consuming public, avid for heroes, going to understand a man who forsakes fame simply because the idea of crippling himself, perhaps losing the feeling in his fingers, offends him deeply?

The pressure of the game did not drive him away. "Sometimes, you find that you like those extreme pressure situations," he said. "You like the responsibility. You know, sometimes the most terrified people do the best work."

The heat of the public spotlight burned him more than the heat of the mound. "You are part of an entertainment," he explained. "But you are not an entertainer. That is unnatural. But I enjoyed doing it . . . probably even more than the fans enjoyed watching. I thank them for enjoying it with me."

Even in that Southern California media whirl, Koufax maintained his privacy by refusing to do otherwise. "If you want your life to be private, it can be," he said. And that's that.

That wall of privacy is not topped with Ted Williams' barbed-wire snarl but with a gentle, disquieting smile. Where was Koufax for seven years from 1972 to 1979? "Wherever I wanted to be . . ."

Koufax, in his blank-faced, enigmatic moments, can seem like a man protecting an enormous and simple secret that is more important to him than it could possibly be to anyone else. Like some adventurous introvert in a Joseph Conrad novel, he seems to have glimpsed a sobering heart of darkness either in himself or in the world.

When someone praises him too much, Koufax gives a weary, knowing look and says, "Who are we talking about? I don't think I know this person."

When a man says, in passing, "You know, Sandy, I think if I had to be interviewed as much as you, I'd crawl in that trunk."

"I'm tempted," says Koufax gently.

Yet, at other times, Koufax seems comfortably ordinary recycling the driest baseball cliche as though it were new. The clue, perhaps, is that Koufax has seen through the veil of his game. A sport can be extremely difficult without being extremely important. Baseball could fascinate him, but not control him.

"It is unfair to make comparisons. I don't want to be compared to anyone," he said, as though saying it one more time is unlikely to change anything. "I am just myself . . . the same person I have always been."

And who might that fellow be—that chap who retired at thirty, who has lived in blessed gossipless solitude with his wife since, and who has returned to baseball with such natural ease? That central inviolate self remains as untouchable as a Koufax fastball, as admirable as a Koufax curve.

Islamorada, Miramichi, Bangor, and Winter Haven

For five years Ted Williams was away from the hunt that he loves best. He had tried to satisfy himself with the fly cast at dawn, the down-turning flick of the wrist and the splash. In winter he lives in the Florida Keys, trolling for bonefish near Islamorada. In summer the spiky air of Canada calls him to Miramichi to pursue the Atlantic salmon, greatest of game fish. And in the fall the woods of Maine are lovely, dark, and deep. What better, for a man without promises to keep than to set out early from Bangor with gun on arm.

But what of spring?

For Williams the month of March was always one thing: Open season on pitchers. The Splendid Splinter—age sixty—leans against the batting cage again. Once more The Kid is a hunter of pitchers, training his favorite pack of hounds: the hitters.

Here in the spring-training camp of the Boston Red Sox, Batting Coach Williams is at home the way few men are anywhere, the way he is in only one other place—in a fishing boat on a lost lake.

These wild animals of Winter Haven fascinate him. Williams, professor emeritus of hitting, presses his face against the mesh of the batting cage as these brutish critters pass in revue before him. The lynxish Yaz, the ponderous Boomer, the bristling Rice, the fierce Fisk, the wild and untamed Hobson: each is a separate specie of homo homerus (home-run man).

Ostensibly, Williams has been hired "to help the rookies and minor league kids any damn way I can." But Williams has not had this sort of marble to chisel in half a lifetime, not since the late forties and early fifties when Williams, Pesky, Doerr, Stephens, and Co. produced 1,027 runs in one year.

As soon as a Bosox regular becomes restless and discontent, Williams approaches, delighted to take the thorn from a swing.

"Come on, Fisk, you idiot," stormed Carlton Fisk, lashing in the cage.

"In the spring you always feel betwixt and between," commiserated Williams. "The darn pitchers are ahead of us.

"Your hands aren't cocked in close enough. They're too high and far away," said Williams, grabbing Fisk and wrestling him into the proper position. "How can you feel quick and explosive if you're not compact? Am I right? Am I right?

"I missed baseball," said Williams, who had been out of the sport since managing the Washington Senators in 1969–71 and Texas in 1972. "This is the uniform I should never have taken off," Williams added, meaning the Boston red, white, and blue. "You're always a fan of this game after you've played it. You enjoy being around it, listening to the young guys in the clubhouse. This is my chance to be up close to the game for a few weeks. I'll leave when the rookies are shipped out. But it's enough to give me an interest in the game again."

The Red Sox players are glad to have him as up close as he wants to get. Home-run king Jim Rice has carried The Book (Williams' *My Turn at Bat*) with him everywhere since he broke into the league. Dwight ("Dewey") Evans calls Williams "a genius and a great guy."

When Williams played a challenge tennis match against Carl Yastrzemski, 240-pound George ("Boomer") Scott volunteered to be ball boy.

"Ted's never been this sweet-tempered for this long at a stretch in his life," joked one front-office man.

"He's mellowed a lot," said Coach Johnny Pesky, a longtime friend. "But his enthusiasm for the game hasn't. He brings that sharp mind to everything. It isn't just the rookies who are in awe of him. A lot of us have always been."

Williams is just as prone to feats of skill as ever. "Hear that airplane engine?" Williams will say. "Bet I can spot it before you do." And, of course, he does.

Many a bet was made on how long Williams could resist getting into the batting cage himself. That didn't last long. "I waited for a warm day with nobody around, then took a hundred swings," said Williams.

"I'd have paid to see it," lamented Evans. Only a few did.

"He wore that indoor pitching machine out," marveled rookie Chuck Rainey. "Nothing but line drives. Nice easy swing.

"Somebody switched the machine to curves. He took one, then said, 'Oh, breaking balls, huh,' and he lined them all over the place. It's like riding a bicycle to him. He'll never forget."

Two stupid questions follow Williams everywhere—one joking, one serious. Will he make a comeback as a DH? Will he manage again?

Such constant petty prodding has driven Williams back to his fishing boat before. But he tolerates fools more generously than he once did.

"No comebacks," he said. "I wouldn't want to tamper with the mystique of my last at bat [when he homered]."

Once, Williams might have snapped, "What the hell's a mystique?"

Manager Don Zimmer, who calls himself, "just a .235 hitter with a metal plate in his head," can be thankful that Williams has finally convinced all comers that he is not after Zimmer's job.

"I have absolutely no interest in managing anywhere again," said Williams. "I'll come back as the season goes along to see a hitter who's struggling. But I won't do it too often. I want my summers the way they are."

Williams silently snaps his wrist in the imaginary two-part motion of a perfect fly cast. Miramichi is waiting. "A thousand salmon in one summer," he said. "That's my goal."

Williams still has his old sore spot—vanity.

Comparisons with Rod Carew, who once hit .388, annoy Williams. He will not point out, but his old friends are anxious to, that when Williams hit .388 at age thirty-eight his slugging percentage was 200 points higher than Carew's was in '78, and his on-base percentage 100 points higher.

"Ted doesn't think a comparison between a man who has less than 100 career homers [Carew] and one who had 521 is any comparison at all," said a Williams friend of twenty years.

Williams' other no-touch area is his separation from his third wife and their two children who live in Vermont, while Williams remains in Islamorada.

"There isn't anybody in the game today who's near Number Nine," said Pesky. "Willie Mays was the last one who had that kind of presence."

Williams is an American original—independent, still fiercely private, a paradoxical conservative renegade. He leaves the Winter Haven clubhouse in garb that would draw stares if he were selling bait on a pier. His toes-up tennis shoes are worthy of comedian Prof. Irwin Cory. His baggy khaki pants are too short and his old baggy sweater too long. In other words, he looks great.

Scott, in his huge rings and necklace of "second basemen's teeth," is demonstrating his stance to the great man and insisting, "I'm one of the greatest hitters who ever lived."

"Well," grinned the amused Williams, "you'd be a hell of a lot greater if you'd open up your front foot so you can clear your hips and get that big rear of yours into the ball."

Scott, who challenges anyone who mentions his weight to a point-blank duel with Louisville sluggers, dropped his jaw and said, "Show me what you mean, man."

Williams and Scott start the eternal wrestling match, Williams not only talking theory but trying to transmit the subjective feel of a proper swing by twisting and shoving and adjusting Scott's body.

"Am I right? Am I right?" badgered the grinning, excited Williams.

"Right on, Number Nine," said the Boomer.

Why Baltimore Wins More Games Than Anybody Else

Pennants are won in March. The Baltimore Orioles are conclusive proof of that statement.

From 1960 through 1981, the O's have won far more games than any other team in baseball, finishing 552 games over .500. They eclipse the second-best club, Cincinnati, by nearly 50 games.

The Orioles don't do it with money or attendance or publicity or a beautiful stadium. They rank in the middle of baseball in all of those areas. The most basic reason for their superiority, say the O's, is always the same: Fundamentals are the Orioles' edge.

"What is a baseball fundamental?" says Ken Singleton. "It's any baseball act that is so simple that the man in the stands thinks, 'I could do that. Why can't those big leaguers?'

"Fundamentals are the easy plays and the basic thoughts that we work on more than any team. From the seventh inning on, we make those plays, the other teams don't, and we win again."

"Baseball is pitching, three-run homers, and fundamentals," says Earl Weaver, the manager with the second-highest winning percentage in the twentieth century. "For instance, the most fundamentally sound player in baseball might be Jim Palmer. What I've always appreciated about Jim is the enthusiasm he brings to our fundamentals. He doesn't need them, but he realizes they are a necessary evil. He leads by example. I appreciate that," Weaver says with a straight face. "Be sure to talk to Jim."

"God, don't talk to me about fundamentals," rails Palmer, sweat still pouring from two hours of fielding bunts, covering first base, backing up bases on cutoffs, and, finally, running eighteen foul-line-to-foul-line wind sprints. "So dull . . . so dull. I hate fundamentals. Cursed Oriole fundamentals . . . I've been doing them since 1964. I do them in my sleep. I hate spring training."

Ah, fundamentals, the castor oil of baseball.

The term "fundamental" is one of the vaguest, most ubiquitous, and least understood in baseball. But it's simple. "Baseball is richer in 'situations' than any sport," says Ray Miller, Baltimore pitching coach. "What's the score? What's the count? Who's on base? How many outs? For every baseball situation, a player must have a conditioned reflex for every play that can happen. Those conditioned reflexes—those basic situations and the plays that grow out of them—are the fundamentals.

"Just being smart and alert isn't always enough. You want your players to react to those familiar plays without thinking. It's conditioned reflex . . . over and over."

"Extra bases and extra outs, that's what fundamentals are all about," says Weaver. "You want to make the other team earn all four bases, and you don't want to give them any extra outs."

Although it is not as universally understood as it should be, baseball is a game of "big innings." In a substantial majority of games, the winning team scores more runs in one inning than the loser does in all nine. Fundamentals are the plays that minimize your opponents' big innings, while maximizing your own. The Orioles not only understand this, but preach it as gospel.

"When Earl goes to the mound in a jam, he always says the same thing," Miller says. "He tells the pitcher, 'Stay out of a big inning. Take the out if they'll give it to you. Don't worry about one run.'"

"Our whole objective," says Singleton, "is to make the basic plays, never give up a cheap run, and keep the game under control. We wait for the other team to give us an extra out, or put extra men on base with walks. We'll have more chances to explode because we'll make less of those mistakes that open up a big inning."

"What distinguishes the Orioles is that they have a whole theory of how the game should be played," says Miller. "You feel it the first day you're in the organization. It stretches down to the lowest rookie at Bluefield [in the minor leagues]. We may not do things the right way, but we do 'em the Oriole way. And, in the end, that's just as good."

Oriole fundamentals lend a sense of order to the entire organization. "It almost irritates other players," says Singleton. "They'll ask you in August, 'Don't you guys ever throw a ball away? Don't you ever miss the cutoff man?'"

That sense of order and control and restraint runs, like a baseball Ten Commandments, through the Oriole's system. For exam-

ple, "On the sacrifice bunt, we'll always grab the sure out," says
Weaver. "If you play for one run early in the game, you'll end up
losing by one run. We will never turn down an out and take a
gamble."

"We tell all our pitchers the 'pick-off' is an incorrect name,"
says Miller. "We are not attempting to pick off runners. We are
trying to make the runners worried and defensive on the bases.
That's enough. There is not now, and never will be, a pick-off play
worth throwing the ball away."

To many players, becoming an Oriole has been a sort of revela-
tion. On the first day, they are handed an organizational book
that outlines the Oriole way to do everything. It is a proof of
something they suspected: Baseball can be simple.

"That book is under lock and key in my home," laughs Miller.
"Nobody gets it away from me.

"It's no accident that the same few teams keep winning, like
the Orioles and Dodgers and Reds. They are the best fundamental
teams. Clubs like Cleveland and San Francisco keep watching
their players become all-stars as soon as another organization gets
them. Wonder why that is?"

When Frank Robinson, after twenty-five years with the Reds
and Orioles, became manager at Cleveland, he was stunned to
learn that the Indians taught the game differently at every level—
or, rather, didn't teach it at all. "I was teaching fundamentals to
big leaguers," says Robinson.

Robinson was spoiled. He figured every pitcher knew, from the
first day of spring, that after covering first base to take a throw,
the next move is always to turn to the left quickly and face the
infield. Why? So that if there's a fast runner on second base he
can't score on a routine ground out. In just such small ways—
dozens of them—a team gains a sense of composure and mutual
trust.

"One bonus of longevity is that you can do everything the same
at every level from rookie league to majors," says Weaver. "When
a Mike Flanagan or Eddie Murray reaches the big leagues, they already feel at home. Organizations that change managers at the
top every year also have to change at the bottom every year, too.
How can their young players have a sense of continuity?"

The Orioles don't worry about the athletic feats that beat them.

A home run against them, or a shutout, only produces a yawn. They know they aren't the only team with talent.

Because the Orioles are so self-assured in fundamentals they can afford to be fascinated with the nuances of the sport.

In the first game of spring training, the Orioles were tied, 4-4, in the eighth inning. A Bird rookie outfielder, Drungo Larue Hazewood, overthrew the cutoff man while trying to nail a runner going first-to-third on him. The throw bounced crazily into foul territory as the go-ahead run raced home. But, the O's pitcher—a veteran—was down the left-field foul line, backing up the play. The runner was out at the plate. The O's won in the ninth.

"Didn't take long for us to start playing Oriole baseball, did it?" Singleton says, grinning. "You can practically go a whole season without seeing our outfield throw to the wrong base or miss a cutoff man. But when a rookie screws up, there's our pitcher, practically sitting in the box seats, so he can back up the play."

It dismays the Orioles that the trend of their game is away from fundamentals, rather than toward them. "I could understand it fifteen years ago when I started pitching," says Miller. "We had so many rookies in camp that the Giants gave me Number 465. With that many players, who has time to teach? In seven years in the Cleveland organization, I never remember working on a bunt play. In spring training, we'd run, shag flies, and cover first base for three days—those were our fundamentals for the year.

"Today, the minor leagues are much smaller, so you ought to be able to instruct more. But most clubs don't. They spend their money on free agents, or else they teach baseball as though it were football. Everywhere—in colleges or pros—you see weight-lifting equipment for baseball players," says Miller. "I disagree with that overemphasis. I tell my young pitchers, 'Son, in this game, it's never going to be a third-down-and-one.' You don't hit off tackle in baseball, and you can't play the game with your teeth gritted. Muscles are fine. But this is a game of relaxation, condition reflex, and mental alertness."

If you want to see weight lifting, go see the Chicago White Sox or the Texas Rangers—teams with talent and muscle but ridiculously inept at fundamentals.

An Oriole spring training is an education in the minute technical secrets of how to make the basic plays correctly.

"Show the glove early," a Bird coach yells to a young pitcher covering first. That is to encourage the first baseman to make the underhanded toss quickly. If he doesn't see the pitcher's glove, he hesitates.

"Pull it in," another coach calls out to a pitcher fielding grounders, then wheeling to throw to second to start a double play. "Catch, pull in, look, step, throw."

By pulling the ball in to the belt buckle—almost going into the pitching stretch position—the pitcher composes himself and gets into the most familiar throwing position.

"That's why we never throw a ball into center field," says Miller.

As each Oriole finishes his batting-practice swings, he follows a base-circling ritual. After sprinting to first, he takes a lead, then steals second on the next pitch. He takes a lead at second and imagines breaking for third on a sacrifice bunt. Finally, he breaks for the plate, then retreats, tags up at third and comes home on the first available flyball. This endless drill begins the first day at Bluefield and continues right through batting practice before World Series games.

"We score a lot of runners from third base on infield grounders with one out," said Frank Robinson, now trying to teach fundamentals in San Francisco. "That's because we're aggressive and practice it. The runner's front foot should hit the ground in a running stride just as the pitch crosses the plate. That's what everybody practices in BP."

"Our strongest fundamental is probably our sacrifice bunting in the late innings of close games," says shortstop Mark Belanger. "Getting the bunt down to move the runners is becoming extinct. Some teams practice it seriously in March. We practice it seriously before 162 games.

"On the other hand, our weakest fundamental is certainly defense against the sacrifice bunt. With more Astroturf fields and more trick defensive plays, teams have proved that you can nail the lead runner more than anybody ever thought. But Earl is so adamant about taking the 'sure' out that we seldom gamble for the lead runner even when we could get him."

"You'll never see *all* our infielders moving simultaneously to defense the bunt," says Robinson. "Too many things can go wrong. It's not worth the risk. Just take the out."

If the Orioles have one huge advantage, it is their total commitment to play as a team. "Most good fundamental teams are unselfish teams," points out Miller. "With a man on second and none out, every player in our organization is under instructions to take one shot [swing] at moving the guy to third by hitting to the right side. On many teams, it's a half-hearted effort—a foul ball —because the guy doesn't really want to give himself up. He wants that hit for his batting average.

"The first day I was with the Orioles in AAA, we had a guy named Robby Andrews, who was leading the league in hitting, reached out for a curve in the dirt so he could give himself up. When he came back to the dugout, twenty-three guys were beating him on the back. I said, 'Hey, what's this? It must be baseball.'"

Fundamentals are infectious. They become a teamwide obsession, almost a badge of honor. Even the most obvious chores become part of a ritual of success.

Some teams, for instance, make fun of the Oriole doctrine— which goes back more than twenty-five years to Paul Richards— that pitchers must run.

Oriole theory says that when the legs, which have 60 percent of the body's muscle, get tired, something must compensate. So the arm gets hurt. "It's an illusion that our pitchers get stronger as the year goes along," says Miller. "The rest of the league just falls by the wayside. The Rangers run very little because they say it's too hot in Texas. But they have to pitch there. And every winter their staff goes back under the knife."

Oriole pitchers are so religious about their running (though they profess to loathe it), that they grouse whenever their slave driver of the day is a minute late to oversee them.

The key to getting a player to love his castor oil is to prick his pride. In 1978, the O's had a poor, frightened outfield. In 1979, it was competent, and even occasionally good. The reason: Frank Robinson went back to fundamentals in spring training. "They were praying that the ball wouldn't be hit to them," says Robinson. "I stirred their pride, convinced them they could enjoy the outfield if they *wanted* to catch the balls."

Robinson even invented a new teaching technique, eschewing those traditional, lazy 300-foot fungoes that coaches hit. "Man, anybody can catch those. They retard you because you get false confidence. We had to get to work," he says.

So, each day, Robinson and his outfielders stood just 150 feet apart as the coach hit grounders and liners to the edge of their reach. "They could get more work in less time," the coach says. "They could hear me when I had something to say. Because they had to run hard, short bursts, they could work longer without tiring. At that shorter distance, I could hit accurate enough fungoes that every play was difficult, instead of a lazy shag. They learned to see the ball come off the bat, and they got more excited the more good catches they made.

"People made jokes and asked, 'What do you need an outfield coach for?'" says Robinson. "Well, our outfield did not lose one game for us the next year."

The tactical implications of having a fundamentally sound team are wide-ranging, but they have the greatest impact on pitching, which of course, is the Orioles' trump.

"The first thing we tell our new pitchers," says Miller, "is that now they have eight guys on their side. If they will just make the other team hit the ball, we'll catch it for them. Avoid walks, avoid home runs, and let the fielders do the work."

The ultimate Oriole pitcher is Palmer, who makes the game look effortless, who seldom strikes out anybody except in a jam.

"Palmer is the greatest 'situation' pitcher I've ever seen," says Miller. "He never makes the two-run pitch. He makes them beat him on a single and one run at a time. Most of the homers he gives up are solos because he only works to their power when the bases are empty."

At heart, the Orioles have operated for the last two decades on the assumption that baseball is a game of basic situations and fundamental plays. They seldom stop studying their game. In the Oriole clubhouse is a TV set, attached to a videotape machine. Recorded are all the pitches of the previous game, spliced so that a three-hour game can be reviewed in thirty minutes, every pitch seen from directly behind home plate. The Birds gather nonchalantly around that TV, but the banter is the stuff of pennants.

"Hey, ol' [Nelson] Norman's got himself a new stance," says Tim Stoddard, watching a replay of a game against Texas.

"But he can't handle the jammer," mutters Rick Dempsey. Heads nod agreement.

"Here comes the Doctor of Leather," laughs a Bird as gloveman Pepe Frias steps to the plate.

Frias steps deep in the bucket while fouling off a Steve Stone pitch.

"Pepe no like that big curveball very much," says Dave Skaggs.

"Watch," says Stone. "He doesn't like this next one much either."

Suddenly, the realization grows that every player in the room recalls every pitch—its sequence, its location—from an exhibition game in Florida.

"Did you hang this next forkball?" Singleton asks Stone.

"Yup," says Stone. "I hang one in three. This is the one."

"Hey, somebody call me when [Johnny] Grubb hits his three-run homer," announces Palmer. "I want to see where that pitch was."

But Grubb hasn't hit a home run this game, Palmer is told by an outsider.

"Sure he did," says Palmer. "He hit two of 'em. One off me and one off Stony. The wind just happened to blow 'em back in the park and Singleton caught them at the wall. You know, the wind's not always going to be blowing," says Palmer. "This is a good chance to find out where his power zone is."

Slowly, the Orioles dress, preparing themselves for their game of fundamental plays and fundamental thoughts. What base do you throw to? Who is the cutoff man? Who backs up? Which direction do you pivot after tagging the bag? What is Nelson Norman's new stance? What pitch can't Pepe Frias hit with a shovel? What pitch don't you throw to Johnny Grubb with men on base?

All these things can be practiced in advance or known in advance. They require neither great talent nor great intellect. They may seem exotic, but to a big leaguer they are fundamental.

The fan, as he leaves the park, remembers the towering home run, the acrobatic double play, the blazing fastball that struck out a dozen helpless batters. The players love the spectacular, too. The patois of the game is full of "dingers and taters," "heaters and hooks." Some teams love the sublime too much. "Boston never wins it all," says one Oriole, "because they can't be bothered to play dull baseball." But the best players, the best teams, usually digest the game and then dream about it, at a different level.

They grumble about the sacrifice bunt that was popped up, the pitcher who forgot to cover first, the cutoff man missed, or the catcher who called the wrong pitch.

Perhaps more than any of our other major sports, baseball rewards the mundane and the extraordinary in almost equal measures. That, mayhap, is why free agents have altered the game's competitive balance less than expected.

Willie Mays climbing the fence or Mickey Mantle hitting the upper-deck facade in old Yankee Stadium are what first attracted us to the game. But, year after year, it is the subtle, yet totally accessible fundamentals of the game that keep us attached to baseball as we see common sense, alertness, and perseverance rewarded, while the slipshod is relentlessly punished.

The Big Bang Theory and Other Secrets of the Game

Earl Weaver's curses, his beer, and even pieces of his uniform hung in the air in his small office. "You're all a bunch of second-guessing idiots," the Baltimore manager informed the reporters cowering over him.

"Anybody who wouldn't have done what I did in the eighth inning *isn't a baseball person.* I know in my heart what's right. I do what *I* want. Always. That's why there are 1,100 wins around here. That's why we can go without a single victory for the next three years and I'll still be over .500."

The managerial dervish subsided. "What I did today was absolutely basic," said Weaver, suddenly calm. "But you'll never understand."

The secret of baseball had been on display and, as usual, no one noticed, except a few old hands in each dugout.

Boston led Baltimore by a run in the eighth inning. Baltimore had a runner on third base with 1 out. The Saturday crowd, led by a drunk taxi driver standing on the dugout roof, cheered and chanted. They didn't have a clue.

The Orioles' Rich Dauer was due to bat against Red Sox reliever Bob Stanley: righty versus righty. The Orioles sent up lefty pinch hitter Terry Crowley. The Bosox countered with southpaw Tom Burgmeier. Baltimore pinch-hit for the pinch hitter, sending up righty Lenn Sakata. On the surface, this was the ritual Dance of the Percentages between two veteran managers. But why were the Orioles standing on the lip of their dugout screaming in rage? Why was the home-plate umpire shoving Boston catcher Carlton Fisk from the mound to the plate with both hands?

The Red Sox infield played in on the grass. As the pitch was thrown, the crowd went silent. In sports, there is a moment too rich for noise—the heart of the matter. Sakata dribbled a grounder to second. The runner stayed at third, and Sakata was out at first. Boston's defense returned to normal. The next Oriole grounded out. The potential big inning had died. Objects were smashed in the Baltimore dugout. Boston won, 1–0.

Once again, nobody guessed the secret.

How are baseball games won? How should they be watched? And how, ultimately, can they be understood? Like burglars, we search for the tools that will let us steal a few of the true gems of the diamond. An inventory, please. First, the conceptual jimmy that allows us to pry ajar the door of the vault: the Big Bang Theory of Killer Innings. Then, the lever that pops open the safe: a grasp of the overall, semiconscious theory of team building and how it interlocks with the game's crisis points. Next, the dark lamp that lights the inside: the fundamentals of the sport. Finally, the skeleton key to the baseball strongbox: the mystical scorecard.

But before we try to break in, we must first case the joint.

The locker nearest Weaver's office belongs to Coach Ray Miller, the team's unofficial interpreter of Weaver. "Earl's mad because he knows he was wrong," said Miller. "But what *really* makes him hot is that he can't explain the reason he was wrong. Earl thought he had trapped Zimmer in a mistake, but it backfired."

Normally, Weaver would have let Dauer hit against Stanley, ignoring the righty-lefty game. Although Dauer had been only 1-for-12 in four futile years against Stanley, in his previous 11 games he had hit .432. But, unexpectedly, the Red Sox had forgotten to warm up Burgmeier. As Dauer stepped to the plate, in the bull pen Burgmeier had just stripped off his jacket. Weaver's eyes popped. "Terry," snapped Weaver to Crowley, "hustle up there to the plate. They'll have to pitch to you. Burgy's not hot yet. This is what we've waited the whole damn game for. The gun is loaded. And it's pointed at them."

But Boston veterans know something about guns, too. Perez visited the mound. Then Fisk ambled out. The Orioles were apoplectic, especially Weaver, who would have raced out for a toe-to-toe—except that would have wasted more time. Finally, the umpire shoved Fisk back toward home plate. Then Zimmer headed toward the mound, moving slower than a groundhog burrowing from the dugout. By now Burgmeier was ready. Zimmer waved his left arm. The bullet had been removed from the Baltimore gun and replaced with a blank named Sakata.

"That one at-bat was the ball game," said Weaver later. "The SOBs stalled us out of a game."

Inside major league dugouts, there is a common assumption that seldom escapes: Baseball is a game of big innings. In a majority of games, the winning team scores more runs in *one* inning than the loser does in *nine* innings. To grasp the game, we must start there.

In baseball, all moments are not of equal value, or even equal potential. In games of continuous action—football, basketball, or hockey—a player can score only one goal on any single play, no matter how spectacular. A baseball player can produce *four* runs on a grand slam, and many other hits produce two or three runs on one play.

Look at the World Series since 1960. In those 133 games, the winning team followed the Big Bang Theory by scoring as many— or more—runs in one inning as the other team did in the whole game 106 times: 80 percent. In 75 games the winner scored more runs in one inning than its foe did in all nine. In only 27 games did the big-inning notion not apply. That breakdown—75-30-27— is worth considerable cogitation.

From a technical and psychological standpoint, almost everything contributes to a multirun inning, *once the rally is underway*. With the bases empty, the initiative is with the defensive players. They choose the pitch, the tempo, the defensive alignment. Only a home run can change the system—and that's only worth one run. But, as soon as the first runner gets on—especially if it's the lead-off man—the balance is changed. Infielders must hold runners, or fake the hold. They must move in, either to make the double play or cut off a run at the plate. Holes appear in the defense, pitch selection is restricted, the leverage of a full windup is removed, percentages deteriorate. And the more men on, the worse the odds become. Breakdown begets breakdown. Suddenly, it is the offense that can force defensive mistakes—with a steal, a bunt, a sacrifice, a hit-and-run. Hitters on the bench tell each other, "Get him out of his windup, then get him out of the game."

Of all the game's well-known strategists since the introduction of the lively ball in 1920, perhaps only one has stubbornly stuck with the one-run-at-a-time theory of baseball from dead-ball days.

That fellow, Gene Mauch, has the game's most perplexing record
—no pennants and twenty fourth-place-or-lower finishes in twenty-
two years. Certainly, current managers who have distinctive styles
have spun their theoretical webs around the assumption that explosive innings are vital—or, as Weaver, who hates the thought of
giving up an out with a sacrifice bunt or a "caught stealing," puts
it: "The answer is a single, a walk, and a three-run homer."
Tommy Lasorda, George Bamberger, Dick Howser, and Don Zimmer are men who build their teams, down to the twenty-fifth man,
with the idea of power preeminent.

The most improved team of the 1980 season was the New York
Yankees, thanks to Howser's commitment to the platoon home-
run power theory and the big-inning approach. "We're a slow
team," said Howser after the Yanks finished tenth in the AL in
runs in 1979. "We need more one-swing, then-trot innings."
Howser created a hidden sort of muscle by platooning lesser-
known high-homer-per-at-bat players at first base, left field, designated hitter, and, when injuries struck, almost any other position.
"All of a sudden, we looked just like Baltimore in '79," said Graig
Nettles, "when they had Roenicke-Lowenstein in left, May-Kelly
at DH, and nobody knew where all the homers [181] came from."
The Yanks hit 189 homers and led the majors with 103 victories
in 1980.

If baseball has seen a new tactical twist in the last fifteen years,
it is that the all-out baserunning blitz is consonant with big-inning power baseball. The most adamant proponent of "Lumber 'n' Lightning" is Pittsburgh's Chuck Tanner, whose 1976 Oakland A's stole 341 bases, while his 1979 world champion Pirates
had the game's best blend of speed and power throughout the
lineup. When they were in Cincinnati and Kansas City, Sparky
Anderson and Whitey Herzog believed that, in the era of Astroturf, taking the extra base on balls hit to the outfield opened the
floodgates.

The play-offs and World Series of the past several years have
been showcases for these styles. The 1975–76 Cincinnati Reds and
the 1977–78 New York Yankees mixed their homer power with so
many first-to-third singles that, at times, they seemed to be running a private relay race. Cincinnati did it with team speed.
"Teams get real sick of seeing us flying past second," bragged An-

derson. By contrast, the Yankees were deep in bat-control artists—Thurman Munson, Lou Piniella, Roy White, Willie Randolph, and even Mickey Rivers—who loved to hit-and-run or hit to the opposite field. The key is to have five or six players in the same lineup with similar, linked skills.

The result is to establish a sense of momentum, of increasing pressure on the defense. The motto: Get the most runs from the least base hits. By going first-to-third, or first-to-home on a double, you can score a run with one less hit than your opponent needs. Two singles and a sacrifice fly or ground out is an easier task than three hits.

Interestingly, Tanner, Anderson, and Herzog have been baseball's most conspicuous Captain Hooks—managers who embrace the idea that there is nothing sacrilegious about using three or four pitchers in *one* crucial inning. Tanner used his trio of Kent Tekulve, Grant Jackson, and Enrique Romo 250 times in '79. It took baseball a century to wise up, but once a blaze of base runners has begun, the best way to douse the flames may be with a bucket brigade of firemen.

The underlying assumption is simply this: After all the broad tactical groundwork of team building and game strategy has run its course, there remains the moment of truth with one pitcher and one hitter facing each other with the big inning at stake. "There's only one important thing in managing during a game," says Weaver. "When the crisis moments come, especially in the late innings, have you held back the right man for the right spot? Do you have your gun loaded for that one big shot, or did you pull the trigger too soon? On the other hand, if you wait *too* long, the game's over. You still got your key bench guys sitting next to you, and you ain't fired a shot."

In other words, with a runner dancing off third base and the game on the line, do you let Dauer hit against Stanley? Or do you send up Crowley and hope that Burgmeier can't get warmed up in time? Or do you get stuck with a .212 hitter named Sakata batting against an All-Star named Burgmeier?

The strategic grist of the 1979 Series was Weaver's sending his lefty-righty platoon of hitters against Tanner's bottomless store of relievers (including Don Robinson and even Bert Blyleven, as well as The Big Three).

One of the advantages of platooning, of building a team with many interchangeable parts is that it counteracts the use of overpowering specialty relievers. When a Goose Gossage or a Tekulve arrives, just wheel out the left-handed half of the platoon and you aren't so badly overmatched.

An ideal example was the eighth inning of the fourth '79 Series game when Tekulve came in with the bases loaded, only to find the Baltimore gun loaded—six runs worth. Lowenstein for Roenicke (2-run double). Smith for Dauer (intentional walk). Crowley for Skaggs (another bases-loaded double). Nobodies pinch-hitting for nobodies—but every one with the odds on his side. The side-arming Tekulve was neutered and Baltimore led, 3 games to 1.

But as the Series progressed, Tanner got better at catching Weaver in the platoon switches. The offense can flip-flop top-to-bottom only once—you have only enough bench people to load up once. But the defense can change pitchers—or, just as important, threaten to—many times to tilt percentages back its way.

"The problem," growled Weaver, as the Series slipped away, "is that, in a short series, they have so many good pitchers in their bull pen that you can't get the matchup you want as often. You don't even force them to make all the moves, *because you know they can.*"

The ninth inning of the seventh game was a textbook tactician's dream. In the top of the inning Weaver used five different pitchers against five consecutive Pittsburgh hitters in what seemed a defiant parody of the way the Bucs had lengthened their already long bull pen by using starters in relief.

But this was Tanner's night. Weaver had used all his big-inning trumps trying to build rallies in the seventh and eighth. Tanner had played right-left-right by summoning Robinson, Jackson, and Tekulve in relief of starter Jim Bibby. By the last of the ninth, Baltimore was helpless, out of moves. Right-handers Roenicke and DeCinces had to lead off the last inning of the season against the scythe-like Tekulve, a man neither could hit with a tennis racket. They both struck out, without so much as a foul tip. It was simply the curtain drop on a seven-act tactical play.

So now we have a feeling for baseball as a whole. But how do we focus on the specifics of this game, this day, this minute, so that we recognize its secret as it is happening? Or just before it happens?

Other sports have an impenetrable mystique. Baseball offers insights. Even as we are watching it, we can dissect the game, then reassemble it to a better-understood whole—with the simple scorecard. Or, at any rate, a slightly elevated form of it.

How you keep score means nothing. *Why* you keep score means everything. The texture of the game itself—its pace and flow, its strategies and hidden foreshadowings—is camouflaged within the scorecard. The observant fan does not decide on a cabalistic method of keeping score with an eye to digging the meticulous scribblings out of a box decades hence. Better than nostalgia is a note-taking system that helps light up the game in progress.

What trends and keys you study, and when you decide to make special notes, are the difference between a casual recorder of numbers and one who really sees. A typical ball game is primarily dead time begging to be condensed. Any game that has more than a dozen key moments is one whale of a game. Remember that the birth and death of rallies (the Big Bang Theory) are what separate the winners from the losers. Underline all outs that are made with two or more men on base, or with a man in scoring position. Then you and Joe Choke will be the only two people in the park who know he stranded ten men. Reggie Jackson once stranded nineteen runners in a 3-game series and nobody noticed until he mentioned it. Note with an asterisk all innings that end with that symbol of defeat—men left in scoring position.

(The importance of hitting in the clutch is so disproportionately vital that Seymour Siwoff of the Elias Sports Bureau has kept secret stats in recent years that he sells to some major league clubs. His computer breakdowns of players' performances in every at-bat of the season—average when batting leadoff, average with men in scoring position and less than two out, etc.—are an underground legend. Ask Siwoff about his private cottage industry and he will say, "What secret statistics?" Ask almost any major league general manager and he will talk about the trades—like Bill Madlock to the Pirates in '79—that were predicated on Siwoff's statistics.)

How does one value conventional statistics in light of the Big Bang Theory? For one thing, batting average is less meaningful

than on-base percentage, since on-base average is a far better indicator of a player's ability to foment or maintain a rally. Also,
slugging average grows in importance because it is the extra-base
hit that maximizes a rally.

The eternal game-within-a-game—pitcher versus hitter—is the
constant subject of scrutiny in the dugout. Consider: It is a rare
player, usually a marginal one, who cannot tell you every pitch
that has been thrown to him—in order—for the last week or more.
Ask Kansas City's George Brett, in the midst of a 51-for-100 batting tear in his .390 summer of '80, when he last swung and entirely missed a pitch, and he will say, "Last Saturday in New York
. . . Doug Bird . . . slider down and in . . . I got out in front
. . . top hand rolled over." Similarly, it is a rare pitcher who can't
recall all 120 pitches of the game—and the reason for each. Contrary to the conventional wisdom, major league players are *not*
casual about their craft. If anything, they are almost frighteningly
obsessional about detail. Situation, sequence, result: bottom of the
third, two on, fastball up and in, soft line single to left. That is
where they live, and have lived, since their first day in Pawtucket.

To really see the game, stop noticing *where* the pitcher is being
hit and concentrate on how *hard* he's being hit. Underline all
well-hit balls in a specific color (carry different color pens)—twice,
if they are crushed. Merely scanning the scorecard can show that a
pitcher working on a shutout has, in fact, lost his stuff and is living on borrowed time. Several seasons ago, Jim Palmer pitched a
one-hitter in which there were 14 hard-hit outs. His first voluntary
comment after the game was, "That was the worst one-hitter in
history. Those people had no idea what they were cheering."

One tactic, above all others, opens up this undisguised game.
Keep track of telltale pitches. Just as a game has a few crucial
plays, so it also has a limited number of crucial pitches. On the
normal ball park scorecard there are five seldom-used columns
marked "AB-R-H-RBI-E." Use them to keep track of the pitches
to each hitter. As soon as each player's time at bat is over (and
you're marking down "6-3" or "K"), write down the final count in
those unused columns. The only other time to make notations in
those columns is when the count reaches 0-2 or 2-0. Just put a
check mark in the appropriate box for 0-2, or an X if it's 2-0. If

those checks don't lead to victory, and the X's to big-inning doom, you just scored a game that was a fluke.

So what do you have? Nothing less than the total number of pitches thrown by each pitcher and his ratio of balls to strikes. (For fanatics only: Indicate a 2-strike foul ball with dots in the proper box.) You know who is taking or fouling off pitches and being a pain in the neck. And you've also identified the over-anxious chap who's made 4 outs on 5 pitches. In short, you've got a gold mine equal to the normal scorebook itself.

Why bother?

Quite simply, to acquire the ego-building illusion that you can sense what is unfolding better than anybody else. Enough even to get a pitch ahead of reality.

Players do it all the time. A sixth sense, somewhere between informed anticipation and eerie premonition, is one of baseball's charms, as well as the proper justification for its constant lulls. That slow tempo which maddens the philistine is an abundance of rich gaps that allow us inside the game. When the 1977 Red Sox hit 33 home runs in 10 games—a streak not even approached in baseball history—certain players were so "wired" that they could predict homers for certain others. "It wasn't anything vague, like 'Yaz'll hit one today,'" says Rick Wise, then a Sox. "It wasn't even enough to call the at-bat. You had to get the feeling and call the exact pitch. It got pretty spooky."

Last season, in a press box in Milwaukee, a reporter idly perused his cluttered scorecard. The Brewer starter, although leading 1–0, was being hit harder each inning as he fell behind on more and more counts. The reporter noted how Al Bumbry, in his first at-bat, had flied out to the left-field fence on a 2-0 fastball. He noticed that, thanks to six 2-strike foul balls by stubborn Rick Dempsey, the Brewer pitcher had thrown more pitches in getting one out in the sixth than he had in getting three outs in any other inning. The count was 2-0 on Bumbry again. The pitcher's curve was erratic. He had to throw a fastball from the stretch because runners were on base. The fuse had reached the dynamite. The press box was semi-asleep. The reporter nudged the Milwaukee chap next to him and said quietly, "This pitch. Left-field bleachers."

Bumbry hit the next pitch into the left-field bleachers while the clairvoyant was still dreamily pointing there. It wasn't a cure for cancer, but it was a nice moment.

The most important secret of baseball isn't fundamentals. Nor the way that keeping score—even every pitch—lets us watch those key at-bats with a special private anticipation. The most important secret of baseball is that we can get so close to the game's skin that we can hear it breathing.

Baseball's true secret is that, for those who appreciate and value it, it has no secrets.

April

How Baseball Helps the Harvest or What the Bay of Pigs Did to the Bigs

The sugarcane fields are ablaze in Pinar del Rio, their scorching sweet smoke rolling down the barrancas, a sign that the rich, hard weeks of harvest have come. Cuba has two obsessions, two sources of sustenance, two causes for annual celebration: sugar and baseball. Both have reached their season of fruition. Both are on fire now—cane by day, baseball by night.

"That's one sugar on Juan Castro," crackled the voice of Sala Manca, the baseball radio announcer for all Cuba. "The fish has bitten the hook."

From easternmost Point Maisi to the Isle of Pines in the west, perhaps half of Cuba's 9.6 million people are listening to Sala Manca's voice as he tells them in his rolling, idiomatic Spanish that the count on Juan Castro is 1 strike. In the batter's box in Pinar del Rio Stadium, Castro steps out. The bases are loaded and so is the air—with a crescendo of sound. Women beat on 20-gallon tin cans. Enormous air horns, outlawed as hearing hazards in the U.S., pierce the lush night. It takes three men to lift the largest horn. The leader of the trio is still in his cane-cutting field clothes with gaucho straw hat. He smokes a foot-long Cuban Hupman cigar and smiles blissfully. Banners flap above the Pinar dugout: "Juan Castro, with your home runs, you put rhythm back in the dance."

Castro fouled the second pitch into the crowd. "Two sugars on Castro," Sala Manca tells Cuba. "Now the fish is in the pan."

The crowd of 30,000 *beisbol fanaticos* filling every bench seat in the beautiful, spanking modern stadium, pleads with Castro. The precious foul ball that Castro had hit into the stands is thrown back into play. A soft ripple of cheers acknowledges the gesture, for baseballs, like many commodities here, are hard to come by. A man in white gloves—so that only clean hands will touch the ball —collects the *pelota* for future use. The moral mandate to return fouls is just one Cuban incongruity to northern eyes. All fans get in the stadium free—first come, first seated. Cows graze only a few feet away from the open stadium gates, and occasionally must be dissuaded from wandering into the park.

Once inside, the single-deck stadium offers no advertising, no ushers, no concessionaires, no hawkers, no pantyhose night, no exploding scoreboards, no inessential public-address announcements. The game is the only focus, and it is played quickly—usually in two hours or less. Strong, sweet hot tea is passed through the stands in small cups during the middle innings. A few drink Cabeza de Lobo—Wolf's Head—beer, but they do it surreptitiously. Baseball is thought to be sufficient inebriation for any Cuban.

The Havana manager, hoping to squeeze the 2-strike tension tighter around Castro's throat, calls a long mound conference with his pitcher, Juan Pedro Oliva, brother of former big leaguer Tony Oliva. The party caucus at the hill is enormous—six players and a manager. But Pinar del Rio shows Havana what a real conference is like: All three base runners, two coaches, the on-deck hitter, and the manager surround Castro at home plate, patting him on the back, giving advice. If Havana can have seven on the mound, Pinar can have eight at the plate.

Finally, all four umpires—dressed in outrageous raspberry suits so they look like four fat popsicles—congregate on the mound to break up a meeting that now seems to have enough members for a *coup d'etat*. Sala Manca tells the masses every detail. In the morning at 5 A.M., the laborers will be back in the cane fields stripping the burned leaves off the cane stalks with their machetes. Until sundown, they will work, often scrambling in mountainside fields. The baseball games at night are their release, their joy.

Sala Manca knows. The Cuban Government knows. "Baseball helps the harvest," says that other Castro, Fidel. "It is tied to the heart of our economy." When the "Game of the Night" has ended, Rebel Radio will flash around the island, picking up other games in progress until the last out in Cuba has been recorded.

"Will the fish be fried?" asks Sala Manca, as the huge conferences disperse. "Will it be three sugars on Castro?"

Castro lunges at a curve, catching it flush on the fat of his aluminum bat. CLANK! Although his swing was off balance, the lively metal bat and the even livelier Batos ball produce a soaring fly to the left garden. The white baseball hangs high in the constellation-filled Caribbean sky, flying toward the only two signs.

(One says, "Harder work produces better-quality tobacco" and is signed with one word, "Fidel." The other is a 40-foot-high mural of a local revolutionary.) Cuban crowds never make a mistake on flyballs. It is shameful to stand and scream for a flyball that dies at the warning track. Only Sala Manca is extended the privilege of doubt.

"*Se va, se va* [It's going, it's going]," he screams as an estimated 5 million Cubans listen. "*No se va* [It's not leaving]. *Se, se va* [Yes, it is]," he plays the cat-and-mouse game.

The crowd roars. The ball disappears over Fidel's name on the sign. Sala Manca cannot keep his secret any longer.

"Good-bye, my dear Lolita," he says, laughing to show that he knew it was a grand-slam home run all the time.

So no one cares that a marriage of an aluminum bat, a rabbit ball, and a short fence (345 feet to left-center) have combined to create this moment of madness. Cubans demand excitement, scoring, base stealing, strategy—therefore, all the conditions of the Cuban game promote offense. A 1–0 pitchers' duel is worse than cutting cane. Fans leave early en masse in disgust.

A grand slam like Juan Castro's produces a minute of near-national euphoria. All along the winding 200 kilometers of road from Pinar del Rio to Havana, people are in the streets, at gas stations, in front of diners, listening and cheering. This ball will not be returned by the children outside the stadium.

The noise in the Pinar del Rio stands is shattering. This has always been called the "Cinderella Province" because it has produced great athletes despite its rural spareness, its ancient housing, its legacy of brutal labor in the cane and tobacco fields. It has been a generation since the Vegueros (Green) had a champion. Good players, *si*. Island-wide supremacy, no.

Now they have a champion. When the youthful Pinar fuzzbeards (average age twenty-three) startled the nation by winning the eighteen-team Serie Nacional in March, there was a holiday in the province. Cane cutters, with their machetes raised, formed a phalanx of honor to escort the team into town. People rode horseback, the players stacked themselves on jeeps. Beer and rum and pork and dancing filled the streets all night.

On this night, the greeting for Juan Castro as he runs out his grand slam is a continuation of the same celebration. Pinar del

Rio has moved up into the rarefied air of the Serie Selectiva—the six-team national World Series when the stars of all eighteen provincial teams are consolidated. Beyond all expectation, Pinar now leads the Serie Selectiva, as well, holding a cane-stalk-thin 2-game lead over the menacing maroon-clads of Havana.

Before Juan Castro reaches second base, the entire Pinar team has exploded from its dugout and waits for him—not at home plate, but strung out the entire length of the third-base line. As soon as Castro's foot hits third, his hand is grabbed in the first of twenty-five soul shakes. At the plate, the three men who were on base wait with their arms linked around each other's shoulders. They are bouncing as they wait to give Castro his final embrace.

It is only the first inning.

It would dismay Cuba to think that any country could match its love for baseball. Relative to its population, this nation is convinced that neither the United States, Japan, nor any Latin neighbor is its equal in per capita frenzy—either in playing the game, watching it, or dissecting it. Baseball in Cuba is a unique three-part blend, as pungent as the land's omnipresent espresso coffee. That mixture is one part century-old tradition, one part artistic Latin temperament, and one part first-generation communism. No other country offers the old game in such a challenging and often perplexing form.

More than a hundred years ago an American Merchant Marine ship sailed into Matanzas Bay. On a hilltop overlooking one of the most breathtaking natural harbors in the Caribbean, the U.S. sailors planted a huge seed exactly the size of a baseball. On that hill above Matanzas, a town called "the Athens of Cuba" for the beauty of its setting, the islanders built their first baseball stadium, Palmar de Junco, and inaugurated it in 1874. Today, Palmar de Junco is a preserved relic, a museum, an academy for young players of the Matanzas province. During its first hundred years, the park played host to scores of legendary Cuban players from Adolfo Luque (194 major league victories) and Martin Dihigo (Hall of Fame), through Camilo Pascual and Minnie Minoso, down to the last prerevolutionary contingent that included Tony Perez, Mike Cuellar, and Luis Tiant.

One need look no farther than ancient Matanzas to discover the importance of baseball in Cuba under Fidel Castro. The town itself is as physically repulsive as its setting is magnificent. Public housing is Cuba's major embarrassment, and no better example than Matanzas need be looked for. The one-story row housing makes Appalachia look like a resort. The people in those houses, however, are fiercely dignified. The gutters are spotless and the children who pop out of the dismal doorways are like so many neat pins.

In the midst of this cramped world of narrow streets, tiny and overcrowded houses and antique U.S. automobiles of the '40s and '50s, rises the Estadio Victoria de Giron—a 30,000-seat memorial to Cuban baseball and to the American defeat at the Bay of Pigs. The park looks a bit like Chavez Ravine with a hint of the enclosed coziness of Fenway Park. That is to say, it is more pleasing to the eye than half the stadiums in the U.S. majors. And it also looks like it cost more to build than all the pinched houses in Matanzas.

Baseball may be the only facet of Cuban life that comes close to transcending politics. Other sports bear the stamp and rhetoric of a severely disciplined party line. There is an approved state way to do every push-up, and if a child anywhere in Cuba chins himself, there seem to be two adult trainers on hand to graph his progress.

Baseball, however, has a degree of autonomy. True, Cuban sportswriters have been instructed to stop using personal nicknames since the team, not the individual, is of primary importance. "We must help the people to learn to think collectively," says Cuban sportswriter Jose Luis Salmeron.

Also, Cuban pitchers who are yanked by their managers or players or who are called out wrongly by umpires show incredible restraint in sublimating their anger to respect for authority. Cuba's top hitter, Wilfredo Sanchez, was once called out by a "blind" umpire in Matanzas when he was safe by a yard, leaped high in the air, spun around, and made the psychic transformation from complete disbelief and fury to resigned composure before he returned to earth. He walked off the field without any show of displeasure except that four-foot vertical catapult when he first saw the umpire's thumb.

The contrast between crowd behavior in Cuba and in its spitting-distance neighbor, the rowdy Dominican Republic, is almost total. The Dominican Republic surpasses even Puerto Rico for incipient fan violence, fields ringed by police, and a suppressed sense of danger.

Cuban ball parks may be the only ones in the hemisphere that combine rabid partisanship, ferocious noise, and umpire baiting with a sense of total personal security. The crowd has its right to yell, "We are being robbed," and, "We are playing nine against thirteen." But when the ump has heard enough, he calmly raises a hand like a school principal and the sound turns off like a faucet. It is an impressive and somewhat unnerving sight. Even after a controversial game, the umpires walk slowly, face up, into the crowd, without a policeman in sight. The children throw harmless wads of paper . . . at their feet. Whatever subtle political and psychological realities may lie below the surface of baseball under Fidel, the exterior of the game is idyllic.

All the Cuban players must work at other jobs. Many also continue their schooling through their twenties. Members of the national team, which has won six of the last nine world amateur titles, supposedly work as dentists, accountants, dock workers, and the inevitable legion of physical education instructors.

No Cuban baseball player has publicly said he has any interest in U.S. major league money in twenty years. On the contrary, Cuban stars spit out the word "professionalism" like a curse. If their stream of pro patria words is said with anything other than considerable conviction, they are even better actors than athletes.

The unpaid Cubans say they play for pride, patriotism, incalculable public adoration, and government fringe benefits that would seem paltry to a Big Ten football player. Nevertheless, even more unusual than the Cuban players are the fans of every hue of pigmentation coexisting in the stands, without a hint of an argument, other than in jest. And without a gendarme, an usher, or any official personage in view.

Like the fans of Puerto Rico, the people of the Cuban provinces split their parks down the middle into cheering sections. But unlike Puerto Rico, they throw only words across the dividing line.

"I have no interest to play anywhere else," says Cuba's top hitter, Wilfredo Sanchez, thirty-one, whose .332 career average is the highest in Cuban history. "We give to the people and they give us back things that cannot be measured.

"We all await the day when we can play against the North American Great Leaguers. We know that they are better than us. We have much to learn from them. And perhaps they have things to learn from us. We have many stories to tell each other."

That is why the first week of April 1978 was a time of subdued mourning for Cuban baseball fans—in other words, the entire population. That was to be the occasion when the North American "Great Leaguers" would send the most magnificent team ever assembled to their island.

Finally, Sanchez—the lead-off man called "Hit-Fredo"—would get to bat against Nolan Ryan.

Cuba's astonishing boy manager, Servio Borges, who had already led the national team to six world amateur titles in a ten-year career that began at age nineteen, could match strategy with Billy Martin.

The Mr. Everything of the Pearl of the Antilles, nimble short-stop Rodolfo Puente, could draw his magic line in the box with his bat, from the right-front corner of the plate to his right toe. Would the Americans know what it means? Could Joe Morgan really be better than Puente?

El Gigante del Escambray—the Giant of the Mountains—the slugger known only by his last name, Munoz, could join forces in the power slots with two other muscle men known throughout Cuba by one-word names: Cheito and Marquetti.

Could the almost mythical catcher that this nation has never seen, Johnny Bench, stop the thefts of Vicente Anglada? And could the battalion of sluggers from the north intimidate the pitching staff of junk-balling southpaws in the Mike Cuellar mold, and side-arming righties with corkscrew deliveries like Luis Tiant?

Cuba, after an almost twenty-year wait since seeing its last Great Leaguers, was as prickly with anticipation as the ceiba tree. All 65,000 seats in Havana's Stadio Latinoamericano would be distributed free, on a merit basis, to the citizens judged by their local communities to be the best workers, revolutionaries, and comrades.

The people—who knew? perhaps a million strong—would gather in the Plaza de la Revolucion, between the marble statue of the poet-martyr Jose Marti and the grotesquely huge mural of Che Guevara, to inspire their players.

"Surely the Great Leagues cannot be afraid of losing," said top Cuban official Fabio Ruiz.

When the year comes that the United States and Cuba finally meet, in the sport that is the titular National Pastime of one, and the de facto national fanaticism of the other, both sides probably will have a shock. Cuban fans and players have little conception of the power of Stateside hitters and the speed of the best fastballers. Despite this, it is possible that a Cuban all-star team would be considerably better than the customary appraisal that Cuban teams are at the Triple-A level, at best. Put all squads together, and the Cuban national team would have excellent speed, defense, hitting-for-average, bunting, and relief pitching.

"We believe that the real quality of baseball is in the Great Leagues," Cuban Manager Borges says modestly. "Nevertheless, I would not agree to give a player-by-player analysis of my team. That is one advantage I should like to keep, should we ever meet. We know you far better than you know us."

Ironically, Cuba's best player, right-fielder Sanchez, is his country's most candid evaluator. "Most of our pitchers throw the fastball and curves. Nothing else," says Sanchez. "We know that pitchers in the Great Leagues throw sliders, screwballs, sinkers, knuckleballs, and other pitches. We have those here, too, but not as much."

Sanchez, one of four outstanding brothers, epitomizes the best of Cuban players, while also typifying the norm. The grinning, smooth-skinned Sanchez seems too young, too unpretentious, too funny, too free of cares to be the top star in a nation addicted to baseball for a century. Yet, it is characteristic that Cuban baseball stars carry their fame lightly.

"It is said that the Cuban team has exactly as many managers as there are people in the population," smiles Borges, the real manager of that team. "I try to apply the same rule that I give my players: You can only be a hero in relation to yourself, not to the demands of others.

"After every game," Borges says, with a grin, "I have nine and a half million people waiting outside the stadium who want to explain to me, for the good of Cuba, what I did wrong."

Sanchez is probably the best unknown player in the world—
unknown, that is, outside Cuba, where every child past diapers
knows that Sanchez:

- Has the highest career batting average in Cuban history, .332.
- Has won six batting titles.
- Is Cuba's first 2,000-hit man.
- Has a .388 lifetime average in international play as lead-off
hitter and top base thief.
- Once came within inches of starting the only quadruple play
in history (4 outs) with a great outfield catch.

"Yes, we almost got four legal outs on one play," Sanchez says,
laughing. "But as it turned out, I became the only man to start a
triple play which drove home the opposing team's winning run."

That near-quadruple play, certainly the most spectacular unknown play ever, captures the central threads of current Cuban
baseball—recklessness, speed, superb defense, and fascination with
rules and strategy.

The 4-out play, explained, becomes stunningly simple to baseball aficionados and stays forever unintelligible to the rest of
humanity. Any Cuban school child, for instance, could explain it.

With the bases loaded, none out, tie game, Sanchez made a remarkable catch in right-center field. The runners on first and second bases ran on the line drive up the gap, and were trapped far
off their bases as Sanchez pegged to second and the relay was fired
to first. Triple play: one flyball caught, two runners doubled up.

Meanwhile, however, the alert runner on third base had tagged
up and crossed home plate before the final (third) out at first
base. Since the final out was not a force play, the run counted.

Here, the play takes on what might be called The Cuban Di-
mension. The manager of Sanchez' team appealed the runner's
tagging up at third, claiming that he had left the base a split second before the catch.

Few managers would know that such an appeal play could result in a legitimate fourth out, thus nullifying a vital run. Except,
that is, in Cuba where even the hounds lying in the road would
know.

In the confusion, one umpire signaled that *fourth* out, while
the others upheld the run. Finally, the run was upheld, and it cost
Sanchez' team (Matanzas) the game, 3–2.

"Such a play would severely test my theory of managing," says Borges. "Even if, inside, you are like a volcano, you should be like a serene lake on the outside. You must be inexpressive because what you reflect penetrates the others. What I do," he says, with a mischievous smile, "is pull out my hairs one by one from under my cap when the players are not looking. I will be also the youngest bald manager."

Borges' position in Cuban sports life is an apparent incongruity on the surface. He wears jeans, an old "Cuba" zipper jacket, tennis shoes, and a '50s hair style that makes him look like a slightly tougher Sal Mineo stepping straight out of West Side Story.

Yet Borges is not merely the manager of the national baseball team, but the Director of Sports for the entire country, a mammoth job of coordinating programs in a score of sports in fourteen provinces. Over half-a-million Cubans play some form of organized baseball, and almost all are in some way under Borges' young eye.

The boyish figure in blue jeans sits in a marble-and-mahogany office worthy of any oil company executive. The signs on the doors speak of "people's committees" and the like, but it is obvious that Borges is the man who can put his sneaker up on this desk anytime he wants.

When Borges speaks he seems even more incongruous. "I was a bad player myself, so it will be no surprise if I also become a bad manager," he says. "No hit, no field, and now no manage." But in a moment he turns serious. "I do not think that sport is like art," he says, "I think that sport *is* art. Every sportsman becomes a creator in every act.

"We deal with techniques that might need scientific and mathematical study. That is one side. Cuba makes strides every day melding science and sport. We use computers to study motion and angles of stress and maximum techniques. But we must also find a way for emotion and inspiration to conjugate themselves with art. We cannot be robots. Science, art, and inspiration," he says, lifting a marble cube on his desk and revolving it in his fingers to look at the various sides. "Those are the components."

Borges begins to laugh at his own philosophizing. "We must not make sport too difficult," he says. "Take the signs of a baseball team—steal, bunt, hit-and-run. It is much better for both teams to know the signs, than for neither team to know them."

Borges and Sanchez are both first-generation products of Fidel Castro's fiercely competitive athletic meritocracy based on the double dictum: "Sports is the right of the people," and "I cannot conceive of a young revolutionary who is not also an athlete."

On that day when America's Great Leaguers finally find their way to the elephantine Stadio Latinoamericano here, they will be met by a tangled nexus of baseball fever and radical political fervor. The Benches and Jacksons need look no further than the ball park itself to see the juxtaposition. The grandstand has 35,000 prerevolution seats which look like a block of Cleveland's sprawling old Municipal Stadium. The outfield is ringed by 30,000 modernistic bleacher seats built by "voluntary" workers' cadres in the twenty-first-century style of Anaheim.

The major leaguers also need not worry too long about bringing back a Sanchez with his name on a contract. "Why would I want to leave my country," says Sanchez, disbelievingly. "The last time Americans came to my province it was the CIA landing at the Bay of Pigs. When we captured them, they all said they were cooks.

"That was long ago. Now even we think that is funny. When the Great Leaguers come, we will welcome them and be their cooks. We hold no hard feelings."

Wilfredo Sanchez smiles to himself. This blazing light shining under a bushel in the Caribbean, has, like many others, planned his welcome for the Great Leaguers for many years, slowly cooking, cooking. This profound desire to see the Great Leaguers in the flesh is only redoubled by the fact that all word of the capitalist majors has, ostensibly, been kept out of Cuba for two decades. Those here who remember America's Hall of Famers, or played against them, are revered like venerable saints.

Take Connie Marrero.

The old Washington Senator pitcher takes a drag on his black cigar and looks down at the tips of his bowling shoes. "To Mickey Mantle, you must keep the hard slider inside and up," says the senior citizen Marrero, as though both he and Mantle were about to meet once more in Yankee Stadium. Marrero jams the cigar in his mouth and imitates Mantle's compact stance. "Too many muscles in the arms and shoulders," says Marrero, demonstrating how Mantle's swing often swept underneath Marrero's nasty slider.

"That's left-handed," says Marrero, holding up his stogie between two fingers as his young Matanzas pitchers listen with eyes wide. "If you throw him that pitch when he bats right-handed, he will hit it on the roof.

"Curves low and away right-handed," said the shrunken, white-haired man, snapping his meat hook of a right hand with its cigar-thick fingers in the curveball motion.

Marrero's eyes snapped like his fingers. "I always had the good luck with Mantle. But Ted Williams . . ." he shook his head. "When you talk of Williams, you must stop the conversation." The Matanzas players—infants when Williams retired—nodded in agreement.

"The first time I pitched to Williams, in 1950," said Marrero, flying back half a lifetime in a blink, "he fouled off two sliders and I struck him out on a knuckleball."

Marrero grinned. "Theodore hates the knuckleball . . . and the slider. But he learned to hit them, anyway. In Boston, he hit two home runs off me in one game. One slider. One knuckleball. After the game, he put his arm around me under the stands and said, 'This was my day.'"

"I told Williams," said Marrero, "every day is your day."

This is the way Cubans talk about the game they love far more than any other—with patiently told tales and infinite detail. This, sadly, is the way they can no longer talk about the Great Leagues.

"We have little information," said Marrero, pitching coach for Matanzas, with a resigned air. "How is my friend Bucky Harris?" he asked of his manager for all five Washington seasons.

"He is dead," Marrero is told.

"Si, si," said Marrero. He expected as much. Like most Cuba baseball lovers, Marrero has cut "North America" out of his heart so that it cannot haunt or hurt him.

But the old stories, all antedating the 1959 revolution, he will not give up. Young Cuban players can see Mantle and Williams and Willie Mays in their sleep. Members of the older generation have passed down their lore, their idiosyncracies, even their batting weaknesses.

After all, this nation worships subtlety in its baseball. Marrero was once given a standing ovation for his windup. The crowd was on its feet cheering Marrero's head-bobbing gyrations before he ever released the pitch.

"That's true, that's true," said Marrero. "It is easy to teach the curve, impossible to teach brains. I still pitch batting practice and fool them. I smoke these cigars," he said, "to keep my arm young."

Cuba has two distinct baseball generations: one that remembers and one that does not. It is easier for the youngsters, the first-generation revolutionaries, who can say with the conviction of lifelong acculturation, "We have no interest to play in the Great Leagues or to know more of them. We are doing the work of the revolution. We love it."

But for those over forty, the words and the facial expressions that go with them are more ambivalent. The tug of the Great Leagues is still there.

"This was a good time of day for me," remembered Marrero, standing in Matanzas Stadium at dusk. "I would stand in the tunnel behind the plate where they would not notice me, and watch the Yankees take batting practice. If you watch long enough, suddenly it comes to you . . . the pitch they do not like, the sequence that will deceive them, the pitch they love to swing at but do not hit well."

"I have lived two lives," said Andres ("Papo") Liano, called "The Torpedo" a decade ago when he had the best record in Cuba (13-2), including a no-hitter. "One before the revolution and one after." In that first, Liano lived for baseball, even working his way up to an expense-paid visit to the States to try out for the Giants. Those were free and easy days. "The great hitter, Don Miguel Cuevas, kept a notebook on every pitcher in Cuba. He wrote down every pitch he ever saw," said the gentle Torpedo. "So one day the pitchers stole his book and it was passed all over the country until every pitcher had read what Cuevas had said of him.

"It did not help at all. Cuevas knew everything about us, but had written down nothing whatsoever about himself."

Now, in his second life, Liano is associate director of the 2,000-student Sports Academy in Havana, the institute that is to be a model for sports schools in all fourteen Cuban provinces. "We grew up swimming in a muddy hole and playing baseball with sticks and rocks," said Liano, looking at the enormous new institute for which he is the No. 2 man, with 169 coaches teaching twenty-five sports. "No one could ever have imagined this . . . a school where talented children come when they are eight years old and stay until university."

Lazaro Perez was the first great Cuban player to reach his peak just as the northward flow of Cuban baseball players was cut off by Fidel Castro after the Bay of Pigs. For fifteen years, Perez caught every game for the Cuban national team that has not lost in the prestigious Pan-Am games since 1967. Of all Cuba's players, Perez is known for his inspirational play away from Cuban soil. "It is better," Perez said, "to have the enemy right there in front of you. It is hard to drive yourself to the fullest against your countrymen. Yes, I am what you call a 'clutch hitter.' "

The measure of Perez' tangled fascination and antipathy for the Great Leagues is his fierce desire for one exhibition against the Nortamericanos before he retires. "I have never wanted to sell myself for money," he said proudly. "But I have waited for years to play against the professionals." Perez touches a tuft of white hair that has sprung up on his forehead like a spot marking a Thoroughbred horse. "The fastballs of the years have done this," he said. "I don't think there is much of me left. At last, I am feeling old. But for one game against the Yankees," he said, not distinguishing if that is a team or a nation, "I might still be young."

The Cubans who migrated toward the Yankee dollar right after the revolution are viewed with a mixture of wry contempt and not entirely open-handed forgiveness. "Dagoberto Campaneris and Rigoberto Fuentes were the last two," said Juan Ealo, the legendary former Cuban manager, using those players' full names, not the Americanized "Campy" and "Tito." "We were playing in Costa Rica on the day of the Bay of Pigs attack [Cubans call it 'Victory of Giron'], and American scouts offered three players contracts," said Ealo. "Both Campaneris and Fuentes were young, second-string players. They knew no better and they left. But our best pitcher, Joe Mitchell Pineda, understood that you do not sign yourself away to a country at the very instant when they are invading your homeland."

Ealo paused in a story that may or may not be embellished at the edges. "I still have Pineda's unsigned contract framed on my wall at home."

Both Campaneris and Fuentes have returned to Cuba in recent, more relaxed, years to visit their families. "I spoke to Fuentes on the phone before he returned," chuckled Manuel Gonzales, head of the international amateur baseball governing body, IBA. "I told him, 'I understand that since you have gone to America you now wear eight rings on your fingers and have your hair in braids. If you return to Cuba with your rings and braids, your father will choke you.'"

Gonzales munched on his cigar. "Fuentes returned with his hair cut and no jewelry. It was a wise decision."

It is a point of honor in Cuba to show a lack of interest in the Great Leagues. Nevertheless, Cuban knowledge of American players is enormous when it is considered that virtually all information is by word of mouth. Cuban TV, radio, and the official newspaper, *Granma*, report not a word about the majors.

Reggie Jackson's home runs, Nolan Ryan's strikeouts, Joe Morgan's multiple gifts are all familiar knowledge, although the names are all given hallucinatory Spanish pronunciations. Burt Hooton becomes Bob Houston, and Joe DiMaggio can become absolutely anything.

"You see, we are kept well informed," said Cuban sports reporter Jose Luis Salmeron, recounting Jackson's three home runs. But the U.S. baseball information is only skin deep, even with the most passionate fans. Bruce Sutter and his new pitch, the split-finger fastball, fascinate the manager of the Cuban national teams. "We must find out about this new weapon," he said. "Are the American hitters plotting to murder him?"

Perhaps the unsurpassable symbol of the love-hate relationship that Cuba's over-forty fans feel toward the Great Leagues is a nervous, wizened gentleman named Edel Casas. Casas is seen as one in an endless series of proofs that Cuban socialism can overcome any obstacle in one-upping North America. Edel Casas is Cuba's one-man library on baseball history—American or Cuban.

No American trivia expert could surpass Casas on the genuinely trivial. He knows the date of every well-known American baseball happening from Johnny Vander Meer's no-hitters to how many thirds of an inning Walter Johnson pitched in the World Series of 1924 and 1925.

Each day, he studies the Agence France-Presse reports so he can stay current. "Ask Campanera [comrade] Casas *anything*," smiled Cito Perez, director of sports propaganda.

The human library blinked and smiled. "Ah, Washington," Casas said. "Only one world championship." And he is off and running, reciting events before his birth. At last, Walter Johnson has won on Earl McNeely's hit. Casas stops his recitation.

"Wonderful, wonderful," everyone tells him.

"McNeely's bad-hop hit struck a famous pebble," Casas is told. "Washingtonians say they would bronze that pebble if anyone had been able to find it. Was that pebble in front of first, second, or third base?"

Casas seems justifiably hurt by such a sneaky, such a trivial question. "Second base," he says, tentatively. And, of course, incorrectly.

"Marvelous," he is told. "That's right."

The little middle-aged man relaxes. His performance cannot trip him up in front of his superiors.

"I want very much for the United States and Cuba to have an exchange of games," he says.

"You see, I have never seen an American Great League game with my own eyes."

All of Us Bear the Marks of the Lash

If baseball will give Washington no Opening Day, then let us declare one for ourselves.

Once, Opening Day lived here. It was Washington's World Series, the capital city's bonus Christmas. For one afternoon a year, Washingtonians were first citizens of the baseball state, while the rest of America waited to be franchised.

The presidential inaugural was the dawn of the year's better half—a cherry blossom declaration of independence from winter, a springtime bill of baseball rites. It was a holiday too rich to do without, so let's not. If we cannot have a fresh first pitch, then let us relive the last one.

Turn back the clock to April 5, 1971—the date of the last real Opener. All since have been ersatz.

Look at that strange extinct species—the Washington Senator box score. The names—Frank Howard, Mike Epstein, Dick Bosman, Paul Casanova—still have an eerie freshness, since no other names have pushed them from the heart.

Instead of an Opening Day of pomp, let us have one of candor. It is impossible to slander the dead, so let us exhume the Nats and let them tell us who they really were, now that they feel free —released by time or retirement—to tell larger pieces of the truth.

What was that Opening Day, and that last Senator team, truly like? And what have the years since brought the former Nats?

The nine players in that starting lineup have scattered like a supernova explosion. Among them they seem to have covered the gamut of baseball and life experiences.

"All of us bear the marks of the lash," said Epstein.

The two Nats most opposite in character—Curt Flood, the brooding Othello of his sport, and Paul Casanova, the game's ebullient man-child—have both gone through bankruptcy, deep bitterness, and expatriation.

Flood has emerged scared and wary—a living witness to what happens to rebels. His Supreme Court lawsuit opened the floodgates of free-agency, but he has tasted not one dollar of it.

Casanova runs a disco in Caracas, Venezuela, and still shows American visitors the scar on his elbow, saying, "My throwing arm is better now. I can still play."

Yet another Nat—Joe Foy—has survived both alcohol and drugs. Now, his once-formidable baseball talent wasted, he finally lives the straight life—attending college and counseling wayward children in the South Bronx.

On the other hand, two Nats quit baseball on their own terms, hanging up their spikes before the game could can them—Tim Cullen and Epstein. Both have become far greater success stories in the business world than they ever were in baseball.

"I couldn't be making more money if I were Jim Rice," said Epstein. "After baseball, business has been a reprieve."

Both then and now, the most closely observed actor in the cast is Frank Howard, the 6-foot-7 former manager of the San Diego Padres.

"A lot of guys from that old Senator team are watching Frank real closely to see when he gets a managing job," said Bosman, who now works for an automobile dealership in the Washington suburbs.

"They may see him as a ticket back to the majors as a coach," said Bosman. "I'm not one of them.

"When you shut the door on baseball, you have to keep it closed or it will never let you go. You just gotta go with the cards left in your hand even if you're not crazy about them. You look at 'em. You play 'em."

That is the long, hard lesson that almost every man from that Opening Day lineup must face continually with each passing year.

☆ *Toby Harrah* ☆

No Senator remembers that last Washington Opener with half the clarity of the leadoff man—Toby Harrah. It was his first major league game.

"I can remember the entire lineup," said Harrah, and he does, rattling off numbers one through nine in order

Harrah's debut came on one of those perfect days for a rare Senator triumph, an 8–0 shutout of the Oakland A's, who would go on to win 101 games. It was a day when everything worked out properly. The sun shone, the stadium was full, Richard Nixon couldn't make it.

"I got a hit off Vida Blue and scored the first run of the season. You know, to this day, I still wear out Vida Blue," said Harrah, now going bald but still beaming at the memory. "That was some thrill for a kid who still carried Mickey Mantle's picture around in his wallet.

"I couldn't believe I was playing shortstop for that team. You know, I'd made 52 errors at Burlington the year before . . . threw everything hard as I could. No one expected me to make the team," said Harrah.

"I looked around me and there was Denny McLain who had won 31 games and Frank Howard who could hit a ball farther than any man alive, and the manager, Mr. [Ted] Williams. Jeez, it still gives me a kick.

"Washington was such a beautiful city in the spring. It's still my favorite town. I had so many relatives come visit me that summer that I could have passed for a guide. I took 'em all to the museums and art galleries and to that big graveyard across the river. You know, I'd go out there to watch the changing of the guard."

Harrah, from rural La Rue, Ohio, may have been the all-time appealing green rookie. "He was just a wide-eyed country kid . . . lost at the plate," recalled Bosman. "Every time he threw to first, it was an adventure. You wondered if it would go eighteen rows up in the seats or hit you on the pitcher's mound."

To Harrah, that adventure was pure joy. "What a great team to break in on . . . it's the most fun I ever had on any club. We really communicated. I remember that before our first road trip to New York, Tim Cullen came up to me and taught me how to tie a necktie. I didn't know."

Harrah learned everything as quickly and compulsively as he did the double knot. Each year, he improved dramatically until, by the end of '77, he was generally considered the best shortstop in baseball.

"I hit 27 dingers [homers], drew 109 walks, drove in 95 runs . . . sure I was the best in the game," said Harrah, just talking facts. "People didn't have much choice but to say it was me. The numbers said so."

Then came the crash. In 1978, he and his wife, whom he married two weeks after that '71 Opener, were divorced. "Knowing how Toby takes everything to heart," said Bosman, "I assume that explains his bad year [.229]."

Harrah, who moved to third base in the 1978 season, has since been traded to the Cleveland Indians.

"I pity Toby," said Bosman, a former Indian. "That town will beat you down. It's a tough place to get yourself back together. God, what a hideous ball park . . . The Dungeon, we called it . . . The Mistake by the Lake."

"I'll make it," said Harrah, who has leveled off as a steady veteran. "I've learned that you can never stop believing in yourself in this game . . . because you're the only one that does."

☆ Curt Flood ☆

For Curt Flood, nothing is more painful than thinking back to April 1971. It is like asking the survivor of a shipwreck to recount his weeks adrift in a lifeboat.

"Pressure," he said softly. "Pressure and tension . . . that's what I remember. It was tough. I had been out of the game for over a year because of my lawsuit against baseball and the reserve clause. That spring was a big year for me, the first chance I'd had to play.

"I knew all along that those few weeks were the time that was going to decide whatever was going to happen to me right down to this moment, actually," said Flood.

Flood, dressed all in black that spring, was a solitary Hamlet-like figure—one slender, rusty, center fielder standing against a century of baseball tradition. Not one other player in baseball took his side. Like a leper, he was not vilified, simply avoided.

Flood only returned to baseball from Denmark because owner Robert Short's contract offer of $110,000—half of it in advance—offered some hope of keeping his head above water financially.

But, two weeks after that Opening Day, Flood had given up hope. His court case had suffered another defeat and would have to be appealed to the Supreme Court—more expense. His wife was seeking support for their five children—an expense he could no longer meet. And his batting average had sunk below .200. His spirits were far lower.

Flood fled to Madrid, later tended bar for more than a year on the island of Majorca.

"After I went back to Europe, I had plenty of time over the years to think about whether I gave up on my comeback too soon," Flood says now. "I'm sure I was right. Those young kids were running all over me."

Now, Flood, born in 1938, looks older than his years. He is frequently on the defensive, as though questioners were trying to catch him in some innocent mistake to make him look a fool.

During the 1979 season, he returned to the baseball scene briefly as a radio color announcer for the Oakland A's—a bizarre connection since owner Charlie Finley is the No. 1 victim of the free-agent system that Flood helped create.

"You seldom see a man's basic character change, especially a strong character like Flood, a genuinely thoughtful rebel," said Epstein. "But when you see Curt Flood today, you see a man who has been tied to the mast and has taken one lash too many."

That is as close to a candid comment on Flood as anyone on the baseball scene is likely to make. His continued financial precariousness, in an age of free-agent millionaires, is a bitter irony that cuts several ways.

Despite all his suffering for his convictions, Flood at least has the solace of seeing that his ideal of justice triumphed—although he speaks very softly on that subject, too.

"I believe that free agents have helped the game," he said. "It was the only equitable thing, that everyone get a fair share. Someplace along the line in baseball history, the people on the field, the actual entertainers, had to be included in the picture on a fair basis.

"I don't blame the owners for trying to keep a lock on their game. Maybe I would have too, in their position.

"It took baseball a long time to realize who the people were who were the source of the profits."

Then Flood grows quiet, tries to think back to his last Opening Day. "I don't even remember whether we won or lost," he said. "I just remember the strain.

"You say the President wasn't there that day? Well, if the President didn't come, why was I there?" It is a subdued, intellectual's wry joke. But it is good to hear Curt Flood laugh once more.

☆ *Hondo* ☆

"When I think of the old Nats, I'll always think of Hondo," said Bosman. "He was that team.

"I don't remember him leading the league in homers and RBIs [44 and 126 in '70]. I remember some darn foul ball landing in the upper deck and there's Frank Howard running into the left-field railing chasing after it. Some people laughed at that kind of hustle. Well, that's just the way the man lived and played. Put him on my team every day . . . give me the guy that dies with every defeat.

"When you looked at Hondo, you said to yourself, 'Take a lesson.'"

No figure, not even that of Williams, was as dominant on those Senator teams as the Washington Monument.

"We were all castoffs, all of us scrapping," recalled second baseman Cullen. "It was Frank who set the tone. He's the reason we were always a hustling, close-knit team . . . even when we were lousy, we played the game right."

"We always had a few guys on those Washington teams that weren't playing with a full deck . . . especially that last team after all the crazy trades," says Howard now. "And, brother, I was one of 'em."

If the Nats played hard on and off the field, the Gentle Giant was the prime mover.

"I had to cook for that son-of-a-gun," said roommate Bosman. "We'd have four guys at the table for a noon breakfast and Hondo'd say, 'Bozzie, why don't ya throw on about eighteen eggs and six or eight steaks.'"

When Bosman served the Bunyanesque breakfast, Howard would insist, "Now you guys take all you want . . . hey, take some more now . . . okay, everybody got enough?"

Then Howard would simply take the main serving bowls and eat whatever was left—usually the bigger half.

"I'll never forget," said Bosman, "he'd always finish by saying, 'Anybody doesn't want one of them steaks, you just flop that thing over here on my plate. The big boy might have to crank out another one [home run] tonight.'"

Perhaps the only Nat with mixed feelings about Howard is Epstein, who played in his shadow and, some Nats say, could not help being jealous.

"I remember one of those congressional baseball games when some representative from Oregon was in the locker room talking to everybody," said Epstein.

"He'd say, 'Hello, Big Mike, how ya doing? Where's big Hondo?'

"So there's Hondo sitting in the corner smoking, and the congressman goes over and slaps him on the back and says, 'How are you doing, Big Frank? I'm Joe Blow from Oregon.'

"And Hondo turns around, kind of caught by surprise, and says, 'Glad to meet ya. I'm Frank Howard from Ohio State.'"

Epstein paused, shaking his head. "To me, that's Frank. He was always s-o-o-o-o concerned about being nice to people . . . going more than halfway to make them feel good. But sometimes Frank was so concerned about being a nice guy that he wouldn't hear what you were saying. He'd miss the whole other half of the conversation.

"We had an ex-relief pitcher come by the clubhouse one day and Howard said, 'How are ya doing?'

"And the guy answers, 'Well, my wife's in the hospital.'

"But Hondo doesn't hear him. He just says, 'Good, good, glad ta hear it.'

"Then the guy goes on about how he's out of work and you're afraid he's going to jump off a bridge, and Hondo keeps right on saying, 'Good, good. Great to see you.'"

Howard, by contrast, has only fond memories of Epstein, pointing out the high expectations that burdened him and the first baseman's chronically bad eyesight.

Howard, typically, even goes out of his way to praise Williams' managing, which drew few raves.

What about the modern player with his multiyear contract—can he play as Howard once did?

"Well, that's the one thing you do wonder about," he said. "Not the ability."

☆ *Mike Epstein* ☆

Once, while walking through a Boston hotel lobby, the late Nat coach Nellie Fox spotted a painting of a sad clown holding a base-ball bat.

"That," said Fox, "is Mike Epstein after we have gotten our butts kicked, 15-2, but he has gone three for four."

"No truer words were ever spoken," said Bosman, remembering the incident. "There was always a lot of serious bad-mouthing of Epstein by the rest of us. He could never accept his role on a team. He always thought of himself as the star, even though he wasn't. He couldn't accept the fact that he had to be platooned against left-handers and had to be taken out for defense.

"There just wasn't a whole lot positive about the guy . . . you always felt that ego.

"When he was traded to Texas, he said he wasn't signing until they moved in the fences. I can remember him on road trips. Everybody else slept till noon. He'd be up walking the streets at six A.M. or reading a philosophy book. He was just goofed up."

As Epstein, a graduate of Berkeley, might say, "*de gustibus non disputandem est.*" Or, there's no disputing taste.

"I never thought of myself as a ballplayer. I would never allow myself to," said Epstein, who lives with his wife and three children in San Jose, California. He owns a yacht and has a hand in so many businesses—real estate, manufacturing companies, cattle ranches—that he has to slow down to list them accurately.

"There is a crossover point, a real juncture, where you stop thinking of yourself as yourself and start thinking of yourself as a ballplayer," said Epstein.

"In another field, that might be acceptable, but baseball is transient. You know it from the first day. It's too easy to become trapped by living high on the hog. I never let myself become suited to the baseball life.

"I've seen it happen to a good friend of mine—Ken Holtzman. I once told him, 'Kenny, you sound just like a damn scared ball-player, worrying about how's my arm and what will I do if I can't make a comeback.' You can't let the game destroy your independence and self-reliance."

Epstein is such an oddity among baseball players—a slugger who was a guide on Wyoming antelope hunts in the off-season and had a passion for flying planes—that he says, "Yes, people looked at me like something of a Martian. When I was in the minors [where he was named Player of the Year], I threatened to sue my [parent] team [Baltimore] for a million dollars if they didn't trade me. I guess it started then."

Despite that distance that he fought to keep, Epstein says, "It's hard to call your baseball days memories because they are so vivid. They almost cut you. You never get on the same interpersonal plane with people that you did in baseball. Sometimes when I meet guys I played with, I get to laughing and storytelling until the tears come to my eyes. I know I'll never get on that level with a group of people again."

For Epstein, the Washington years were bad years. "Hunters say that the only interesting guns are accurate," said Epstein. "Perhaps the only interesting teams are champions. Most of my good memories seem to be from my two years in Oakland."

Epstein's Senator torment was his tag of "unlimited potential."

"First day in spring training with Williams, he's walking around with his entourage of eighty writers . . . you know, letting the world know that Teddy Ballgame is back . . . and I hit six batting-practice pitches in a row into the palm trees.

" 'That's my prodigy,' said Williams. 'That Epstein ought to hit forty homers a year.'

"From then on, I always felt that nothing I did was enough. People compared me to Mickey Mantle, and I knew I couldn't carry his jock. When I was playing, nothing was ever good enough for me. I probably tried too hard for my own good.

"Now I finally have perspective. I realize I was really a bear-down guy. How much better could I have been?

"You can't get more out of yourself than there is in you. I wish now that I could have been more loose, that I could have opened up more. But it always seemed like somebody else was riding the crest of my wave. At thirty-one, I finally said, 'The hell with it.' "

That was the best move of Epstein's life. "Business turned out to be my talent. I am my own self-limiting person now. In baseball, I wasn't the controlling factor."

Although Epstein says he is now "financially established for the rest of my life," he still maintains that "baseball was the hardest thing I ever tried to do. Everything after it has been easy by comparison."

Oddly, the one Senator that Epstein says, "had one of the most dramatic effects on my life," was Williams.

"He didn't teach me about hitting," said Epstein. "He taught me about life. Ted showed me what it meant to totally commit yourself to excellence. Ted was like one of those toy robots that keep walking into the wall, backing up, then banging into that wall again."

☆ *Joe and Denny* ☆

Of all Bob Short's reclamation projects, all his attempts at salvaging what he called "damaged goods," Joe Foy and Denny McLain were the most extreme examples.

Both arrived in the spring of '71 with big question marks. Both had been sent to psychiatrists—Foy by previous clubs, McLain under orders from Commissioner Bowie Kuhn after it was revealed that he carried a gun and consorted with bookmakers and borderline underworld figures.

They were absolute contrasts in that weird Senator clubhouse—McLain the center of every controversy, Foy the loner in the corner.

"I wish Joe Foy well," said Bosman. "I hope he's alive. I never saw a guy with so many undertones of a lost soul. There was a lot of good in the guy, basically, but he traveled with such a bad crowd that at first I was afraid of him.

"When he came to us, we knew he had problems. His career was obviously on the fence. You'd see the people who met him at the clubhouse door and you'd say, 'Good Lord, there can't be much good in those folks.'

"Hondo and I tried to encourage him to straighten up, but . . . I'll always remember Joe Foy as this tremendously talented guy sitting on a locker stool smoking a cigarette and looking at everybody out of the corner of his eye. And all the time the talent just dripping away from him."

Foy's slide into first, alcoholism, then drugs, was doubly painful because he left in his wake a succession of people, like Epstein, who swear, "He was really a great guy. We were both from the Bronx and we had a lot to talk about."

"Joe had a likable temperament when he was with the Red

Sox," remembered one Boston official. "He was the only black guy on our AAA team, but he'd look up in the stands in the wives section and say, 'Guess which one I'm married to.'

"One night we were greeted at the airport by five thousand people during the Impossible Dream of '67, and all the players were afraid of the crowd, asking where the police were. Joe Foy stood up with this wonderful kid's grin and said, 'Take me to my people.'"

"Joe's problem was just that old peer-group pressure," said Elliott Maddox. "I always liked him, but there was nothing to do for him."

Now, nothing needs to be done for him. Foy, with the help of two brothers who are New York City policemen, has not only beaten his problems, but has been counseling kids in his home town. He is a regular at Yankee Stadium, bringing caravans of neighborhood children with him to the ball park. He is also a student at Lehman College in the Bronx, a four-year liberal arts school.

It cannot be said that McLain's non-baseball trip has been as successful.

"You have to talk about two people—Denny on the mound and Denny off it," said Bosman. "I couldn't help but like him, he was such a riverboat gambler. He was born to go out on that mound and set up hitters to make fools of themselves.

"McLain had more savvy and guts than a whole staff of pitchers. A guy would hit one eighteen miles foul in the upper deck, and McLain would start talking to him and cussing him, and he'd strike him out on the same pitch.

"But you should have seen him and Williams. The sparks flew from day one. If one guy said it was light, the other would call him a liar and say you couldn't see the hand in front of your face.

"One day, Denny was getting killed. The infielders were catching 'em out of self-defense and the outfielders had to get oxygen between innings," said Bosman.

"Well, Ted yanks him and McLain coming in yells about, 'What is all this six-inning shit!'

"McLain goes down the tunnel cussing and Ted's right after him. The whole bench followed 'em down the runway just to watch. They stood toe to toe and screamed for five minutes.

"After that, Ted left him out there to dry up and flake away a few times."

McLain was also the founder of The Underminers, a fraternity complete with initiation ceremonies, that was half-seriously dedicated to undermining Williams' authority.

"I met McLain years later," said Maddox, "and we both started yelling, 'Hey, come here, you Underminer.'"

That sight of the 6-foot McLain has changed considerably. "He must weigh 350 pounds," said Epstein.

McLain has tried to get his finances back in the black by promoting minor league ball clubs. His success has been mixed, his travels extensive.

☆ *Cazzie* ☆

No Nat is remembered as fondly by his old teammates as Paul Casanova.

"If he's got a disco in Caracas," said Cullen, "then it's the best spot in town. Cazzie could always pick 'em."

"Cazzie was a prankster, a spender," said Maddox. "Water beds were just coming into fashion in '71, and Cazzie got a new one every week. He had one in the bedroom, one in the dining room, and a mini water bed in the bathroom. He'd walk down the street and say, 'Gotta get another water bed.'

"Cazzie was always the center of the party, the center of the 'fox' hunt. Once we got on an airplane and he had a tape deck with three speakers. He put 'em all over the plane."

It surprises none of the Senators that Casanova squandered his money, once declared bankruptcy, and refused to believe that the game he loved so openhandedly had no more use for him after the Atlanta Braves gave him a pink slip.

"The game changed him, the money changed him, and the breaking balls changed him," said Bosman.

"Somewhere in South America," said Epstein, "you could find a very handsome but rather disappointed man."

That, however, is not the way those who saw him in Washington will remember him.

"Cazzie wasn't teachable as a hitter. He just didn't have the

mental tools," said Bosman. "He was a wonderful physical speci-
men who just loved the game more than life.

"But Cazzie always had trouble with the signals. He thought
one finger for a fastball, two for a curve, and three for a slider was
tough. He'd call all fastballs if you let him. If you tried to change
the signs with a man on second base—you know add or subtract
by using the glove as an indicator—well, you could see the smoke
rising from the top of Cazzie's mask. The wood was burning."

In Venezuela, where Casanova still plays winter ball, he is as
popular a figure as ever—6-foot-5 and radiant as he stands in the
door of the Baseball Disco.

"He seems very happy," said one Washington magazine writer
after searching him out in Caracas. "He will not let you talk
about anything but baseball."

☆ *Elliott Maddox* ☆

One locker was different in the '71 Senator spring-training clubhouse—the one with the "Free Angela Davis" sticker posted over
it.

Elliott Maddox, now wise in the ways of the world, is still a bit
startled that, at twenty-two, on a team run by arch-conservative
Williams, he would smack the most radical college-kid slogan
imaginable over his cubicle.

"That got quite a few stares," said Maddox, a graduate of
Michigan. "It was easier for the team to put its thumb on me
then, keep me from saying political things, because I was young
and not established."

Then he laughed. "But no one has ever totally kept me in
check."

Maddox, a natural leader, some say clubhouse lawyer, was at
the center not of the Senators' black contingent, but its biracial
cast of rookies that included Harrah, Jeff Burroughs, Lenny Ran-
dle, Pete Broberg, and Dave Nelson.

If there was a team within the team, it was the infants. "We
were all babes in the woods together . . . we were so close it was
amazing. Most of us still are," said Maddox.

"We discovered all the spots on the circuit together. I don't
think we ever took the team bus back from Fenway Park. It was

too close to Kenmore Square and all the college kids. That was perfect for us."

Maddox seemed so mature for his age, that it sometimes did him harm.

"Ted took me out of the lineup that spring and put in Larry Biittner," recalled Maddox.

"I asked him, 'Why are you taking me out?'

"He said, 'I want to look at some of the young players.'

"I told him, 'Ted, I'm twenty-two and Biittner's twenty-five.'"

Everywhere Maddox went, he found what he saw as an *ancienne regime spectre* in the manager's office—first Williams, then Billy Martin.

"Martin seemed to follow me from team to team," said Maddox. "I'm the only guy to get traded by the same manager three times."

Baseball seems to have forgotten Maddox—bad knee, bad head —that's the rap.

"I have my health back at last, but now I don't have a position. I'm not happy," said the bright, gifted outfielder, who seems never to have really been content.

"Just say, 'I'm available.'"

☆ *Tim Cullen* ☆

Tim Cullen—"The Worm"—only needs to look down the block to see the precarious past that he chose to leave and the comfortable present that has turned out to be his reward.

Cullen, who quit the game at thirty—going directly from the 1972 World Series to retirement—is now a successful trader of listed securities in San Francisco.

Whenever Cullen wonders what he has left behind, he looks down the street in Lafayette, California, at ex-Nat Del Unser.

While Cullen is deep into his second career, Unser is still holding on to his first one by his fingernails as a Philadelphia utility man who hit .153 in '81.

In '72, after being traded to Oakland, Cullen was sent to Des Moines. It was the beginning of the end. Apparently.

"That was it," he said. "I couldn't take anymore of that. Bad lights and [6-foot-8] J. R. Richard looking down at you from the mound like he was going to reach out and shake hands.

"I learned to hit in those few months in the minors. I concentrated out of terror, and it made me a better hitter."

By season's end, Cullen had been recalled and was playing in pennant-race games, hitting a creditable .261, and finally taking the field in a Series game. "It was like a career in one season," he said.

Cullen knew when to quit. The tiny second baseman had minted a seven-year big league career out of as little raw ore as any man. "The Worm had next to no tools," said Howard, "but everybody admired him."

At his best, Cullen once made only three errors in an entire season. "I didn't play enough games for the Golden Glove, though," he said. "That's what I always wanted."

On the other hand, at his worst, Cullen once made three errors in one game. "When I came to bat, the Washington crowd gave me a standing 'boovation,'" said Cullen. "I think that's the only time they ever stood up for me."

In the ninth inning of that horrific game, Cullen almost made a fourth error—which would have put him in the record books. "I fielded it with my arm pit," he said. "The Worm always had good hands."

After such a career, Cullen was accustomed to hard work. He never figured life was easy. When he saw a chance to get into block securities trading with Dean Witter, he jumped.

"I was lucky to find something else I could do," he said, humble as a utility infielder. "I really knew nothing else besides baseball and the securities business."

☆ *Dick Bosman* ☆

"Sure, I remember that Opening Day. We had lost our last fourteen games of the previous season, and I went out and beat Vida . . . shut him out," said Bosman.

Then he paused for effect. "Of course, we didn't know who Vida Blue was. If we'd known he was gonna go out and win his next dozen, we might not have touched him."

In many ways, Dick Bosman was the epitome of the Senators—a quintessential baseball player. He once won the AL earned-run title, and he pitched a no-hitter. His best year was 16-12. But Bosman, like the Nats, was always trying to win with one hand tied behind his back.

"Bozzie had guts and control, and he'd fight you," said Howard. "He just didn't have much of a fastball."

So, when the end came, baseball said good-bye to Bosman unceremoniously—pink slip. "Charlie Finley just cut my throat and left me to bleed," said Bosman. "Didn't can me till the end of spring training when it was too late to catch on anywhere else."

Like so many others, Bosman is sure that the last one or two decent years in his arm never were used. They just atrophied and died. Now, it is too late to worry. It makes no difference now.

"At first, being out of the game wasn't so bad," said Bosman, who lives in Woodbridge, Virginia. "There was no home-town team, so I didn't feel it."

But now the newspaper sits by his breakfast plate every morning. "There are those guys you played with grinning up at me from among the palm trees every day," said Bosman, who wishes he had never seen a sports page.

"It hits you every day. If you play a kid's game for years, really give it your life, then have to walk away—well, anybody that says it doesn't rip 'em apart . . . 90 percent of 'em are lying," said Bosman.

"The real world wears on you more than the game ever did. There's more stress. They say that the game teaches you character. Well I don't see it. Baseball really doesn't teach life at all. Maybe it *is* life, but it doesn't teach it.

"I talked to an old friend the other day and I told him, 'The difference between us is that you grew up working and I grew up playing.'

"Just because a ballplayer sweats, he shouldn't kid himself that it means he's working. It's just hard play.

"I once asked Marvin Miller [players association lawyer] why he kept working with ballplayers," said Bosman.

"He said, 'You guys keep me young. You actually believe the party is never going to end.'"

Where Did You Go? Out. What Did You Do? Baseball.

I was a baseball boy, one of the last. I look at myself in the mirror now and see a dying breed. I grew up without a uniform. The streets and alleys of Capitol Hill were my diamonds and stadiums.

"My seniors," a grizzled college baseball coach once told me proudly, "have played organized baseball for fourteen years. Some of them were in uniform before they were eight years old."

What my baseball days lost in organization, they made up for in memories. Twenty-five years ago baseball ruled the streets of Washington as surely as basketball does today. There was only one national pastime then; any game in which a sphere was hit with a stick was it.

Before high school brought me a jersey with a number on the back, I had already lettered in lineball, workups, hotbox, five hundred, alley hardball, whiffleball, and the city's ultimate test of boyhood—one-on-one stickball at fifteen paces.

Before I ever shaved, I knew the ground rules and the social decorum of four distinct baseball universes—the inner city (stickball in the alley), the suburbs (whiffleball in the backyard), the summer camp (softball on the diamond), and the farm (hardball in the field).

None of my city neighborhood friends had ever heard of country boys "chunking walnuts."

Few of my St. Stephen's School friends in Alexandria ever wrote home from camp that they had just given up a home-run hit "into the Mattaponi River."

Moreover, my buddies at Camp Whitehall in Tidewater, Virginia, had never seen a real "three-sewer spaldeen."

And none of my August friends in Selbyville, Delaware's chicken belt, had ever seen a hardball thrown through the stained-glass window of a church while President Lyndon Johnson was taking communion.

In fact, I was exposed to almost every sort of baseball except Little, Pony, and Babe Ruth Leagues. In my boyhood, no adult told me what position to play or made me take a three-one pitch. The kids I played with had figured out what the children of the Bad News Bears never understood—that adults were the natural enemy of kids. Perhaps I never "got baseball out of my system" because no adult ever had a chance to drive it out.

Baseball was never work or practice or the big game or trophies. It was adventure.

I brought into adolescence with me all the survival techniques of the world of disorganized baseball. Before the glass from a shattered windshield had stopped falling, I knew how to be in another taxi cab zone. I could scatter and regroup fifteen minutes later in another neighborhood after the police car came to clear the kids out of the streets.

I learned how to spot the kid who would steal the ball, then beat you up if you chased him down. Any guy with purple shoelaces in his black hightop tennis shoes was up to no good—unless the sneakers were Chuck Taylors. In that case, you could trust him with your glove, even if his shoelaces were green.

Play stopped in the presence of anyone named Turk, Junior, or Tyrone—unless he could tell you where Butch Sewell lived. In that case, he was all right, too. If he did anything to you, you could get Butch to put him in the hospital. My career in disorganized baseball began in Eisenhower's second administration. It lasted a dozen years until Ike's grandson, David, challenged me to the unofficial stickball championship of our college.

In the beginning, the wall of my house on Lexington Place, fifty feet high and covered with ivy, was enough of a companion and adversary. For every thousand throws that the wall returned as flyballs, the ivy would eat one. I walked past that wall years later and a hardball, wrapped in ancient black masking tape, dropped with a soggy thud at my feet like a belated apology.

From the evil, ball-devouring wall, I graduated to playing catch in the narrow one-way street in front of our house. There I learned about hundred-dollar windshields and character.

For a year I suspected that I had magic powers. If, after making a wild throw, I winced hard enough and summoned sufficient terror and penitence, the ball would mercifully, harmlessly, thump on the hood. It was sin, remorse, confession, and forgiveness condensed to microseconds and the arc of a ball.

One August day my dispensations were exhausted. When I reached the wounded DeSoto, I knew I would never doubt the efficacy of prayer again. I had destroyed perhaps the last windshield in Washington divided in the middle by a metal bar.

The way I slunk home, the DeSoto might have been pregnant. But the young psychologist suspected he would survive. I was reasonably sure I was worth a hundred dollars to my parents, though at ten how sure can you be? "Dad," I began a speech I still remember, "I just broke a windshield, but it was only half a windshield . . ."

Of all life's crucial decisions, it is perhaps easiest to know when one has outgrown one's own block. I homered through the window of the house across the street—a thrill. But when I broke the same window again, it was time to move on.

With my exodus from the block came long afternoons, whole Saturdays, days with a kind of freedom different from anything since. The only law of those days was not to walk farther from home to play than you had strength to walk back. It was the special exhaustion and liberty of a boy, completely dependent for everything, walking enormous distances home through the city, after twelve home runs, certain that dinner was waiting.

On cold, overcast fall days when baseball should have been over for weeks, the front door would open after those long walks like an oven full of light and familiar smells.

My alley was still good enough for playing catch unless the ball slipped and went in old Mrs. O'Hara's yard. Then we never saw it again. She loathed noise and waited on her back porch for our mistakes. No one ever beat her to a ball.

Our other fear was Mrs. Wade's tin garage. If a low throw skipped past us, crashing like a cherry bomb into the tin door, a voice from my back porch would call all that ruckus inside for a piano lesson.

Away from Lexington Place—its windshields, old ladies, and pianos—I searched for the perfect alley. I was sure I would recognize it on first sight. Even now from the top windows of the Library of Congress Annex looking east, I can see in the maze of streets, all the secret, personal fields that others simply call urban decay.

Once I thought I had found my Polo Grounds. A wide, long,

impeccably clean alley with sheer walls on both sides, no yards in sight, and not a single broken soda bottle. I knew something had to be wrong, and it was. The neighborhood was too "good," the ritzy home owners had rabbit ears, and the police who rousted us from the parks patrolled that alley like we were the Mafia.

Just as well I never found a spacious diamond. Cramped quarters were better for games with only half a dozen kids. I never saw eighteen kids come together spontaneously for a game in my whole childhood. We would not have been interested in a game where you just played seven innings and only came to bat three times. We got to hit that many times in a good inning.

It is hard to recall how tiny those brick, city fields were. Not long ago I took a shortcut through a narrow, twisting alley that popped out onto Constitution Avenue. The alley seemed alien, yet I had subconsciously known where it came out. "I must know you, alley," I thought, "but who are you?" I walked back up it. Slowly the street lifted its mask, like Barbara Stanwyck at a costume ball.

Congressmen, their aides, and bureaucrats live there now. The Restoration Society has put its little eagles on the doors. Twenty years ago that same neighborhood was not so swanky. The same big, old houses were probably worth $20,000 then, not $200,000. But their back steps were friendlier. We sat on them between games chewing up those awful miniature wax bottles with the syrup inside. Penny apiece. Loved 'em.

Now the garage in center field, all of a hundred feet from home plate, has bouquets of dried flowers and many-colored corn hanging on it.

Because of the size limitations of the streets—only New York was built with stickball in mind—most of my baseball had to be played in the mind. The street game broke the sport into fragments. Hotbox was for baserunning; five hundred was shagging flies and hitting fungoes, while whiffleball and stickball were batting practice.

If I wanted the game complete, I went to books. *Iron Duke* and *The Warren Spahn Story* were consumed in one day. I died as the Keystone Kids fought up through the minors. When High Pockets was beaned, I got a headache.

Finally, my father, who worked at the Library of Congress,

smuggled me into the off-limits-to-the-public stacks. There in a musty corridor of deck 29 with GV862 overhead, my father said those fateful words, "Okay. Here is every book on baseball ever written. Don't go blind."

My devotion doubled. In the mornings I rose before the paper boy to play catch against the front steps, and after dinner I fielded many a lazy bouncer off the garage wall.

My grandfather began to wonder if I would come to a bad end. When I visited him in Selbyville, I stood in his front yard and fungoed walnuts at his barn by the bushel with a broomstick. "Is that boy still chunking walnuts?" I could hear him ask as I played out entire World Series in my head with the landing of each smashed walnut signifying a different play. Then I gathered the half walnuts and "chunked" them.

Selbyville meant hardball to me. Those country boys were the only group of twelve-year-olds I ever met who weren't fazed by being hit in the ribs by a fastball. My suburban friends would play catch or shag flies, but when it was time for a game, they wanted to use a softball or plastic whiffleball. In the city a baseball was usually thought too valuable to risk losing. We played with tennis balls or rubber spaldeens. But the boys of Selbyville played hardball, and I always hated to leave.

The farmland boys also lacked the fierce prejudices of the city. They accepted me and my family and my funny city talk immediately. In the mean Washington streets we weren't that generous. An immigrant youngster named Ladislaw Turlicki wanted to join in our games but fled in the face of the nickname we gave him: Coleslaw 'n' Turkey.

The zenith of my baseball career came when I was fourteen. Johnny Bench, Carlton Fisk, and I were all born in the fall of 1947. I have never been jealous. For one thing, I had my six weeks of glory at Camp Whitehall in summer 1962.

In those five-inning, after-dinner twilight games, I was a scourge. I have since convinced myself that the reason that fair Whitehall switched from baseball to softball soon after was that all the "Chiefs," as the thirteen-to-fifteen-year-olds were called, went home and told their parents they would never return if they had to bat against me again.

In a dusty drawer of my parents' den, in the yellowing archives of an only child, is a batch of letters we campers had to write home every Wednesday and Sunday ("no lunch without one") to convince our parents we were still alive.

"Dear Mom and Dad . . . Pitched another no-hitter today," says one letter in a large childish hand, blasé as Catfish Hunter talking to a stewardess.

One pitch epitomized that summer. David Kirby-Smith, also fourteen, the great-grandson of the Confederate Civil War general, stood in the right-hand batter's box. This boy knew no fear. Kirby-Smith was a terrible baseball player, but we loved him. His credentials for boyhood were impeccable. He had once chased what we all fervently believed to be a poisonous water moccasin into its reedy lair with only a stick for weaponry. Kirby simply exclaimed, "When am I going to get another chance like that?" When indeed.

So, naturally, he preferred to let my best fastball hit him in the knee rather than move six inches. He slowly crumbled into a sitting heap with a smile on his face. He never complained, certainly never cried, and the next day, when his knee was swollen and purple and you could see the stitches of the ball in the horrid flesh— well, he was even more pleased about it than I was.

I was next to the best thing a boy could be; I was the kid who could throw a fastball that did genuinely awful things. Kirby (we became friends; I pulled the thorn out of his batting stance and taught him to hit) was the boy who could get hit by that fastball and laugh. That was better.

I won the best-athlete-in-camp award that summer and sat on it and broke it on the way home. It was a symbol. Like many a little leaguer, I had thrown out my arm with too many curves and too many innings. Or maybe I just stopped growing. I had never put those pickup games into their final, permanent perspective until a Whitehall friend asked me not long ago, "Do you remember Dubby, the kid you always struck out?"

"Yes."

"Well, he's a brain surgeon now."

By the time I reached high school the next year, with its pitching machines, chalk baselines, paid umpires, dugouts, and graded infields, I was ready to leave the games of kids behind. Those years of organized baseball, with a big league bird-dog scout in the stands a couple of times to see someone else, are sprinkled with vivid moments of pleasure and pain. Those games remain indelible, but they were also the only times that baseball ever made me want to cry, except perhaps from an unnameable happiness on a spring day. The years before—the spaldeens, the whiffleballs, the walnuts—were just a patina of contentment that coated my childhood.

I retired in the middle of an unspectacular college career. I had more luck hitting books than balls. Nevertheless, I still felt the desire to swing at something in those first weeks when winter finally left the Massachusetts hills.

In the late sixties when SDS was considered politically middle of the road on my campus, it was hard to find other twenty-year-olds who wanted to play stickball. But gradually we discovered each other—Eric Landis, a bulldog catcher from the Bronx, a tall pitcher named Lewis, and a big-eared poli-sci major named Eisenhower. Landis and I stood Lewis and Eisenhower one balmy day for what we could safely call the Amherst College stickball championship. No other teams were entered.

We laid down the ancient rules: tennis balls and sawed-off broomsticks at fifteen paces. No gloves, no hitting to right. Then the local ground rules: liner past the pitcher a single; a one-hopper against the dorm in center a double; hit the wall on the fly for a triple and on the roof a homer. Of course we old pros did not even have to say, "All grounders and pops fielded cleanly are out. Pitcher calls balls and strikes."

With the small ball and the close pitching distance, it was the traditional afternoon of blurred fastballs, sharp curves (the kind we could never have thrown with a baseball), and the sound of swishing sticks. When our arms were all pronounced dead, we quit.

I don't remember the score or who won, but I remember my last home run, a towering poke to the dorm roof off David.

I always said you couldn't learn real stickball on the South Lawn.

Rookies in God's Country

Every summer, as soon as high school graduation is past, young men pack their gloves and flock to these little towns in the Appalachian Mountains—Bluefield, Pulaski, Covington, Marion, Bristol. In appropriate isolation, tucked in the folds of these big green hills that locals call "God's Country," the youngest and rawest of professional baseball players take their first plunge into the deep water of pro ball.

It is a summer of truth, a gathering of fastballs and fast feet. The Appalachian League, one of baseball's rookie leagues, is a place for major league bodies and high school minds. For some it also is the place for homesickness and loneliness, for finding out that a lifelong dream is a delusion, for bus rides and boredom and fast food three times a day. For others, "God's Country" begins to look like heaven as they find out they actually may be among the elect.

The lead-off batter of the Appy League opener one season a few years back at Calfee Park in Pulaski, Virginia, was a small Bluefield Oriole shortstop named Hunt Mitchell III, a sweet-faced teenager with braces, just two weeks out of Landon School, one of Washington's most exclusive private schools. Back home in Washington he had been the cat's pajamas, hitting over .400 at Landon, stealing two bases a game, and tearing up adult Industrial Leagues. He was twice all-Metropolitan in soccer and a football hero to boot.

In Pulaski his name was greeted with stony silence, until one fan bellowed, "Runt Mitchell! He looks like a runt."

The fan was a crew-cut, lumberyard worker, Jerry Stout, known for years to Pulaski fans as the Red Chicken. Like Grelber in the Broomhilda comic strip his specialty has always been the "free insult." The Red Chicken had entered the ball park, early, anxious to start the baiting. When Mitchell came to bat to open the Pulaski-Bluefield game, the Chicken was in fine fettle, sitting in the back row of the third-base seats like a fat-and-happy mudlark, a box of popcorn on his lap and a rolled program in his back pocket.

The 5-foot-8, 155-pound hitter would have liked a walk, but the loud fan didn't want to allow it. He told the rookie umpire to "get a miner's helmet" and "turn on the lamp" so he could see those strikes the Pulaski pitcher was throwing. Mitchell tried to check his swing on the third pitch but popped up weakly. The glorious first time at bat of his pro debut, a moment Mitchell had worked years for, had come and gone.

Like most of his fellow rookies, Hunt Mitchell has lived baseball as long as he can remember. In Landon's yearbook is a picture of Mitchell at age five in a baseball suit. The boy began switch-hitting soon after and has played baseball almost every day, summer and winter, in a league or clinic for more than three years. On that same yearbook page, Mitchell quoted painter Vincent Van Gogh, "The best way to know God is to love many things."

Mitchell, the only player in the rookie league with a "III" after his name, has always been a child of affluence, an honor student, and the sort of clean-cut student athlete to whom college admissions officers and employers love to say "Yes." Why is Mitchell, the smallest player on the Bluefield team and a fellow who has only hit one out-of-the-park home run in his life, playing the roulette wheel of minor league baseball—committing his whole life to baseball, he says—when so many safer and richer roads seem open? What is he doing in the Appy League, with its legends of 21–18 games, teams making 15 errors, Steve Dalkowski striking out 18 and walking 18 in the same game?

"Since I was eleven, I've wanted to be a major league player. I've always been small. It's never bothered me." Mitchell plans to go to college in the off-season; the Baltimore Orioles have guaranteed to pay his college tuition as part of a modest bonus. "I will get a degree, no matter how long it takes," he said. Mitchell knows how to put his best foot forward. He paid his way to a Puerto Rico tournament during Christmas vacation. He returned to Puerto Rico in March, during spring vacation to avoid the Washington weather. On both occasions Mitchell ended up working out, not with his peers, but with major leaguers and ex-major leaguers.

Mitchell's parents were asked, "Is this what you want for Hunt?" Anyone who knew the Mitchells would know better. Dr. George H. Mitchell II captained the 1950 St. Albans baseball team. His wife pitched in a softball league until her son was sixteen. For years one of the familiar scenes at Landon was Dr. Mitchell hitting fungoes to his son until after dark. When young Mitchell was drafted seventh by the major league Orioles, "I think Dr. Mitchell was happier about it than Hunt," said the Landon athletic director.

Yet the man most responsible for Mitchell getting a shot at the pro ranks was Edsel Martz, coach of the Martz Insurance team in the Maryland Industrial League. When the little shortstop attended his first Martz practice, it was pouring rain and Martz was giving the pitcher heck for not throwing strikes. Between Martz and Mitchell was established a deep bond, between the crusty old major league bird-dog scout from the School of Hard Knocks and the baby-faced private-school kid from a place that says you're in "Form VI" instead of 12th grade.

All the differences between the two were on the surface. The Bluefield Orioles saw why the first day Mitchell showed up for their ten-day preseason indoctrination. Infield coach Chico Fernandez, an old major league Oriole, saw through the good manners, the polish, the name, and the correct grammar. "The kid is hungry," he said. "He's not afraid of nothin' or nobody." Of course it did startle Fernandez when Mitchell began talking to him fluently in Spanish.

Waiting for the rookies when they get off the old Piedmont double-prop plane in Bluefield are Paul, Chico, and the Rabbit— the coaches. All have left thatches of their hides sticking to the thorny bushes that lead to the majors. No player can possibly have a disappointment they have not felt, a desire to quit that they have not fought back.

Fernandez made the parent Oriole club for one year (1968) at twenty-nine, but was beaned and almost killed the next year. He was in a coma for eleven days. It took a year and a half for him to learn to speak again. "I forgot two languages," he says, with a tight smile. He now has a steel plate in his head.

Ray Miller, thirty, is the Rabbit, the Orioles' roving minor league pitching coach. Big and handsome, he threw his slider and spitter ("I called the pitch myself") past minor leaguers for ten years, averaging over a strikeout an inning. He pitched successfully in every AAA league, but not one game in the majors. "I was never in the right place at the right time, but I'm not bitter. I still love it." Rabbit's goal now is to make the big-time as a pitching coach. "I keep a team loose, listen to problems, give advice. I'd like someday for people to say that when I walked into a room, it lit up."

Manager Paul Flesner, twenty-eight, is a rookie like his players. Now he has Fernandez and Miller to help him, but in a few days they will move to another minor league team to instruct and evaluate, while Flesner remains as "father, big brother, and clergyman" to his twenty-five away-from-home players, according to Oriole farm director Jack Pastore. "I put their diapers on and take them back off," said Flesner.

An Army hitch helped keep Flesner from playing in the majors. His nerves and temper are near the surface and he demands respect. His hair is thinning, and he doesn't like to be called an "old infielder." His favorite drink is called an "Aluminum Nail." Flesner should not be in danger of rusting.

Pastore says his trim young manager has given up a "good deal" in an attempt to reach the majors by the manager/coach route. "Paul divorced a girl who was worth several million dollars," said Pastore. "The old story . . . her old man wanted Paul to come into the business and quit baseball. Paul wouldn't. He's always been his own man."

Flesner, Fernandez, and Miller are all true products of the game. Miller, for instance, believes "There ain't a left-hander in the world that can run a straight line. It's the gravitational pull on the axis of the earth that gets 'em." So when his pitchers run wind sprints, he either lines his lefties up on a hill to balance their gravitational field, or else puts them all on the right-hand side. "If you don't," he says, "they'll whip out your whole line."

Flesner is a student of signs. He vows to keep them simple, unlike Hal Lanier, one of his old managers, who had different signs for infielders, outfielders, and pitchers. "If the bases were loaded, he had to give signs in four different directions."

Above all, the Bluefield coaches have mastered the minor league art—pace. "After you've done anything fifteen hundred times, it's like brushing your teeth," said Miller. "There ain't nothing to do in Bluefield except go to bed," said Pastore, "and there's no hurry about that."

Unfortunately, the rookies, who stay in the Bluefield College men's dorm, have not learned the trick. "This place drives you batty," said third baseman Don Kuhnhoff, from Los Angeles. "You can sit and watch the coal cars go by." Few have a television or an auto. They must walk a mile or call a cab to get to the nearest cheap restaurant. The cab costs three dollars. "I could get real tired of that," said Kuhnhoff. Most of the players' rooms are still bare of decoration. "We like the shag concrete rugs," said Kuhnhoff. Some, like L.A.'s Randy Checkos, are homesick. "I miss the smog," he said. "I've been throwing up ever since I got in this clean air."

Farm director Pastore knows from experience that time and the season will drive away most of the blues. "After the season starts they can move into town out of the dorm. After the girls come out of the woodwork, they'll be all right."

Mitchell plans to stay in the dorm. "When the others leave, it should be nice and quiet," he said. He has not noticed the boredom since he's been busy keeping a book of notes on what his instructors teach every day. He also likes to be with old friends he made in school, guys named Faulkner and Twain. Mitchell also enjoys polishing his Spanish. It's been his biggest pleasure, after baseball. "I like the sound of it," he said. "It's a kick. It is, it really is. The Latin players don't know too many people, and they appreciate me interpreting, sort of. I eat with 'em. They're nice guys."

Foremost in all minds is winning a starting job. All know that if you can't burn it in Appalachia, the majors are out the window. Nevertheless, one Bluefield rookie admitted, "Whatever happens, the folks in my town will always say, 'That boy spent some time with the Orioles.'"

Surprisingly, Pastore says his toughest problem is not telling players they are being let go. "They want to cry," he said, "and you tell them that's not weakness. That it's not degrading for a man to cry. You point out the experiences they've had. The friends and contacts they've made. You're doing them a favor when you cut them. You tell them to get into a normal life as quickly as possible." The real soul-troubling problem for Pastore is the player he does not cut or demote, though he knows he will never make the majors. "We're stealing time from this young man to keep him around for organizational purposes."

The box score in the Bluefield *Daily Telegraph* one Friday morning read: "Mitchell, ss . . . 4-0-1-1." The box score was just the first of hundreds that await Hunt Mitchell as he steps into baseball's grist mill. Yet when the other nights, the other fields have long become impossible to recall, some second of that first pro game may be as vivid as breakfast.

Perhaps it will be his first hit, a double up the left-field alley that drove in the first run of the Appalachian League season in the third inning and silenced the Red Chicken. But just as likely, an older Mitchell will remember the hurried throw he shouldn't have made that skipped past first for an error. Or the embarrassment of being picked off second after his first hit.

To the experienced eyes of the Oriole organization little of that mattered. Rabbit noticed that Mitchell once went to the wrong cut-off spot. Flesner liked the way he covered third once to surprise a runner for an out. Pastore, the man who matters most, "liked his range" but added, "Of course, we hope his arm will get stronger."

All the major questions will remain unanswered for months and perhaps years.

"I'm glad it's over. I was so nervous," said Mitchell. Still exhilarated, and with $13 meal money in his pocket for two days on the road, Mitchell grinned, "It's my father and Mr. Martz I have to thank for being where I am today."

Some would say that Hunt Mitchell is a young, unmade man in the deepest netherworld of baseball. However, to Mitchell no prospect could seem finer than playing 70 baseball games in 71 days. He hasn't seen Covington, Marion, or Johnson City, yet. Each one seems like the gate to heaven.

Hunt Mitchell played four years of minor league baseball, then retired, graduated from the University of Maryland, and is now an investment counselor. However, he did make the majors—for one day. "One Friday afternoon in September, Toronto let me work out with the team. I took BP and infield before a game against the

Yankees. It was great. Rick Cerone, who was with the Blue Jays then, gave me a pair of spikes. Still got 'em."

Does Mitchell ever wear them? "I think about playing now in a good amateur league. I still get the itch."

May

Growing Up with the Game

A dozen miles outside the Washington Beltway, the land escapes from the tight grip of man, and basically, by the time you get to rural Charles County, is returning to nature. It isn't beautiful yet, but it's getting better.

By the time you turn off the main drag in the little Maryland town of Waldorf—left at the brick police station, then a hundred yards back across the railroad tracks and into the clearing in the trees—you have, in a few minutes, left the capital of the United States and traveled to America.

"Chaney Field . . . Home of Waldorf Little League . . . Enjoy Coca-Cola" proclaim signs at the entrance to the five small baseball fields with a dirt parking lot in their midst.

This is baseball at the bottom line—simple, unadorned, economical, every penny counted, but perfectly satisfactory. If you're a kid and you want to play baseball, here it is. But no come-on, no frills.

A foul ball can reach the railroad tracks. A forest of electrical transformers—the town's power source—looms above the old trees.

The infields are hard, baked dirt full of pebbles, but no rocks or glass. The outfields are splotchy grass, but green. The waist-high cyclone fences surrounding the fields have no fancy distance markers. There are no lights. Get finished by sundown.

The chalk scoreboards aren't used. The bleachers are half-full when they hold a dozen parents. This is word-of-mouth baseball.

"What inning is it? . . . What's the score? . . . Who's winning?" a player asks his mother in quick succession.

And he's the pitcher.

"Coach," pleads an eleven-year-old whose back is barely big enough to contain the uniform words Ken Dixon Chevrolet-Buick-Honda, "somebody's got to help me. Scott just filled my batting helmet with dirt."

This is partly baseball, but mostly growing up, mostly one of those few remaining places where everybody gathers to pass on the tribe's collective sense of itself.

Teenage girls ignore the three games that are in progress simultaneously, instead grooming each others' hair, or wandering off to sit on big, old red-with-rust oil barrels to share a soda with a boy.

Everywhere you look, there are unselfconscious rituals, rites of passage, and a gentle, unhurried symbolism.

Slide into home and get a strawberry on the hip as a badge of courage. Get hit by a pitch and bite your lip to keep from crying.

"I've got to throw this ball out of the game," the ump announces to the little crowd as the dented batter limps toward first base. "It's flat on one side."

The child laughs to keep from crying. The hops here are half-true, just like lots of things in the hard-working, when-do-I-get-my-break life hereabouts.

"Don't flinch. Hang in there," a father yells to his second baseman son. "You have to face the hops." These fields are like gardens where the bumper crop is vignettes.

The Lions' catcher comes to bat with the bases loaded and an adult fan whispers to him in the on-deck spot, "Boy, if you hit a home run, I'll give you a dollar bill."

"You don't have to do that," says the team's coach to the man. "I give any of 'em five dollars for a home run."

As the hitter gets to the plate, a woman's voice cuts through the drone of chatter, yelling, "Come on, baby. Throw to the mitt."

Of course, it is the mother of the twelve-year-old pitcher, and the hurler in question really is her baby.

Thus do we learn the importance of games, and the winning of them.

It is probably silly to search for rights and wrongs in something so true to the grain of daily life as summer, baseball, and Fourth of July week. These scenes don't leave us with moralisms, but with memories.

The air toward evening, as the sun starts to go down, is full of humidity, dirt hanging in a haze, and the over-powering, over-sweetness of chlorophyll and pollen. It is so delicious, so redolent of childhood, that a sneeze is a relief—a return to the present.

In a time that insists we live by decades—that we clutch at the fifties, sixties, and seventies as they leave us behind like perplexed hitchhikers—these fields are a testament that things change with a merciful lassitude.

"Kids never change. They're already great. Neither do the adults. They're sometimes a pain," said Waldorf umpire Joe Brown, a wholesale glass salesman.

"Adults take it too serious. The kids understand," says Brown. "Last week, I had two good catchers working in front of me. Whenever either one of 'em was hitting—so that all three of us were at the plate together—we all took a vote on the balls and strikes.

"I told 'em, 'Boys, we gotta do this quick, so the people won't start to wonder,' " Brown said, with a laugh. "They called every darn pitch right. I never had to break a tie.

"One of 'em turned to me and said, 'Well, Mr. Brown, I guess I just took a third strike.'

"I told him, 'Yes, I guess you did.' "

That sort of innocence seldom lasts too long. At what Waldorf calls the "major league" level of nine- to twelve-year-olds, you can vote on the calls. But don't try it on the adjacent field where the thirteen- to fifteen-year-old "Senior" Little Leaguers are playing.

"I called one the other night that the 'Senior' catcher didn't like. He went out and talked to his pitcher. Next pitch—a letter-high fastball—came in and he never tried to catch it. It hit me right in the chest protector.

"I warned him, but he did it again. I went to his coach and said, 'Your catcher has to move to another position, or I'll put him out of the game. I didn't come out here after working all day to be used for target practice.' "

At the nine-to-twelve stage, however, baseball is still a cherub game, for the most part.

True, as the Jaguars and Pirates walked off the field this particular evening, one angel yelled at the other, "We'll get you nitbrains next year." "Yeah, well who won this game, huh?" inquired the other cherubim.

However, a few feet away, the Lions and the Carruth and Son Concrete Dodgers had just ended the final game of their regular seasons. The Lions, bound for the glory of the play-offs, invited the Dodgers to share in an enormous chocolate cake.

"Well, another season down the drain," said a small defeated Dodger, glove in one hand, napkin with cake in the other.

"Did you make all-star?" asked a girl of the same age, but much taller.

"Nah, but I will next year," said the boy, turning to his father to ask, "What's for supper?"

"Spaghetti."

"Uuuuuughhhh," he said, as though it were fried catcher's mitt.

"Big strong baseball player won't eat spaghetti?" asked his dad.

The big strong baseball player wolfed down the remains of his cake, sensing perhaps that, if left uneaten, it might become a casualty of the bargaining process.

While the Dodgers disbanded, the Lions held a team meeting.

"We'll practice for the play-offs at my house," said the coach. "If you can't come, call me. Does everybody know my phone number?"

Without a cue, the team chanted the correct phone number in unison. How come Billy Martin couldn't get the Yankees to do that?

"Everybody try to be there," interjected a very young and perhaps overly enthusiastic assistant coach. "This is a once-in-a-lifetime shot, guys. Trophies and everything."

The Lions, by and large, seemed to look on the remains of the chocolate cake as more of a once-in-a-lifetime shot. After making sure no morsel remained, the pride of Lions meandered over to the last inning of the senior game between the Route 301 Seven-11 Pirates and the Anderson Hardware Brewers.

They might as well have walked into another world.

Instead of pitches that looked hump-backed and friendly, here the ball whistled and swerved. The collisions at the plate that looked so amusing among twelve-year-olds looked extremely different at fourteen.

The Pirates and Brewers ended their evening in a beaut of a rhubarb when the last out of a one-run game was called on an obscure appeal of an interference decision by an umpire. Nobody understood anything, so everybody got mad.

Various coaches did their Earl Weaver imitation. The two umps, with no tunnel to flee toward, had to explain the unexplainable to every concerned parent as they walked toward their cars. A multitude of imprecations, on the order of "You stink" and "It's all fixed," were muttered loud enough for the umps to hear.

The mothers of two players had to be separated by their husbands when one said, "Well, I wouldn't want to win like that," and the discussion began to escalate.

While the adults calmed themselves, the unruffled children discussed more important matters.

"Is that a ten-speed?" one boy asked another on a bike.

"I thought you guys were baseball players," one player teased two boys who were wearing jacket patches for a soccer team.

"We had a better soccer record than you guys had in baseball," answered the other.

Had they been the directors of this particular area's fiercely competing baseball and soccer youth programs, it might have been time to call for lawyers.

Instead, the baseball player grinned at the soccer player and said, "What can I say?"

The biggest field was empty except for one child too young even for Little League. He had no uniform, just a ball and glove.

On the mound, he toed the rubber, looked in for the sign, imaginarily took his stretch, held the runner on first base, then threw his best fastball half-way up the backstop.

Slowly, he walked in to the screen, picked up his ball, and walked back to the mound.

The sun was a deep red in the top branches of the trees. The heavy smell of summer and dust was on the diamond.

The small boy doctored the hill, then looked in again for his sign.

He was in a big jam. And, at the rate things were going, it might take him until dark to work his way out.

Glove's Labor Lost

Each spring, when the ground loses its threadbare look, I wonder if I should buy a baseball glove. It is a quick, fleeting thought, "And what would you do with it?" I ask myself, and that is that.

For so many years the five-finger, Warren Spahn 300 with the trapper's web came up out of the wintry basement with a string tied around it and an old ball clamped inside the pocket. Pulling that string was a truer sign of spring than any robin.

My first glove, a parental gift at age eight, is now only a blurry memory, less vivid than the cowboy guns and garbage cans that I cherished at an earlier period. It was a very dark infielder model and it lived a hard life.

It was once soaked in linseed oil, because in the first stages of my growing addiction I confused linseed with neat's-foot oil, the proper glove preservative.

My rather academic parents thought linseed sounded foolish enough to be correct, so into the oil bath went the new glove. The linseeded glove quickly dried up, cracked like a stoned windshield, and literally flaked away.

During its years of disintegration, I laid plans for a real glove, one that would last a millennium, or at least until high school.

While the first glove was just another toy to be misused, the second, bought with money I saved for over a year, fell somewhere between the last toy and the first personal possession.

Once the money was saved, the shopping began. It took almost as long as the saving. For weeks I was late coming home from school since, after getting off my bus downtown, I would be buffeted by the price tags, models, and signatures available at Irvings, Atlas, and Woodie's. My mother accused me of knowing every glove in the city personally. My father predicted, dourly, that I would grow up and marry a ball.

With a mixture of elation and sadness I settled on the Spahn 300. Before I handed over my thirty dollars to Atlas, I had owned every glove in town, and none of them. Now I had just one. I felt the same paradoxical emotion next when I picked a college.

The new, properly neat's-footed glove slept on my bed at night like a summer puppy and traveled back and forth to school every day, wrist strap looped through belt.

In the alley, beside my house, I saved many a home run from going over a hypothetical outfield fence, and before breakfast and after dinner fielded many a lazy bouncer off the garage wall.

The glove, a ball, and the brick wall of my house, covered with ivy, were my stadium and my major league. When the ball would stick in the ivy, I would dislodge it by throwing sticks and rocks, but only once, my glove. The Spahnie stuck thirty feet up in the ivy, barely peeking out, and my heart hung there, too.

In a still vivid instant, I saw it in my mind's eye lodged there for years, rotting, a testimony to my split-second insanity.

Once retrieved, the glove was never endangered again. I knew, because everyone told me, that it was much too good a glove for a young boy, and I kept it from the careless and uncaring hands of what seemed like hundreds of would-be borrowers. It taught me lessons in saying, "No."

In fact, when my junior high principal, Dick Babyak, sees me now, he still asks, sometimes, "Hey, Tom, can I borrow your glove?"

He still remembers that twenty years ago, when he was my principal, math teacher, and summer camp director rolled into one, I would not let him use it. He wasn't going to get me out in those Sunday camp softball games with my own glove.

The Spahnie stayed with me nearly ten years. I used it in practice in both high school and college, though I used the schools' big first baseman's mitts in games.

Eventually, I lent the glove to Babyak in the summer (to his endless amusement), and by high school I was playing on the same camp counselors' team with him. By my college days he had stepped out of most of the games, unable to hit the ball to the Mattaponi River every time up, as he had once. I inherited his old position.

When I left college, I apparently left the Spahnie behind somewhere. Its role had dwindled considerably. Perhaps I left it on the Theta Delta lawn the week of graduation.

Though service in Vietnam, graduate school, or a job were the uncertain possibilities in my near future, I spent one last summer working in the humid, but still idyllic world of scrapping children and hot macaroni in July.

When the first Sunday softball game came, I had no glove. From the pitcher's mound I watched the twelve-, thirteen-, and fourteen-year-olds running up to bat, tossing down their gloves. I looked for a mitt that seemed familiar, too big for its owner, and almost too well loved.

"Excuse me," I called to a new camper. "May I borrow your glove?"

He looked down, hesitated, then said, "Okay, sir. But take care of it."

"I'm not going to hurt it," I said.

Welcome to the World of Total Average Where a Walk Is as Good as a Hit

For a century, since the 1880s debate over whether a walk was really "as good as a hit" in figuring a batting average, one puzzle has been the granddaddy of them all: How do you measure a player's total offensive ability? Batting average, slugging percentage, on-base percentage, slash-hitting for extra bases, stolen bases—all have their rightful place. But how can their relative worth be balanced and weighed?

Now, we have one simple statistic that comes closer to being the ultimate offensive yardstick than anything before it: Total Average.

In theory, Total Average is elementary, easy, and obvious. That's why it's so hard to dispute. In its results, TA is dramatic and controversial. It illuminates new stars like Rickey Henderson and Willie Randolph, while blowing holes in big names like Steve Garvey and Pete Rose.

Let's start with the theory. Baseball's two fundamental units of measurement are the base and the out. Each base is one step closer to home plate. Each out is a single step nearer the end of the inning. That's Total Average—a ratio between the bases a player accumulates for his team and the outs he costs his club.

To illustrate, take George Brett, the best Total Average player in baseball in 1980. Brett had 109 singles, 33 doubles, 9 triples, 24 home runs, 58 walks, 15 stolen bases, and was hit by 1 pitch. That comes to 372 bases. Thus, the heart of Total Average: All bases are created equal.

Calculating Brett's total outs for 1980 is even easier. Subtract his hits (175) from his at-bats (449) and you get outs (274). Tack on the 6 times Brett was thrown out stealing and add 11 for the double plays he grounded into (since each cost his team an extra out).

Now divide his total bases (372) by his total outs (291) and you get his Total Average: 1.278.

Any Total Average over 1.000 is fantastic, because it means

such a player gets more bases than he makes outs. In baseball history, only seventeen players have had career TAs of 1.000 or better (see chart, complete through 1981).

ALL-TIME TOTAL AVERAGE TOP 25

		Bases	Outs	Average
1.	Babe Ruth	7972	5567	1.432
2.	Ted Williams	6927	5060	1.369
3.	Lou Gehrig	6669	5314	1.255
4.	Jimmie Foxx	6494	5518	1.177
5.	Hank Greenberg	4051	3585	1.130
6.	Mickey Mantle	6400	5738	1.115
7.	Rogers Hornsby	5889	5288	1.114
8.	Ty Cobb	8004	7535	1.062
9.	Stan Musial	7810	7368	1.060
10.	Mel Ott	6838	6610	1.034
11.	Joe DiMaggio	4769	4617	1.033
12.	Ralph Kiner	3885	3764	1.032
13.	Willie Mays	7861	7711	1.019
14.	Johnny Mize	4505	4442	1.014
15.	Joe Jackson	3301	3274	1.008
16.	Mike Schmidt	3463	3455	1.002
17.	Hack Wilson	3319	3317	1.001
18.	Tris Speaker	6705	6766	.991
19.	Frank Robinson	6697	7131	.981
20.	Hank Aaron	8498	8673	.980
21.	Dick Allen	4403	4519	.974
22.	Harry Heilmann	5017	5155	.973
23.	Duke Snider	4937	5078	.972
24.	Joe Morgan	5712	5984	.955
25.	Willie McCovey	5365	5631	.953

What are the virtues of Total Average?

• Players with different styles and strengths can be measured on the same scale. The bunt hit, the walk, the steal, and the home run are all given their proper due.

• The gaudy batting-average stat, which players themselves have long said is grossly overvalued, is brought into perspective. The flashy average, if it isn't backed up by the power, speed, or a batting eye, falls on its face.

• The low-average slugger finds his Total Average depleted by

his many outs. Dave Kingman and Lee May are good examples
from the 1970s.

• The walk (which builds on-base percentage), the most neg-
lected offensive stat, finally is given added importance.

• The strategic trend of baseball for the past dozen years—the
stolen base—is incorporated in a major stat.

• The advantages that a good player on a top team has over an
equally good player on a bad team are minimized by ignoring
both runs scored and RBIs, which are, to a degree, tied to the performance of teammates.

The greatest offensive force ever was Babe Ruth, who was in his
own private Total Average world. In 1920, the inaugural year of
the lively ball, Ruth had the highest TA in history—1.930—when
he had 550 bases with only 285 outs. In other words, he made
roughly the same number of outs as Brett did in 1980 but had almost 200 more bases. Imagine Brett hitting .390, then add 30
homers and 100 walks, and you've got Babe Ruth.

Ruth's TA exceeded 1.800 in 1920, 1921, and 1923. The only
mortal to approach that plateau was Ted Williams, the No. 2 all-
time Total Average man, with a mark of 1.779 in 1941. That season, the Splinter had 482 bases and just 271 outs. Williams hit
.406 and made 20 less outs than Brett did last year, while piling
up 110 more bases. Let's not hear any more Williams-Brett comparisons.

In 1980, only three players, besides Brett, cracked the 1.000 barrier—Mike Schmidt (1.107), Reggie Jackson (1.065), and Rickey
Henderson (1.034). It is a perfect illustration of TA that these
four reached the top in dramatically different ways. Brett, for instance, out hit Schmidt, .390 to .286. But Schmidt approached his
fellow 1980 MVP in TA by hitting twice as many homers (48 to
24) and drawing more walks (89 to 58). Note: in 1981 Schmidt
led the majors with a 1.243 TA and won his second straight MVP.

The contrast between Jackson and Henderson is an even better
example. Sluggers like Jackson have always been given their due.
The skills most often overlooked in baseball are the ability to get
on base and the gift of theft. Henderson epitomizes both. The
twenty-one-year-old not only became the third man in history to
steal 100 bases but, thanks to 117 walks, was the only player in
baseball to reach base 300 times (301). Henderson proves that you

don't need power (9 homers and only 33 extra-base hits) to be a TA superstar. A slightly more modest clone of Henderson is Randolph, the fifth-best offensive player in baseball in 1980 (.965 TA), whose 119 walks, 30 steals, and 282 times on base would have been even better had he not missed almost a month with injuries. (Both, by the way, far outdistance walkless Willie Wilson and his 230 hits—.856 Total Average.)

Perhaps the most persuasive argument for Total Average is the way the cream rises to the top. (See chart of All-Time Total Average Top 25.) TA invariably singles out great performances, which no other one stat does. For instance, the best Total Average performance of the past decade was by Joe Morgan in 1975–76, when he won back-to-back landslide MVPs despite the fact that he didn't lead the NL in any glamour category. In 1976, Morgan's .320 average, 27 homers, and 111 RBIs didn't come close to any of the Triple Crown titles. But because of his 60 steals, 114 walks, and .576 slugging average, he had a Total Average of 1.346—highest of any major leaguer in the 1970s.

It is a convenient coincidence of Total Average that its rating ratios look like old-fashioned schoolroom grades. Any TA ratio above .900 is like a grade of A—you're a star or a superstar. The only active players with a career Total Average in this range are Schmidt (1.002, No. 16 in history), Morgan (.955, No. 24), Willie Stargell (.910), and Jackson (.905). Recent greats like Willie McCovey (.953), Harmon Killebrew (.940), and the vastly underrated Dick Allen (.974) are also in this oughtta-be-bound-for-Cooperstown grouping.

Total Averages in the .800s are like Bs. This is the honors class, the category from which All-Star teams should come. This year only 41 everyday players had TAs over .800.

The bell curve among regulars is largest in the .700s, where your overrated players start to appear. Any player with a TA from .750 down is, at most, a limited, one-dimensional offensive factor. Two examples are Steve Garvey and 1980 NL batting champion Bill Buckner, with Total Averages of .724 and .727, respectively. The durable Garvey has a good average (.304) and fair power (26 homers in 658 at-bats). But he draws few walks (36), seldom steals (6 for 11), and averages a mediocre 1 extra-base hit per 12 at bats. Buckner is a no-walks, no-steals, no-power batting-average specialist. In more basic evaluations, like on-base percentage and slugging average, you can't find him.

If TA has one heart-warming quality, it is the way it exposes bogus averages, like Mickey Rivers' .333 batting average but .729 Total Average. These guys slap singles but never do anything else.

In the Total Average schoolroom, the cutoff for a failing grade, at least for a starter, is probably around .666—or 50 percent more outs than bases. The average TA for the major leagues in 1980 was .656. Any player near that level is no star.

Perhaps the most embarrassing Total Average performance of 1980 was turned in by Rose, with a mark of .634. Many a Phillie fan knew that Rose had suffered a precipitous drop in performance from 1979. But only TA shows just how great: down .228 from a typically excellent .862 in 1979.

In the nether reaches of Total Average, we also find many a middling big name who should be a smaller name. All 96 of Omar Moreno's steals could not raise his TA above .682. The nickname he earned in the 1979 World Series—Omar the Out Maker—still fits in 1980 as he led the majors in making outs with 550.

Who were the truly abominable offensive players of 1980? A couple of All-Stars—Rick Burleson (.622) and Garry Maddox (.603)—barely made it past the paltry .600 level. Several well-known chaps didn't, including Dave Concepcion (.583), Enos Cabell (.562), Bob Boone (.559), Frank White (.559), and Larry Bowa (.540). For the record, the most inoffensive player in baseball (among regulars) was Gold Glove second baseman Doug Flynn of the Mets, whose .255 batting average disguised his ignominious .467 TA. Flynn made 56 more outs than Brett—while garnering 210 fewer bases. We are talking here, you see, about far greater differences in ability among players than most fans realize.

What TA does best is rank players within the same year and the same league. When conditions are similar, it is a hard-to-dispute barometer. What TA does worst is compare players from different eras. When basic conditions for offense change, Total Average, because it combines many variables, shows dramatic differences. For instance, of all the dead-ball greats before 1920, the only two who can crack the TA Top 25 are Ty Cobb (No. 8 at 1.062), and Shoeless Joe Jackson (No. 15 at 1.008). Had Cobb and Jackson played primarily in the 1920s and 1930s, when all conditions for hitting were better than they have been before or since, both might well have ended up in the Total Average Top Five.

Conversely, players like Ruth (No. 1), Lou Gehrig (No. 3), Jimmie Foxx (No. 4), and Hank Greenberg (No. 5)—great as they were—caught much the best of the rabbit-ball age before the dominance of night games, jet lag, relief pitchers, and improved gloves.

Be that as it may, the Top 25 for Total Average is still a vastly more appealing listing of The Greatest Ever than any other statistic can claim. Ruth's superiority at 1.432 is as staggering as it should be. Williams, the second-best slugger in history and the hardest man ever to get out (on-base percentage), takes the second spot, leaving other players of his era—like Stan Musial and Joe DiMaggio—more than .300 behind. A vast gap.

Gehrig and Greenberg tied for the honor of driving in more runs per game than any players in history. The Beast—Foxx—ranks between fourth and eighth in almost every significant career stat from slugging to homers to RBIs to RBIs-per-game to what-have-you.

Mickey Mantle, sixth at 1.115, is the surprise. His enormous walk totals, his speed, and his slugging—in other words, the total skills that made him so breathtaking—raise him higher than he is on any other all-time list. Mantle can stop worrying about how his career batting average dropped under .300 at the end.

The common denominator of those in the Top 25 is their multiple skills. Mantle, DiMaggio, Willie Mays, Musial, and Frank Robinson were all fleet, powerful, complete players in their prime. A nice bonus: TA makes a strong case for three players who have long been left out of the Hall of Fame unjustly—Johnny Mize, Joe Jackson, and Hack Wilson, all in the Total Average Top 20 despite shortened careers.

Is TA the ultimate stat? Probably not. This stat freak himself has put his Total Average through a previous incarnation, one which was less simple and less appealing. A fellow scrivener who thought that, for instance, a walk or a steal ought only count four fifths as much as a base hit might find a sympathetic ear.

Because Total Average measures how well a player does everything, it may not do justice to players whose sole role is to do one

thing well. The most important element in baseball that TA cannot always measure is the ability to drive in runs. In most cases,
the top TA players are also the top run-producers per at-bat. But
each year, there are a few fascinating exceptions—players who are
low in TA but high in RBIs. Why not just call them clutch hitters and leave the mystery intact? Tony Perez (.704 TA, 105
RBIs) and Tony Armas (.732, 109) are the best examples in the
1980 season. For further illustration, Rich Dauer's Total Average
of .586 is awful. What a cold statistic doesn't tell is that in 1980
Dauer hit .336 with men in scoring position—the highest of any
Baltimore Oriole.

Obviously, the purpose of Total Average is not to replace a sensible perusal of all of baseball's valuable numbers. No true fan
would want baseball's rich tradition of esoteric argument to be
diminished by some monster stat. Nevertheless, Total Average
may come closer to illuminating disputes than any single baseball
statistic before it.

AMERICAN LEAGUE TOTAL AVERAGE TOP 10 FOR 1980

		Bases	Outs	Average
1.	George Brett	372	291	1.278
2.	Reggie Jackson	393	369	1.065
3.	Rickey Henderson	458	443	1.034
4.	Willie Randolph	360	373	.965
5.	Ben Oglivie	403	426	.946
6.	Cecil Cooper	393	425	.925
7.	Jason Thompson	294	325	.905
8.	Fred Lynn	269	299	.900
9.	Ken Singleton	376	427	.881
10.	Al Bumbry	404	460	.878

NATIONAL LEAGUE TOTAL AVERAGE TOP 10 FOR 1980

		Bases	Outs	Average
1.	Mike Schmidt	445	402	1.107
2.	Keith Hernandez	398	426	.934
3.	Cesar Cedeno	347	373	.930
4.	Jack Clark	304	330	.921
5.	André Dawson	367	417	.880
6.	Ted Simmons	312	358	.872
7.	Ken Griffey	333	389	.856
8.	Lee Mazzilli	375	349	.854

9.	Ron LeFlore	349	410	.851
10.	Dale Murphy	359	423	.849

TOTAL AVERAGE ALL-STARS

	American League	*National League*
Catcher	Carlton Fisk (.739)	Ted Simmons (.872)
First Base	Cecil Cooper (.925)	Keith Hernandez (.934)
Second Base	Willie Randolph (.965)	Joe Morgan (.805)
Shortstop	Robin Yount (.818)	Garry Templeton (.698)
Third Base	George Brett (1.278)	Mike Schmidt (1.107)
Outfield	Reggie Jackson (1.065)	Cesar Cedeno (.930)
Outfield	Rickey Henderson (1.034)	Jack Clark (.921)
Outfield	Ben Oglivie (.946)	André Dawson (.880)

That First Slash of Grass

Ball parks are a passion among baseball fans second only to the game.

True arrival at a big league ball park begins with the first glimpse of green grass, and not a moment before. The sighting of a light tower in the distance, peering down perhaps over the heads of houses, does not count.

Maybe the butterflies begin then. Tiny smiles begin cropping up spontaneously. The Oh-I'm-not-really-excited walk carries you through the parking lot as the delightful suppression of pleasure builds.

Even the tucking away of the rain check in the wallet, the vendors' cries, and the double-time hike up the stadium ramp are just an overture.

At old Griffith Stadium in Washington that first slash of grass appeared as you passed the louvered grandstand behind first base.

It lasted just a flash, before the crowd, pushing along, swept you past. But in that moment, captured like a freeze frame, you could see the white bag, the coach's box, and that scimitar of dirt called the right side of the diamond.

Those next several seconds—between first glimpse and full view—were a bona fide arrival as the sense of anticipation, carefully kept under control, suddenly welled up and exploded like a home-run cheer.

Doubtless, there are better places to spend summer days, summer nights, than in ball parks. Doubtless.

Nevertheless, decades after a person has stopped collecting bubble-gum cards, he can still discover himself collecting ball parks. And not just the stadiums, but their surrounding neighborhoods, their smells, their special seasons and moods.

Boston's Fenway Park is best on the worst days, in raw misty spring and foggy fall. The streets around the Fens are crowded, narrow, and damp. Taxis blow their horns at the herds of jay-walking Soxers on Lansdowne.

Inside, the emerald field, the royal-blue and blood-red stands, the green bleachers and WALL stand silent under tarp and drizzle just as they did generations ago when Babe Ruth waited for a Northeaster to shift so he could pitch for the home-town team.

Yankee Stadium smells best in October when the armada of hot pretzel sellers rings the walls, plucking at the sleeves of the three-piece-suit crowd that shows for the World Series.

The scalpers and freaks crowd near the ticket windows, one selling tickets, the other trying to steal them. The Stadium is more than faintly criminal. Poverty and violence live just a block away.

But Yankee Stadium digests that squalor like a gouty ward heeler, belches and bellows, "Play Ball."

No park approaches Yankee for bad manners and arrogance. "Be glad you're here," say the white outfield facades. "Get movin', buddy," say the surliest cops on earth.

If Yankee Stadium knows how to be itself only in the midst of turbulence, Baltimore's Memorial Stadium is most comfortably itself with a lonely mid-week crowd of a few straggling thousands.

The brick-and-wood dowager of 33rd Street likes her solitude. No fireworks, no traffic jams, no loud noises, no tasteless getting and spending.

The team that has won more games than any other since 1960 gives nightly seminars in "Baseball, Played Properly." Professor Earl Weaver, proponent of pitching and percentages, sits in his dugout during infield practice and watches the crowd arrive, ones and twos at a time.

"Nice turnout," he says tonelessly, years beyond sarcasm.

The sedate white clapboard houses on 36th Street stare unblinkingly in from beyond the center-field fence. The sun goes down purple and gold, the stars come out, the best rock 'n' roll in the big leagues drifts and echoes around the park.

This is indeed baseball played properly, with only those who truly care in the quiet stands, a grove of pine trees beyond the outfield fence, and Weaver's tomato plants growing in the bull pen.

A continent away, in Chavez Ravine, baseball is played profitably. The most beautiful ball park in the world and the tackiest hard sell go hand in hand, one accenting and exposing the other.

Dodger Stadium in Los Angeles would be heaven, that is, if St.

Peter weren't at the golden gate trying to sell cheap wristwatches.

Chavez is fragrant with L.A. sundown, palm, and begonia. The red clay mixed with the infield dirt, the blue of the walls, and the perpetually filled stands create a rich triple threat of aroma, color, and noise.

It is difficult to introduce 50,000 fans individually during a nine-inning game, but the Dodgers never stop trying. If it isn't sufficient to see Frank Sinatra and Don Rickles in the clubhouse, or Walter Matthau and Harvey Korman sandaled and cutesy in the hot-dog line, the scoreboard has to keep up three hours of non-stop listing of every person in the crowd with a birthday, anniversary, or a bad cold.

"A Dodger Welcome to Heinrich Hilmer of La Jolla."

Some ball parks are made for daylight; others should only come out at night.

The greatest charm of Chicago's Wrigley Field is what it lacks: lights. If the truth be told, Wrigley is not a terribly attractive ball park. Quaint, sure. Beautiful, not really.

The catwalks, the ivied brick outfield walls, the ancient hand-operated scoreboard, the pennants above the center-field fence to show the league standings and whether the Cubs won or lost—all those things sound better than they look.

The bleacher bums are sufficiently demented. Day baseball is what God intended; and the whole shebang is photogenic. And it's nice to be able to see home runs bounce off people's front doors and watch them come out to see what the mailman wants.

But let's blow the whistle a bit. Wrigley Field ain't all it's cracked up to be. From ground level the field looks ratty, the dugouts are embarrassingly cruddy, and the locker rooms are almost shabby.

However, when the sun is bright, the air crisp, and your seat seems closer to the diamond than the on-deck hitter, all is forgiven. So what if the neighborhood is deteriorating, the parking impossible, the scoreboard unreadable? So what if it is impossible anywhere in the park to find out what the actual score of the game is?

The fences in the power alleys are so close you're certain the next man will hit a homer; you're so close to the umpire you can hear him cough; and, suddenly, the crowd decides it will sing a song.

Wrigley Field is great.

But it's not as great as the hideously named Royals Stadium in the Harry S. Truman Sports Complex in Kansas City. For $70 million the Royals should have come up with a better name, something like Waterfall Park. But no price could have built a better modern-style stadium.

However, please go at night.

By day the two-stadium Truman Complex looks like a gaudy, colossal toy that some giant child left in the middle of nowhere.

When the sun goes down and the multicolored outfield water fountains start spouting and the clear midwestern moon starts shimmering on the steel and Tartan turf, even that gauche twelve-story-high Royals-crest scoreboard with the crown on top starts looking classy.

If you're going to shoot 50,000 gallons of water in the air and dazzle it with colored lights, the time to do it is after dark.

Royals Stadium is that rare park that looks stunning from inside, outside, and above. The most distressing tendency of other newly built stadiums is that they look like the Mother Ship from Close Encounters on the outside, then bore you to tears once you get inside.

Riverfront and Three Rivers stadiums are by far the two most conspicuous and jubilant buildings in the towns of Cincinnati and Pittsburgh.

Both are built on the water and from a distance look like blazing riverboats. Both were built with architecture, rather than baseball, in mind. They'll put you to sleep by the fifth inning if the game isn't close.

The Reds' infield is mottled with wear, the second-deck outfield pavilions are monotonous, and all the stands are set inexcusably far from the field.

Baseball always suffers when it is played in a cookie-cutter football stadium, like the ones in Cincinnati, Pittsburgh, and Philadelphia. Kansas City had the right central idea: limit seating to 40,000, but bring the fans close to the action; leave a center-field vista open and enhance it if possible, thereby creating an amphitheatre, rather than a claustrophobic cylinder.

Several rules of stadium building should be carved on every owner's forehead. Old, if properly refurbished, is always better than new. Smaller is better than bigger. Open is better than closed. Near beats far. Silent visual effects are better than loud ones. Eye pollution hurts attendance. Inside should look as good as outside. Domed stadiums are criminal.

For every old park, like Cleveland's decaying Municipal Stadium, which is a punishment to all the senses, there is a regal Yankee Stadium, a glistening Fenway Park, or a dignified Memorial Stadium.

For every new atrocity, like Philadelphia's Veterans Stadium, with its juvenile scoreboard, its rock-hard phony turf, and its baby-doll Bicentennial figures perched in center field, there is a new standard of classicism like Royals Stadium.

The baseball fans' desire to hustle up the ball park ramp and catch that first glimpse of green promise does not fade.

The Best Manager There Is

Ornithologists know Orioles are fond of camouflage. But Earl Weaver is ridiculous. The Baltimore Orioles skipper will go to almost any length to hide himself. To be known thoroughly, to be figured out—he fears—is the first step toward being expendable. A manager needs mystique.

For Weaver, it is not important that others understand him, only that he understand himself. So long as others respect what he does, and gape at his career winning percentage, it suits him just as well if they occasionally are left shaking their heads. Keep 'em guessing. That applies to everyone he deals with: his players, umpires, press, even his bosses in the front office.

It is perhaps Weaver's dominant managerial characteristic that his players seldom think of him in terms of love or hate. Weaver is so candid, yet somehow stays so naturally aloof, that his players regard him not with affection or loathing, but with a strong professional respect and a tepid, unemotional loyalty.

"We're all on speaking terms," says Weaver. Other managers would shudder at such tenuous relationships. Managing is lonely and the need to be loved, to feel that someone in the clubhouse is protecting your back, is almost overwhelming. Perhaps Billy Martin is the classic example of that frenzied insecurity. By contrast, Weaver says of players like Jim Palmer, Paul Blair, Mark Belanger, and Brooks Robinson, "We have had a little rapport. Not too much." That's it. No cheerleading. No gratitude from Weaver for the fame they have brought him. No bouquets thrown to Weaver for the wealth to which he has helped guide them.

With Weaver, the deep lines, the lines of character that run to the core, are all rooted in his twenty-year purgatory in the bush leagues. "You learn the lesson the first day in Class D . . . You're always going to be a rotten bastard, or in my case, a little bastard, as long as you manage," he says. "That's the rule. To keep your job, you fire others or bench them or trade them. You have to do the thinking for twenty-five guys, and you can't be too close to any of them."

The ultimate example of this prickly, adversary relationship is his dozen years Sturm und Drang with Jim Palmer. The elegant, gentlemanly pitcher and the testy, acid-tongued manager are baseball's odd couple. They carry with them countless squabbles and reconciliations, misunderstandings and mended fences. "Palmer airs his opinions on a lot of things," grins Belanger, privy to many a mound SALT talk. "And Earl'll tell you any damn thing he wants to. He doesn't care who you are, and that certainly includes Jimmy. But he expects you to forget, just like he forgets."

"Earl has probably had more fights [arguments] with his players than any manager in baseball," says ex-O Tony Muser. "But the next day the air is clear."

In fact, Weaver practically encourages dugout primal-scream therapy. He and Rick Dempsey have gone so far as to throw gloves, shin guards, and chest protectors at each other.

Why does Weaver tolerate such insubordination—almost prod it into the open? "I thought we still had free speech in this country," he snaps. Then he adds, "A ball club isn't a family, but it's together *more* than a family for seven months. You can't hold your feelings in that long."

If Weaver has one persistent problem, it's that some umpires can't let bygones be bygones as easily as he. "I've talked to Earl about the way he antagonizes umpires. I don't understand his brand of psychology," says Orioles scout Jim Russo. "What really bothers the umps is the things Earl says to them. He has this wonderful grasp of the King's English."

Weaver has, over the years, said an amazing number of memorable things about a large number of gentlemen in blue. Jim Evans: "He's definitely incompetent." Russ Goetz and George Maloney: "They're almost as incompetent as Evans." Hank Morganweck: "The blind one." Ron Luciano: "The worst . . . just a showboat." Armando Rodriguez: "I have to take Elrod Hendricks with me to the plate to talk to him." Marty Springstead: "Not smart enough to remember the rule book."

And, finally, Steve Palermo: "If he ever touches me again without that blue uniform on, I'll consider it assault and his family will have to fly in to see him at Johns Hopkins Hospital."

Believe it or not, umpires have memories.

"Weaver is baseball's Son of Sam," said Evans.

"I hope his teams never win another game," said Luciano, who once ejected Weaver during the exchange of lineup cards.

"Weaver's a pest, an insult to baseball, a clown who goes under the guise of a manager," says Palermo.

Despite this legacy of hostility, Weaver himself considers his temper just another button on his master panel of options. Being in control, even at mock white-heat, is a trump. "The thing that has surprised me most in baseball is the amount of integrity that most umpires have," says Weaver. "It actually took me a while to believe what a good game they'd give you the next night after a blowup."

Nothing is more in character and calculated than the moments when Weaver pulls his own trigger. His rages almost always start as strategy.

When the Orioles are streaking, Weaver effaces himself. "I could stay back at the hotel," he purrs. "They don't need me." However, in a crisis, Weaver inevitably manages his beak off. He takes the wheel and starts gambling, suddenly attracting the attention of defeat to himself. When the Birds win, Weaver never joins in the postgame back-slapping celebrations on the field, considering it a form of front-running. But when the O's lose, Weaver draws the electricity of defeat to himself like a lightning rod so his players can perform in calm.

"That's my job. What the hell else does a manager have to do?" says Weaver.

In the final analysis, all Weaver's acts and antics are subsumed under what he considers his fundamental managerial strength: "My baseball judgment."

"I've been exercising that baseball judgment since I was six years old and every kid in St. Louis argued over whether Pete Reiser or Terry Moore was the best center fielder. Evaluating talent, having a feel for the game, is the heart of the job. From age eight to fifteen, I watched a hundred games a season—Browns and Cardinals. Ran from school with my Knothole-Gang card and saw the last six innings. Here I am, twelve years old, second-guessing Billy Southworth, who's one of the three managers in history to win a hundred games in three straight seasons," says Weaver, pausing slyly. "Of course, I'm one of the three, too.

"I can sum up managing in one sentence. Everybody knows all the strategies. Nothing's changed in a hundred years. A manager's job," Weaver defined, "is to select the best players for what he wants done."

Weaver beams, knowing the complexity hidden in that thought.

"A manager wins games in December. He tries not to lose them in July. You win pennants in the off-season when you build your team with trades or free agents.

"Smart managing is dumb," says Weaver. "The three-run homers you trade for in the winter will always beat brains.

"The guy who says, 'I love the challenge of managing,' is one step from being out of a job. I don't welcome any challenge. I'd rather have nine guys named Robinson."

If Weaver had a conventional theory on anything, he wouldn't admit it, or would twist it to his own hat size. He would rather set his beloved blow-dried silver hair on fire than be taken for granted.

"People say I've never had to manage a bad team," says Weaver who has finished first or second in eighteen of his last twenty-one seasons. "Well, that's the *point*. If you dig hard enough year-round, you should always be able to find players who can do what you want done. They're not all great players; but they can all do *something*."

Weaver's confidence in his own decisions is his trademark. He once watched Mike Cuellar get knocked out early in 13 consecutive starts, before finally removing him from the rotation. Sadly, Weaver said, "I gave Mike Cuellar more chances than my first wife."

"His confidence in you rubs off," says Steve Stone. "Early in the year when everybody was yelling for me to be taken out of the rotation Weaver kept giving me the ball, long after any other manager would have. Now, I think I'm proving him right," said Stone in 1979, when he won 11 games. The next season, he won 25.

No manager is so concerned with that concept of self-confidence, especially as it applies to his substitutes. The O's, who have won 100 games five times in Weaver's first dozen full seasons, have "deep depth" because Weaver adamantly finds spot playing time for his Lowensteins, Ayalas, and Crowleys.

"The man's a genius at finding situations where an average player—like me—can look like a star because a lot of subtle factors are working in your favor," says John Lowenstein. "He has a passion for finding the perfect player for the perfect spot."

This fascination with matchups carries over into the long-range pitching schedule, another Weaver compulsion. He has calendars covered with possible rotations, weeks and months ahead. His players swear that an early-season rainout can make Weaver happy because he knows it will reshuffle his rotation in a series in Tiger Stadium in July.

Surprisingly, Weaver advocates almost no technical theories on how the game is played. "The only thing Weaver knows about a curveball," says Palmer, "is that he couldn't hit one."

"Earl gets coaches who are teachers, then he doesn't get in their way," says pitching coach Ray Miller. "He doesn't tell me, 'Why don't you teach Sammy Stewart the window-shade-release slippitch?' He says, 'Jesus Christ, I'm sick of lookin' at that horseshit changeup. Get him a new one.'" With his absolute faith in his own baseball eye, and his coaches' ability to polish skills, Weaver manages as though victory were an inevitability.

"Patience . . . patience," he often says. "You must remember that anyone under thirty—especially a ballpayer—is an adolescent. I never got close to being an adult until I was thirty-two. Even though I was married and had a son at twenty, I was a kid at thirty-two, living at home with my parents. Sure, I was a manager then. That doesn't mean you're grown up.

"Until you're the person that other people fall back on, until you're the one that's leaned on, not the person doing the leaning, you're not an adult. You reach an age when suddenly you realize you have to be that person. Divorce did it to me. It could be elderly parents, children . . . anything. But one day you realize, 'It's me. I've got to be the rock.'"

Ever since, Weaver has been that little leather-skinned rock. The absolute symbol of that independence—of being untouchable, inviolable, your own man—is money in the bank. The law of the manager's existence is the indignity of knowing that you can be fired arbitrarily. Weaver's pride rankles at that and cash is the solution to the problem.

"I've never been fired from any job," says the meticulously organized Weaver, and he's talking about selling encyclopedias and cars, and being a hod carrier, too. "But I think I've signed my last contract. If AT&T and the municipal bonds don't fall flat, I'll be retired by '83.

"Then, when 'This Week in Baseball' comes on TV, I'll be on the golf course and couldn't care less. And a year after that, nobody will remember Earl Weaver.

"I know exactly what I need to live on, have ever since I made $3,500 a year in '57," Weaver says. "I'm always going to do the same things. I grow all my own vegetables. I stuff my own sausages—pork shoulders should be coming on sale next month. I look for chuck roast on sale to use in stew or grind up for hamburger. Doing that takes time and I enjoy it," says Weaver, who seems to understand that a man is defined by how he spends his time, not how he spends his money.

"I'll have plenty to play golf every day, run out to Hialeah or the dogs, take Marianna out to dinner in Fort Lauderdale, and take a walk on the beach.

"No more guys barreling into my office like Ross Grimsley did one time," says Weaver. "He was screaming, 'You're shafting me. You're shafting me.'

"I asked him how I was doing that," said Weaver, "and he says, 'You're yanking me earlier than any of the other pitchers.' So I told him, 'Do you know why that is, Ross? It's 'cause I think they can get the next man out and I don't think you can.'"

It never gets easier for Weaver. "You step on toes almost every day," he says. "You just step as softly as you can."

The older he gets, the closer he comes to the end of his run, the more money gets stashed away in deferred payments so that he can spend his life in vegetable gardens, on golf courses, and at dog tracks, the harder it is not to find the crotchety Earl of Baltimore appealing. If baseball can germinate genius, then Weaver is the bloom of native American wit and savvy as revealed within our national pastime.

Yet, ironically, baseball may never find quite the right words of thanks to say to Weaver. He is not that sort of man. For his part,

Weaver may find it equally difficult to say good-bye to baseball, no matter how much he protests to the contrary.

"My wife says, 'You spend more time on baseball than you do with [daughter] Kim and me. Do you love baseball more?'" Weaver says. "And that's the second wife talking," he adds, as though anyone who knew the first wife could imagine what she would say. "Well, I told her, 'Without baseball, we don't eat so good.'" Then Weaver says more quietly, "A man and work . . . that seems to be the way it's got to be in this world."

Nevertheless, when the time finally comes to lay that laborious and fruitful work aside, it is doubtful that those who have been close to Weaver for years—those who have been chewed and needled and lectured and even had dirt kicked on them—will know exactly what to say.

Weaver is already familiar with the experience. He sensed it in a complex and revealing moment a couple of years ago when Memorial Stadium was filled on Thanks, Brooks Day when Brooks Robinson retired.

Weaver spent hours wandering around with a yellow notepad, doodling and scribbling. "I just couldn't come up with the words," said Weaver. "I read all the newspapers and remembered all the one-liners, all the praise and adulation . . . they were all true, but what I wrote was so insignificant that it couldn't be said."

So, Weaver threw away the yellow pad. He trotted out to the microphones behind the pitcher's mound, and he was almost in tears. Of all the speakers, only Weaver nearly broke down. He talked about Robinson's generosity toward a nobody manager who was a career bush leaguer. He talked about how he wondered, the first time he gave the "take" sign to Robinson, if he would obey. And, Weaver said revealingly, "I've wondered every time since."

The crowd, restless, did not know quite what to make of Weaver's words, not to mention the almost inaudible, gravelly rasp to which his voice was reduced. When Weaver thanked Robinson for saving his job "several times over the years," it sounded uneasily like the truth and not a speech. Nobody knew what to say. Finally, Weaver blurted out, "Thank you, Brooks. Thank you one million times."

Weaver went and crouched near his team by the third-base bag.

But he remained alone, a little, self-contained man on his haunches. No Oriole said, "Nice speech." Or looked at the manager with his head down.

"I thought of so many things while Brooks was riding around the stadium [in a convertible]," explained Weaver. "What I had planned to say didn't seem like nothin' to me. It wasn't true and honest feeling. So I just did it impromptu.

"No, I don't guess many people knew what I was talkin' about."

Then, Weaver, the man who kicks dirt on umpires, gets booed in rival cities and sometimes in his own—feisty, combative Earl Weaver—said, "I'd like to be like Brooks. The guys who never said no to nobody, the ones that everybody loves because they deserve to be loved . . . those are my heroes."

But when a man spends twenty years in the minors—learning to be an adult, a rock, a leader—the path up and out involves stepping on many toes, even if—like Earl Weaver—you try to step as softly as possible.

The Game By Us

The sandlot veterans have talked it over and they have just about decided that Pickles Smith never really needed that index finger on his left hand, anyway . . .

That's good, because Pickles doesn't have it anymore, not since the jack slipped and the trailer fell.

Smith tried to make light of it. "Just call me 'Nine Fingers,'" he told the guys. But they were worried.

Grown men who play sandlot baseball are a dwindling and close-knit fraternity. When one of their brotherhood is threatened with retirement, either from a sore arm, one too many birthdays, marriage to a good cook, or a falling trailer, the news goes quickly through the Maryland Industrial League.

When Doffy, Barney, One Muscle, and the rest heard that Pickles had cut off one finger, mutilated another and broken a third, they were upset, at least until they got it straight which digit had gotten sheared.

"Oh, the left hand," said one teammate, the forty-year-old shortstop, with relief. "Pickles throws right-handed."

"The index finger," mused Alex, the thirty-seven-year-old designated hitter who stopped one rung shy of Ebbets Field on the Dodger ladder. "Well, Willie Mays never put that one on the bat handle, anyway."

Finally, they had convinced themselves. "That's the finger Pickles needed least," said Alex.

Smith agreed. "I'll be back in August," he told them, and no one was surprised. "Pickles always had a good attitude," said Barney.

Some would question the sanity of these men who play 50 to 100 sandlot games a year for teams with names like Fairfax Furniture, Black Sox, Stroube's Mobil, Atlantic Masonry, or Martz (Insurance) Christians.

That's unnecessary. They question it often themselves. "Sometimes I feel like a prostitute or a junkie with a drug habit," says Barney Gidders, thirty-two, for two seasons a batting-practice pitcher with the Washington Senators, but in recent seasons "the captain of the white boys" on the Black Sox.

"On weekends I'll leave the house at eleven A.M. and get back at eleven P.M. I'll drive maybe a hundred miles to play in a two P.M. and a seven P.M. game the same day. When I get back, my wife just laughs, like 'You big dummy, when are you going to grow up?' "

Nevertheless, it is with sadness, not conviction, that Gidders says he will absolutely retire this year. "Sandlot ball is dying. Even the Black Sox are dying, if not in numbers, then certainly in the quality of players. The guys who really care, who were once professionals, who will spend the time to perfect a pick-off play or a sacrifice bunt or a hit-and-run . . . we're dinosaurs.

"I asked a ten-year-old kid the other day if he played baseball. He said, 'I used to.' God, that made me so sad I almost fell down.

"And my old buddies . . . they play softball now . . . slow-pitch softball."

"They say a grown man is too old to play baseball, but they never tell you what's supposed to take its place," says Alex Harriday, thirty-seven. "There's never a true athlete who has his heart in the game who can just give it up.

"Nothing in this life has given me as many good memories as baseball. I done had so many I can't remember."

Harriday stood under a spreading tree, looking like some lost village blacksmith shoe-horned into a double-knit baseball uniform, as he watched his Black Sox mates play Fairfax.

As the 240-pounder took his vicious practice swings with a weighted bat, giving a little grunt with each, he admitted he did not know the score or the inning, though Fairfax and Black Sox were at the top of the Industrial League.

"I've been up twice. We've got three runs and haven't left many on base. Must be round about the fifth," said Harriday. "If we're trailing in the late goin', then we get serious."

That is all it takes to light the fuse of memory. Despite his years with the old Indianapolis Crowns, his career in the Brooklyn Dodger chain, Harriday recalls every pitch of a game on this same field when his Sox trailed, 11–0.

Bob Avellini, then a shortstop for Atlantic Masonry, later quarterback for the Chicago Bears, started a bench-clearing ruckus.

When it subsided the Sox were riled up. "I hit a grand-slam homer, a line drive up in the trees behind the center-field fence, and we won, 14–12," Harriday said, laughing. "I can still see that pitcher with his head bowed."

With that memory fresh in mind, and a new-fangled aluminum bat in hand, Harriday waddled to the plate and golfed a low curve from the Fairfax pitcher far over the left-field fence.

Normally, running out a home run is not cause for a seizure, but the designated Falstaff returned from his trot in a lather of sweat worthy of a marathon.

Gasping for breath, he looked at the alien metal bat and grumped, "I sound like a one-man Gong Show."

On the Fairfax bench heads were shaking. "Thirty-seven," the Furniture coach Woody Harris repeated Harriday's age. "Time gets away, doesn't it? He still has the fastest wrists around."

Harris knows about time slipping away. Just six years ago he realized that his son, Billy the catcher, had starred in his last game at William and Mary.

So the father simply created a team—Fairfax Furniture—for his son to play on. "Sure, anything wrong with that?" he asked.

If the Washington sandlot game is to keep its flavor and its reputation as one of the East Coast's toughest testing grounds, it is such ex-college players as Harris who will be its lifeblood.

Clearly, at twenty-seven, he does not feel like an addict. "It's a joy to play against the Black Sox," he says, leaving no doubt that Hal Greer, the aged Sox shortstop, Harriday, and Gidders rank high in his Hall of Fame. "I intend to play as long as I want to, just like they have."

Almost every summer night the air is full of their shouts: "Come on, Ox," "Lift one outta here, Ronnie, shoot it up in the light, boy," "Hey, somebody let the air outta No. 5 before he throws one into the seats."

And afterward—after the last murderous hop off a stony-hearted infield, after the last curve in the dirt is called a strike by a blind umpire with sore feet, after the bad lights have turned yet another "kid with a blower [fastball]" into an unhittable Bob Feller— they gather in the parking lot and talk about how long they have left.

Old gloves are thrown in the back seat, bats go with the cracked and taped batting helmets in the trunk. The cars scatter in the night, their headlights a disintegrating nova. No one is heading to an all-night party. Tomorrow is a workday.

"This is where we meet. This is what we have in common," said Gidders. "Just baseball. You start out a prospect, but you end up a suspect."

The night swallows them like age itself. Only the game stays young.

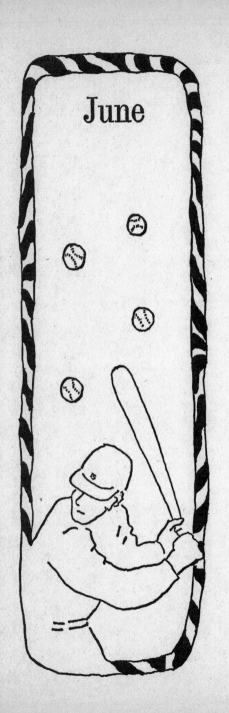
June

Magic Wands and Louisville

Ever since the first caveman picked up the first cudgel, went to his front door and smacked the first nosy saber-toothed tiger in the snout, mankind has known the atavistic power and pleasure of the bat.

From Robin Hood's quarterstaff to Paul Bunyan's ax, men of myth have loved the taper of a handle, the texture of wood grain, the centrifugal surge in the end of a whirling mass. Axes and stout staves have dwindled in everyday use. Now, that ancient inherited desire for thudding force, for an instrument that will deliver a satisfying blow, has descended to the baseball bat.

What familiar sensation in sports is so universal as the pursuit of a perfect bat—the Old Ash, the Lumber, the Good Wood? From the office softball game to the World Series, who settles for the first weapon out of the rack?

Few things feel so annoying as the wrong bat. If it is too short or light, the frail thing seems unworthy of us; almost an insult. If it is too long or heavy, however, it is the bat's fault, not our own lack of strength. "Unwieldy," we say.

"When a bat feels just right, the balance is so perfect that it almost feels weightless," said Baltimore's Ken Singleton. "I've looked all my life for a bat that felt as good as the broom handles I used to play stickball with as a kid in the Bronx."

Call it "My Soul Pole" like Baltimore's Al Bumbry, or "My Business Partner," as L.A.'s Jay Johnstone does, the bat is the most pampered, coddled, protected, and defended piece of equipment in baseball. "If you wanna rumble, just touch my lumber," was George Scott's motto.

Of all the inanimate objects in sports—the balls and boots, gloves and goals, helmets and harness—none is so intensely personal, so surrounded by lore as the ubiquitous Louisville Slugger. Few things look so similar, yet hold such vital, almost mysterious qualities as a barrel full of big league bats.

"Every one feels different, even two bats of the same model," said Yankee Roy White, one of many players who swear they can tell if a stick is a half ounce off specifications. "I once went five-for-five with five different bats. I kept switching 'cause none of them felt just right. After I got to three-for-three, I said, 'Maybe I better keep switching.'"

Tommy Agee, former New York Met, once got the same notion on a grander scale, using 22 different bats on a 22-game hitting streak. "Worst hitting streak in history—23 hits in 22 days," related Singleton, then a Met. "Agee was actually in a slump, but he kept switching bats every day."

S-2, K-55, R-43: These are the "Star War" style names that bats are known by. Those letters and numbers burned on the barrel of each Hillerich and Bradsby weapon are shorthand for length and weight, degree of handle taper, nob style, and distribution of weight. Even here there are superstars: R-116, the original Babe Ruth; O-16, the ever-popular Mel Ott, and the RJ-288, Reggie Jackson's new plaything.

Casually ask a player if that's a P-89 he's swinging and it's a better entree for conversation than a personal letter of introduction from Bowie Kuhn. Lots better.

However, some of the most infamous bats are unmarked or else have phony monikers. These are the outlaw breed.

"Sure, there are guys who will 'fix' a bat for you," says Yankee Graig Nettles. "When it comes back, it's like a Mafia hit gun . . . no serial numbers."

Several years ago, Nettles shattered his bat while hitting a routine flyball against Detroit. Out of the demolished barrel bounced six ultraresilient, ultraillegal Super Balls.

"Bill Freehan was catching, and he dashed all over the place collecting the evidence," said Nettles sheepishly, thinking of those tiny black toys that even children can whack over tall buildings bouncing around home plate. "I guess Bill thought they'd put me before a firing squad."

Nettles, however, knew the rules. Illegal bat equals automatic out. Nothing more. "What the hell," said Nettles to Freehan, "I was out anyway."

Many a well-loved bat is not made entirely of wood. Ted Kluszewski, Cincinnati batting coach, was so strong that he embedded tenpenny nails in his bat barrel for contraband oomph. Many a big leaguer has a "corked" bat or two for special occasions. Or maybe for every occasion.

"Cork a bat?" says Baltimore Manager Earl Weaver. "Easiest thing in the world. Hollow out the barrel with a drill. Fill it with cork. Put the plug end back in and seal it with plastic wood. You can't spot a good job with a magnifying glass. You gotta saw 'em up to find anything."

But Weaver, of course, has never used one of the nefarious instruments? "Never used one?" Weaver snorted. "I played on a team at New Orleans in the minors where every bat on the club was corked. I hit six homers that season . . . every one of 'em in the one month before they found us out. The umpires raided our clubhouse like they were the Untouchables. They destroyed the bats in public, right on the field. I wanted to cry."

Have the Orioles ever used corked bats?

"Never," said Weaver. "However, Norm Cash used to use one against us. We're sure of it.

"You can't yell 'Check his bat' every time a guy walks up to home plate. What's the umpire going to do? Carry a saw? If you're wrong once, then maybe they won't check him next time you cry 'Wolf.'

"But when Cash used to come up in crucial situations in the ninth, a bunch of us would all yell, 'Check his bat.' Norm would turn right around, walk straight back to the dugout and switch bats before anyone could touch it."

Kansas City's Hal McRae, who, along with ex-Royal John Mayberry has long been accused of using bats that would float, had his Louisville Slugger confiscated by the umps. The authorities sawed the weapon into six pieces but found only sawdust.

"My favorite," says Nettles, "is a guy I knew in the minors who had a tube of mercury in the heart of his bat. Mercury's very heavy, so the tube was only partly filled. When he held the bat upright, it felt very light. But when he swung it, the centrifugal force of the mercury whipping out to the end of the bat made it swing like it weighed a ton."

What happened to Mr. Mercury?

"He never made the majors," grinned Nettles. "He had a great bat, but he couldn't hit the ball with it."

Even the universe of perfectly legal bats is far from prosaic.

Frankie Frisch hung his bats in a barn during the off-season to cure like hams. Honus Wagner boiled his in creosol, while Home Run Baker never revealed the ingredients of his secret ointment. Jimmy Frey, former Kansas City manager and minor league batting champ, had a treatment worthy of a bush-league great: Frey soaked his bats in motor oil.

Some players will even smash their favorite bat against anything in sight. "The more you crush the wood on the hitting surface, the tighter the grain," says Johnstone. "The best thing is to find a bat with a knot in the wood right in the sweet spot."

Ah, yes. Tight grain vs. wide grain. Every player has an opinion on which is better. Each has a different theory. Regardless, when a player discovers the bat that was made in heaven for him, he guards it with his life.

"In five years I'm not sure I ever saw Ron Blomberg without his bat," exaggerates an ex-Yankee teammate. "In airplanes, hotel lobbies, I think he'd swing that thing when he was in the men's room."

"If I ever found the perfect bat," grins Johnstone, "I think I'd take it to bed with me."

Perhaps the most cherished of all bats was Jimmy Reese's ancient fungo. Reese, a roommate of Babe Ruth and now a California coach, cut the barrel end of his fungo in half (lengthwise) so the bat was flat on one side, round on the other. With this wand Reese could hit a fly, liner, or grounder to any target inside a hundred yards. Balls thrown back to him, he would deflect with the flat side of the bat and catch harmlessly with his bare hand. Reese even "pitched" Angel batting practice by hitting fungoes from the mound.

One year, Reese tortured an overweight pitcher named Bill Edgerton, making him chase countless spring-training fungoes that were inches beyond his straining reach.

"Edgerton left Reese's fungo in the whirlpool overnight," recalled Ray Miller, Oriole coach. "When we got to the clubhouse next morning, the thing had warped and flared out in all directions like some kind of weird flower. Jimmy just sat by the whirlpool and cried."

Ted Williams valued his bats so highly that he traveled to Louisville in the off-season, went to the factory, and picked out the chunks of ash from which his splendid splinters would be dowled. Williams' technique: Drop the wood on concrete and listen for the sound.

From that day to this, a man's progress could be measured by his bats. A busher settled for standard models. If he reached a big league training camp, his name was stamped on his bats in block letters. When he reached the majors, the block letters turned to script, and H&B took his personal specifications. A star might get his own model number, like Reggie Jackson's recently christened RJ-288.

"I was a block-letter man," grins Baltimore's Weaver. "Still got it in the attic somewhere."

No bats, of course, compare to the bats of memory.

"It doesn't seem to me that the wood is as good as it was thirty years ago," says Weaver. "HB had a fire years ago and I've always wondered if their best aged wood wasn't lost."

Singleton has a more unorthodox theory: "I think they've run out of good trees . . . Sometimes I go up to the plate with a bat that I'm sure God intended to be a chair leg."

Never say that to Brooks Robinson, the old Oriole who never met a bat he didn't like. "My garage is full of hundreds of 'em," Robinson says. "I got the last hit of my career with a bat that had hung over my mantel for sixteen years.

"I took it down one night," said Robinson, giving that universal waggle of the hands that goes back to the Stone Age, "and I could feel the line drives still rattlin' around in it."

Those Who Watch Batting Practice and
   Those Who Don't

All baseball fans can be divided into two groups: those who come to batting practice and the others. Only those in the first category have much chance of amounting to anything.

Those who arrive just in time to hear, "Oh, say can you see . . ." will never truly appreciate what happens after ". . . the home of the brave." Baseball gives up its secrets in dribs and drabs, conceals its tensions and tendencies well. Some say too well. Perhaps no sport rewards its devotees in such direct proportion to the quality of their attention. Batting practice is the Rosetta Stone that unlocks many of the game's hieroglyphics. But "BP," as the players call it, is also entertaining theater in its own right. Finally, and most important, batting practice—including all the fielding drills, pepper games, and pitching warm-ups that fall under that generic term—is a sort of ninety-minute tone poem that sets the mood of the sport.

The fan's leisurely arrival while the ball park is nearly empty, the slowly-paced first hot-dog-and-beer, the meticulous filling out of the scorecard, the calm perusal of the visitors taking their licks . . . all this is part of adapting the spirit to baseball's deliberate speed and its demand for heightened awareness of detail. Especially at evening, when the sky itself darkens like the stage lights dimming, there is a coexistence of total relaxation and keen anticipation that is totally lost on the fan who rushes to his seat to beat the first pitch.

It is commonplace, but essential, to note that the longest home runs, the best outfield catches, the grandest infield pirouettes are almost always displayed in batting practice. The fresh memory of those harshly batted balls and brilliant catches keeps us aware of the potential behind each pitch during the actual game. Surely the gent who reached the upper deck at 6 P.M. can still do it at 10 P.M.

Although batting practice is a circus with many sideshows, the center ring is always the batting cage. The rules of the cage are inflexible; time, down to the second, is of the essence. Each team hits for forty-five minutes and not an instant more. The subdivisions of that forty-five minutes are minutely guarded. A player who takes an extra swing is cursed to his face. A starter who invades the few precious minutes of the bench warmers is threatened with an instant visit to the disabled list.

Only a few princes can ignore the ethics of the cage. Ted Williams, in his later years, disdained the hitter's coffee klatch around home plate, preferring the cool of the locker room. When he stepped from the Boston dugout, the water parted and whichever Bosox had the misfortune to be swinging fled. Williams hit for as long as he wanted and whenever he wanted, then returned to his subterranean solitude. In recent years, Boston's Carl Yastrzemski has tried to cast himself in a similar role—with little success.

"When are you guys going to run that Yastrzemski out of there. He's had sixteen swings already," snaps Boston's Rick Burleson by the Fenway cage, more than loud enough for the Boston captain to hear. Yastrzemski, known for a slight case of rabbit-eared paranoia, anyway, departs in haste, perhaps remembering an incident in Baltimore when the feisty Burleson had gotten in a fistfight with strongman Jim Rice over a matter of just one extra swing.

The batting cage is at the same time baseball's most gregarious gathering spot and also the most serious of workshops. Hitters are that rare athletic breed that must do their plotting in public. "Most of us are constantly changing our stances, looking for different kinds of pitches, trying to protect our old weaknesses and steal a few hits until they figure out our new ones," said Mark Belanger. "Maybe a few great hitters can dictate to the pitchers, but the rest of us have to work on things we'd like to keep secret with everybody watching."

It is as easy to figure out who is hot and who's not, who has changed his tendencies, when a player takes thirty swings in a condensed ten-minute period as it is hard to get a clear pattern from watching the same fellow's four at-bats in the game.

Of all the batting-cage spies, New York's Thurman Munson was one of the most blatant, leaning on the cage for a half hour at a time staring at the stances and swings of the opponents against whom he would call pitches in an hour. Isn't this kind of obvious, like a detective wearing a white suit on a tail job, Munson was once asked. "That might be part of the idea," he said with a grin. Once a crossbar fell off the cage in Memorial Stadium and landed on Munson's head, raising a large mouse, the Orioles awarded the sleuth in their midst a round of mock applause.

For the hundreds of big leaguers who think their "swings" are serious business, there has to be one, Fred Lynn, who steps into the cage with a blank brain and a light heart. "They call me Five-swing Freddy," Lynn said with a laugh. "I don't ask for a particular pitch in a special spot. I don't work on anything or think about anything. And I swing at every pitch . . . even if it bounces. I'm just getting loose and sharpening my hand-eye coordination. I don't always swing at perfect strikes in the game, and the bottom line is that when you finally swing, you gotta hit the ball square. That's all I try to do.

"Five pitches and they're rid of me. I can't think of the last batting-practice pitch that was so wild that I didn't hit it."

To those whose eyes wander from the plate, batting practice offers a panoply of little vignettes. Perhaps an ancient coach like California's Jimmy Reese is running Nolan Ryan into a puddle of sweat chasing his deftly placed fungoes. Perhaps an idle pitcher tries to catch a high fly over-the-head-behind-the-back and manages to get himself conked. Then pretends nothing happened.

For the fan who wants to get a reading on his team's morale, no barometer is better than BP. The pregame ritual is such an accustomed daily event that most players forgot years ago that they are in public. The argument, the glare, the cross words between teammates are almost always exactly what they seem to be. And so are the hijinks, the laughter, the camaraderie. Nobody bothers to fake it in BP.

The manager who stands by the cage needling his players—"Hey, Kelly's hitting line drives. What time is it? Must not be game time yet"—usually knows his players will not suddenly choose this moment to show him up, undercut him as they easily can with a word. And the manager who sits alone usually has his reason, also. So did the beleaguered soul, like Billy Martin during the siege of New York, who hid from the press by shagging fly-balls for an hour and then signing autographs until there was too little time left for an interview.

The athlete, so protected by the shell of professional aplomb that covers any situation on the field, so glib and experienced in showing only one side of himself in interviews, gives at least a glimpse of his disposition in those hours before the game when he acts as though no one could see him.

Batting practice is baseball's gossip mart, its campfire for tall tales. In the wake of a New York blackout, the story that made the rounds concerned the Cubs' wild fastballer, Pete Broberg, who was right at the point of release in the Shea Stadium bull pen when the lights went out. Chicago catcher Steve Swisher, rather in the dark as to whether Broberg had thrown the pitch, winced and held the mitt where Broberg had last seen it. "Smack!" the ball struck dead in the pocket.

Such a yarn, unadorned, is not worthy of the cage. Only the kicker qualifies it. "That," Swisher reportedly said, "was the first time Broberg hit a catcher's glove in six years."

Batting practice presents the baseball tableau on its smallest and most intimate scale. It provides the stuff of anecdote, not myth. Instead of citing great deeds, players are more likely to rest their heads on their forearms as they lean on the cage and discuss their disappointments. Ex-teammates meet again and sometimes find themselves faced with capsulizing the most important events in their lives—a divorce, a bad beaning, a firing—with a quip. "Hey, Billy," a player yells to his old team's coach, "can't you keep your infielders married?"

As soon as a batter catches the assembled eyes by pumping a few into the seats, he is brought back to earth. Brooks Robinson cries, "Put him in the Hall of Shame . . . two o'clock hitter." The old-timers shake their heads and remember names: "Yes, Davey May. Best BP hitter I ever saw. Too bad they couldn't put a screen in front of the pitcher during the game."

The easy hours before the call to arms ("Play Ball") are baseball's pastoral idyll and its guarantee of value. Those who leave the park dissatisfied are usually those who unwisely chose to forsake the game's lazy preamble with its graceful delights. Put 'em all in that Hall of Shame.

The Zen of Rod Carew

Rod Carew sat in the dugout, looking at the drizzle at dusk, watching the steady mist spatter the puddles on the cinder track before him. Other Angels chattered, gossiped, fidgeted. Carew meditated. The man with seven batting titles—the California Wrecking Carew—sat motionless as an Aztec icon, the long delicate fingers of his startlingly veined and tendoned hands barely touching at the tips.

"I can pick out an object—that rock, for instance—and concentrate on it until I feel totally at peace, totally relaxed as though my body were weightless. Hypnosis has helped teach me that," Carew said. "On a bus or an airplane—or right here this minute—I can tilt my head to one side and in a few seconds, I will be asleep. My teammates kid me that I fall asleep everywhere except at bat . . . but it is not a trick. It is a direct reflection of your peace of mind . . . a sort of demonstration to yourself that you have no worries . . . that nothing's troubling you upstairs.

"Discipline . . . order," says the meticulous, immaculate Angel slowly, as though the words were gold and silver held one in each sculpted hand. "These things help you feel good about yourself. No one can give you that feeling. It took me a long time . . . I battled to become myself," says Carew, born in Panama, raised in Harlem, resident of Golden Valley in the Minnesota lake country, convert to Judaism. "Learning to relax . . . to accept things . . . to forgive yourself . . . not to expect to be perfect in baseball or in the rest of your life—I've come a long way," he says. "When I first came to the majors, at least I knew how much of an immature kid I was, how I put myself in moods and then into slumps.

"Now," he says, holding a hand in front of him waist-high, just where he would like every pitch, "I keep myself right here." His hand is without a tremble. It is, metaphorically, the hand of moderation—the rock-steady middle road.

Only the rarest baseball players are watched, studied, openly discussed, and gawked at by their peers. Even within that charismatic elite there is a fundamental division into higher and lower

forms of respect. A few, like Mike Schmidt, Dave Parker, or Nolan
Ryan, are observed for the pure awe-struck pleasure of seeing their
natural gifts, their animal brilliance. These specimens are surrounded by the same nervous laughter heard near tiger cages. A
still smaller number of stars are watched for what might be called
their philosophical disposition toward the game, their mental and
emotional plan of attack. In this category baseball has perhaps
only two everyday philosophers—personalities whose every athletic
gesture is an eloquently wrought embodiment of a deliberate idea.
That pair would be Pete Rose, hustling hedonist, and Carew, the
stoic star. They are baseball's classic Greek types—the Dionysian
and Apollonian performers; the game's pure distillations of fire
and ice. The stocky, swarthy Rose drives a silver Rolls-Royce to
the park. The lithe Carew, with his radiant face, arrives on a bicycle.

Other great players are observed minutely only while perform-
ing. Rose and Carew are analyzed constantly by their fellow major
leaguers even if they are only blending a pregame wad of chewing
gum and tobacco. Character outshines talent. It is no happenstance that both Rose and Carew are being asked to bring their
personalities to bear on their new teams.

The oh-well-we-lost-again Phils need Rose's gumption. The wilt-
in-the-clutch Angels need Carew's grace under pressure. Like teams
that are off to see the Wizard, Philadelphia needs a heart, while
California wants some courage. Anaheim may not quite be the
Emerald City, but two Angels, who lead the team in every major
offensive category, already think that Carew is granting their re-
quests.

Boos leave their brand, repeated failures their mark. Don Baylor
and Bobby Grich, millionaire free agents, both have felt crushing
pressure in their two years as Angels—and both feel it lifting now,
courtesy of Carew.

Baylor, who has borne the weight of great expectations since he
was minor league player of the year long ago, felt so depressed by
Big A boobirds that he asked to be traded. "It was sad," says
Baylor. "I was the team scapegoat, no question."

Grich, crippled by back surgery in '77 for a herniated disk, sank
far lower. By last August "other players actually pitied him," says
Angel reliever Dyar Miller. "He couldn't even make the routine

plays. Guys would say, 'Poor Grich is washed up and he isn't even thirty. He used to be able to do it all.'"

In 1979, Grich has a new Carew batting stance and philosophy. "Another season like '78, and it would have been my last. I'd have quit the game, I think," says Grich. "Now I know I can still play."

Baylor, who gratefully sees Carew all around him—both on base ahead of him and in the clubhouse taking over the pressurized team-leader role—tied a major league record with 28 RBIs in April.

"Rod has taken a world of pressure off us all," says Grich. "He's assumed the burden of the publicity and the pressure of being the top hitter. He accepts it without a complaint. I'm sure it's helped Groove [Baylor] relax."

Groove and Grich, old buddies from Baltimore, fellow Angel sufferers, are in heaven at last, at least in part due to Carew.

"I think we talked about some things in spring training," says Carew evasively. "They had to do too much. They had the big contracts and were forcing themselves. Well, maybe I have the money, too, but it's different."

Different because he is Carew.

"You can't play to suit the public," says Carew. "I watched Harmon Killebrew for years . . . the abuse he took from fans despite hitting over 500 home runs. It rolled off him. He never showed his defiance.

"Maybe the best players develop an immunity to outside judgment . . . they judge themselves. Above all, you must know yourself, know your limits. I absolutely do. If you try to go beyond that, you always hurt yourself. I used to, but no more.

"So I said to some of the guys, 'Put all that so-called pressure and big-money talk on me, because I don't respond to any of it.'"

Grich and Baylor, like the rest of humanity, never have felt that immunity. They marvel at it in their new teammate.

"Carew is so totally relaxed, so orderly, that I just find myself watching everything he does," says Grich. "I started holding the bat relaxed and high like he does, rolling the handle loosely in the fingers, and that relaxation just flowed through my upper body. I've never popped the ball so well."

Carew has also subtly eased Baylor's burden. In essence, No. 3 hitter Carew told cleanup man Baylor he was going to make him a household name whether he wanted to be one or not. "Rod said he was going to be on base so much that I'd drive in 110 runs even if I had a bad year," Baylor, who went on to 139 RBIs and the American League MVP Award, says with a laugh.

Like Carew in one of his meditative trances, the Angels were already glimpsing the future. Baylor would win the MVP; Grich would have his greatest year; the Angels would win their first division championship in history.

From beginning to end the Angels have little doubt who to thank—it is the modest Socrates of swing in the corner, the artist with the angelic face, the quiet man who, it seems, just tilted his head a moment ago and has peacefully fallen asleep.

Georgie Ballgame

George Brett and Ted Williams only have one thing in common: The calluses. In his autobiography, *My Turn at Bat*, Williams sneered that modern players don't have those "real big, hard ugly calluses" that gave him such pride. Batting gloves, bah. Teddy Ballgame took batting practice until his mitts bled. He knew that an honest workman's hands bespoke his trade, and that a hitter's paws should look like the pads on a gorilla's feet. Brett's got 'em. You'd need steel wool and a day's elbow grease to get down to the skin on his palms. His hands are the deeply strained orange-brown of pine tar, dirt, and maybe a little tobacco juice rubbed in over a lifetime.

Those calluses are the outward sign of an inward rage to hit. On rare evenings when Brett has been held hitless in his first couple of at-bats, his Kansas City teammates often hear a horrid smashing sound from the tunnel behind their dugout. It's just George beating a bat against a cement wall in frustrated fury. Only in their raw, sometimes almost antisocial passion to compete are the patrician Williams and the grimy Brett similar. Their theories of hitting, their style at the plate, their whole attitude toward the game, as well as their personalities, are nearly total opposites. In time, their only link may be that, since 1930, they are baseball's only two .400 hitters.

"When Williams got a hit, he gave everybody a lecture on how he did it," said Hal McRae of the Royals as Brett laughed. "When George gets a hit, he just says, 'Gimme another one.' Williams was cold-blooded. Scientific. George is hot-blooded."

"I remember that chart Williams made, showing what he thought his batting average was against pitches in every inch of the strike zone," interjected Brett, shaking his head. "I'd have no idea."

Where Williams was analytical—whether batting, flying a fighter plane, or building a better fishing rod—Brett is a baseball child of instinct and enthusiasm. Because of that, his September 1980 chase for .400 was, in some sense, unfair to Brett, and perhaps even unworthy of him. Williams was always a creature of statistics, a man who divided baseball into the exalted occupation called hitting, and all the rest, which was pointless drudgery, and beneath him. Even that title—*My Turn at Bat*—implied that the rest of any game was superfluous. For him, the solo hunt for .400—just the Kid against those dastardly pitchers—was a proper measure of the man, a heroic crusade full of solitary dignity. By any candid comparison of career statistics, Williams was a better and more powerful hitter than Brett. On the other hand, Brett is a far more complete and entertaining total player than Williams ever was, or even wanted to be. If a general manager were given the luscious choice of picking either the Williams of '41 or the Brett of '80, he might have to think hard, wondering if he preferred self-centered genius or hard-nosed leadership. If Williams was always the stylish flyboy, then Brett is the first lieutenant leading the troops over the top. It is not necessary to have a preference between such contrasts. That is why there is an unpalatable perversity about measuring them on the same .400 scale.

When Rod Carew hit .388 in '77, it was appropriate that these two artists be balanced against each other. Carew was the purist of the place hit and the bunt; Williams was the art-for-art's sake purist of the well-struck pull hit.

But now we have a different situation. Brett, like Pete Rose, is an impurist of the best sort. In a sense, they are baseball cousins once removed. Hal McRae learned the game by emulating Rose when he was a young Red. Brett learned his style by overtly copying McRae when Brett was a young Royal. Theirs is a philosophy that sees a player's skills in terms of function and team result. "I'm a situation player," says Brett. "When the game isn't close, I have a hard time concentrating. When I go to the plate, I ask myself, 'What do we need? A sacrifice fly? A single to move a man from first to third? Do we need a home run to tie the game?'"

Williams was a one-man drama larger than most of the games in which his Red Sox played. He dominated the scene, separated himself from teammates, and made no bones about being a prima donna. When he walked to the batting cage, at a moment of his own choosing, the seas parted, he took his cuts, and left when he was good and ready.

Brett is the melody running through a Royal victory. He

doesn't dominate the game, but blends into it. You must study the action to discover everything he has contributed. Proud of his dirty uniform, bruises, and abrasions, Brett is particularly pleased by his wild extra-base style of running, since like McRae and Rose, he doesn't have sprinter's speed. Brett is just added proof that, in baseball, intensity, adventurousness and seasoned judgment can produce the same results as great talent. Even Brett's father, who was a demon of a stage-door parent, admits that "I always overlooked George. I thought all three of his older brothers had more baseball ability." They probably did.

For those close to the game, Brett has been a half-appreciated treasure for six years. During Brett's chase of .400 in 1980, Royals public relations director Dean Vogelaar could say, "This is the first year that George has started to get the kind of national attention that you'd associate with one of the best players in the game."

To see the true Brett, to see how much more than "a potential .400 hitter" he is, you have to go back to a hot June day before that crazy media chase of .400 began when few eyes were on him and he could be himself.

On a 96° F. day in Kansas City, Brett arrived at the ball park at 2 P.M.—5½ hours before game time, and three hours before most of his mates. First, the ambidextrous Brett pitched batting practice left-handed to a few rusty scrubs who needed extra work and knew they'd be run out of the cage when the stars arrived. Then, Brett shagged their flyballs for another hour after his arm got tired. (Williams came to the park early, too, working on those calluses, but he only took batting practice; he didn't pitch it.) Next, Brett, who is determined to become a Gold Glove third baseman (and isn't far away), took extra ground balls at both shortstop and third base. After batting practice, Brett took infield with the regulars at third, then, when the subs had their infield, he played first base left-handed. Oh, yes, he played the whole game that night and had three hits.

For this man to be the match head of a purely personal fire is something more than incongruous. Brett enjoyed most of the .400 hoopla. "I want to hit .400 more than anybody, even my father," he said at the time. "But it's not going to be drudgery. I'm going to make it fun."

Nevertheless, it does not seem fair to measure Brett by one skill. His highest contribution is an attitude toward the game, a sort of moral philosophy of how a ballplayer should act. Perhaps Brett epitomized his approach—which is not to every taste—in his '76 play-off brawl with Graig Nettles. Each tried to kick the other, as well as punch and gouge. Afterward, Brett said, "One thing impressed me about that fight. Thurman Munson was on top of me in the pile. My arms were pinned, so he put both his hands over my face so his teammates couldn't punch me."

While the aloof Williams with his spotless flannel uniform and the gregarious Brett with his filthy double-knit uniform are sharp contrasts in personality and style of play, they are even more dramatically different as hitters.

The surest way to keep Brett from ever hitting .400 would be for Williams to give him a hitting lesson.

Almost everything Williams preached is anathema to Brett. Williams thought a "flat" swing was a chimera and sought an ever-so-slight uppercut. Brett wants an ever-so-slight downward chop. Williams stood still with his weight slightly back as he awaited a pitch. Brett moves constantly, searching for an "interior rhythm," while rocking his weight completely back in what he, and other Charlie Lau pupils, call "the launch position." Williams stepped directly forward into a pitch, or, perhaps, opened his hips a little so he could "get out of his own way" and pull with authority.

Brett "charges the plate" by standing well off the dish, then stepping toward it as he swings so he actually hits across his body. If Brett used his hips the way Williams constantly preached, he might hit .000.

Williams' bat was vertical; Brett's is almost horizontal. Williams kept his hands free of his body; Brett's are locked in close to his shoulder. Williams never swung at a "bad" pitch, since the strike zone in the rule book and his own strike zone were nearly identical. Brett, who gets only a third of the walks Williams did, has his own strike zone and swings at what pleases him. While Williams was classic and motionless, Brett flutes his fingers on the bat.

Williams, the slugger of menace, was a statue of perfect form. Brett, the all-fields line-drive gap-hitter, stands in the box whirling his bat in an unobtrusive, yet constant circle like a small single-prop plane about to take off. Perhaps most important, while Williams built his own swing and created many of the ideas behind it, Brett had his notions handled by Lau. Williams developed a style to match his own almost superhuman eyesight, his height, leverage, and power. Brett adopted a style Lau created with the average man in mind—a technique that could help the mediocre ballplayer, like the kind Brett was in the minors, become a .300 hitter. Williams, in time of stress, could go back to his own drawing board. Brett must go back to the teacher. Only now, with Lau on the rival Chicago White Sox, he can't.

"I'd like to talk to Charlie," Brett said. "But you can't call up someone in your own league. Charlie used to look at me for one or two at-bats, and he'd spot what I was doing wrong. Now, I may go a week or more before I figure it out for myself."

"Jeeeez, Brett," scoffs McRae, a fellow Lau protégé and the one man who serves as swing doctor to Brett, "you haven't been in a slump in two years. You don't need a coach."

"I feel like Dr. Frankenstein watching his monster on the loose," says Lau.

Where Williams believed that there was a reason for everything, Brett is convinced that there is a mystical element to hitting. "One day, I wake up and I'm hot," said Brett. "I can't explain it. When I'm like that, I get more hits in a shorter period of time than anybody in baseball. I once had three or more hits in six consecutive games [19 for 24]. When I'm like that, I hit any pitch from any pitcher. I can't explain it and I don't try."

For Williams, the closing days of '41 were ones of internal pressure. He walked the streets of Philadelphia long into the night before raising his average from .3995 to .406 in a closing-day doubleheader. A student of the record book, he knew exactly what he was doing and how much it meant. He had discussions with old .400-hitter Harry Heilmann and sought his advice. For Brett, a simpler chap, September 1980 was a chance for "fun" and no particular cause for internal stress. After all, he knew that a .400 average was only one partial measure of what he brings to his game and his team. Told that his statistical line for '80 was almost identical to Heilmann's in '24, Brett got a quizzical expression on his face.

"Who the hell is Harry Heilmann?" said George Brett.

In the end, that insouciance, that almost casual attitude, may be Brett's greatest helper. After all, he already has the only thing a great hitter really needs. He has the calluses.

"Sometimes I Think He's Too Good for the Game"

Frank Howard's left knee is swollen the size of a small trash can. But he won't stop running from the Spokane Indians' dugout to the third-base coach's box. It is a painful trip that sometimes takes more than a minute. Howard looks like Chester in TV's old "Gunsmoke" series, that is, if Chester were in a great hurry and weighed three hundred pounds.

All the nervous twitches and winces of intensity and strain that fans recall with empathy from Howard's home-run days come into play. His neck clenches, his eyes blink and water, his arms pump like Walter Brennan's, and he does a little hop when the pain is too sharp.

"It's nothing much," says Howard, now, in the spring of '76, a rookie manager of the Milwaukee Brewers' top farm team in the AAA Pacific Coast League. "Just a ligament problem. It's getting better. I guess I'm just a worn out old left fielder."

Howard wore out those knees in a noble cause, backing up bases and running out ground balls on Washington Senator teams that were going nowhere. Pete Rose never hustled any harder than Frank Howard, just more conspicuously.

Howard has only one message for his players, and if every trip across the diamond is like a visit to the dentist, then Howard is willing to endure it, if it helps make that point. "Boys," he says, "in this game you never play as long as you want to or as well as you want to. And sooner than any of you thinks, your day will come to get that pink slip that says, 'Released.' When they pull those shades, they pull 'em for a lifetime. When it's over, no one can bring it back for you. It's a short road we run in this business, so run hard."

The Spokane Indians run hard. "He's got us running getting dressed," says third baseman Tom Bianco, in his third AAA season. "We lead the league in hustle, rules, and meetings. We're up to two meetings a day. We even had a meeting after a rainout to go over the rain."

"We call him the three-hundred-pound greenie," says twenty-three-year-old Steve Bowling. "He's better than any pill to get you ready for a game. His energy is infinite."

Just like his strength and his generosity. "He's so big," said Bianco, "he put his arm around me and I felt like a pimple. One day the tractor was broken, so he grabbed hold of the batting cage and dragged it away. Six of us couldn't move it."

Some Indians fear infield practice. "He doesn't know how hard he's hitting those grounders," says Bianco. "One'll hit you in the chest and Frank'll say, 'Are you all right?' and if you say 'Yes,' he'll hit another one just as hard."

"I figure if they get toughened up on hard ones, the rest will be easy," laughs Howard.

The minor leaguers, used to $10-a-day meal money and equally modest salaries, are even more stunned by Howard's largesse. "Nobody can pick up a tab from him," says Bowling. "For a while, if we saw him eating, we'd all pile in and he'd buy for everybody. It got embarrassing, so we stopped."

Nevertheless, the Indians never know when Howard's money clip full of $20 bills will strike again. "He'll yell 'stop the bus. Got to get some beer for my boys. They're playin' some hard baseball,'" said Bianco.

"He'll buy a case for everybody on the bus, then say, 'We got any Coke drinkers?' And he'll buy each of them a six-pack of Coke," said Bowling.

Howard's favorite expression after games is, "How can you wheel that lumber tomorrow if you don't pound that Budweiser tonight."

Howard will not admit to ever having footed a bill, although he mutters, "Aww, these kids don't make any money."

Howard is not trying to buy loyalty. His generosity has always been legendary. He cannot do anything in a small way. He lights his cigars with three matches.

"I was always one of the boys as a player," says Howard, "and I'll manage that way too."

However, the Indians have learned not to mistake kindness for weakness. "Oh, no, don't do that," says Bianco.

"I'll give everybody the courtesy of sitting down and discussing anything with me. I make a lot of mistakes. I'm finding out every day how dumb I am," says Howard, his blue-as-the-sky eyes laughing under red hair, now grown out. "We talk about it, then we do it my way."

"In fourteen years, I've never heard of a manager who showed the players the report he wrote to the big league club after every game," said veteran minor league first baseman Tom Reynolds, thirty-four.

"If I say they played great, I show 'em that," said Howard. "If I said they looked lousy, they see that, too. There are no secrets here. We're all working together.

"I tell them, 'You don't want to play for me. This league isn't where you want to be. I tell every one of them what it takes for them to get out of here and into the big leagues."

"He doesn't play favorites," said outfielder Rob Ellis. "He treats black, white, and Spanish alike."

Howard's temper has only ignited once in Spokane after a team's pitchers threw at his hitters several days in a row. At the next team meeting, Howard announced, according to several players, "The first guy they throw at, we give 'em the benefit of the doubt. The second time, we go right through their lineup—one to nine—and stick [hit] every one of 'em in the ribs. We'll keep somebody warmed up and as soon as they throw out one pitcher, we'll bring in another. We're going to stop this right now, if it costs us a game."

One plunked opponent, the lead-off man, got the point across to the opposition. "It's nice to know your manager will protect you," said a Spokane hitter. "Frank would have carried out his threat, too. He had the bull pen going."

Fortunately, Howard rarely blows his stack. "If he did," says Phoenix Manager Rocky Bridges, "people would be heading for the next train smokin'."

Instead, Howard tries to be low key. "I don't overinstruct," he says. "I had enough people dicker with me when I was young."

Howard, however, does have one pet peeve.

"At first, all the pitchers thought Frank hated us," says pitcher Tom Widmar. All Howard hated, it turned out, was walks—a passion he learned from Ted Williams. "If we walked someone," said Widmar, "we wanted to go to the other dugout."

"What good is it to be able to throw a ball through a brick wall," snorts Howard, "if you can't hit the wall."

As for signs, "I'm not concerned about the other team stealing them," says Howard. "I'm just concerned about us getting them."

To that end, Howard has considered adopting Bridges' steal sign. "He just points to the man on first and goes like this," says Howard, doing a twinkle-toes imitation with his fingers like the "Let-your-fingers-do-the-walking" ad on TV.

Bridges, a legend in the PCL since the day he sprinted out of the dugout, circled the mound twice without talking to anyone, then raced back, has given Howard his managerial blessing. "Big Bird should do good," says Bridges of Howard. "He played the game right."

"I remember the encouragement I needed when I was young," says Howard. "I had no idea what I was doing until I was thirty years old. Like old Teddy Williams says, 'You dumb hitters. By the time you know what to do, you're too old to do it.' When I was a kid I just tried to flat out whale it every time like a crazy man.

"Pete Reiser was my first manager, and I'm like him in temperament—very, very intense. He used to say to me over and over, 'Eliminate doubt. Eliminate doubt. Stay with 'em, kid. Someday you're goin' to light somebody up.'

"That's what I tell my kids now. You've got to come out firing every day. Have pride. Work hard at your trade. If you can't run ninety feet to first base, get out of the organization. Good-bye. Find some line of work where you can goof off. But don't kid yourself. You get in that lunch-pail world and you'll find some real wolves waiting for you."

Spokane players sneak up behind each other and whisper Howard's favorite threat, "Good-bye." It is enough to make any wooden Indian jump.

Howard insists he is "no cop and no baby-sitter." He does tend to his players' private lives, though. In Spokane, he doesn't need to. The only real action is across the border in Spirit Lake, Idaho, at the White Horse Saloon run by Mo Smith, an ex-lightweight boxer. There a man can prop up his feet, listen to country music, tipple tequila, and spit tobacco juice at Mo's two hounds, Homer and Damn It.

Washington's Inland Empire suits Howard perfectly. Spokane is bathed in a crisp summer fragrance of spruce that Howard has loved since he played here for the Indians nearly twenty years ago. Most of the same fans that saw him then are here today, and they still talk about the liner he hit off the left-field wall that bounced back to the shortstop.

"I would like to manage in the majors," says Howard, "or have a coaching job if it were meaningful, not just being a lamppost. But I would never shoot for another man's job.

"I was away from baseball for a year, but it's not something you can get out of your blood. Look what the game has done for me. Twenty years ago I was a shy, introverted kid who didn't know how to hold a conversation with anyone. But gradually baseball brought me out of my shell and taught me to communicate with people. I've traveled around the world a couple of times. It's enabled me to broaden whatever outlook I might have had . . . Baseball's been a good education," said Howard.

"Is it possible," the man who is called the Gentle Giant is reminded, "that you may turn out to be a better manager than you were a player, despite those 382 home runs?"

Howard looks at the ceiling, delighted as much as if he were wheeling the lumber or pounding the Bud. "I guess I never thought of that," he fibs. "For sure I'm no genius. Maybe I'll turn out to be a lousy manager."

Wherever Howard and twenty-one little Indians finish, his players know the quality of the man they have played for.

"If player recommendations would be it, Frank would be in the majors tomorrow," says outfielder Bowling. "We know he doesn't need this game. He has plenty of real estate in Wisconsin. He's just in it because he loves it.

"Sometimes I think he's too good for this game."

Frank Howard was fired in 1981 after one season as manager of the San Diego Padres. "The players took advantage of him," said Padre GM, Jack McKeon. "Frank just couldn't stop being nice."

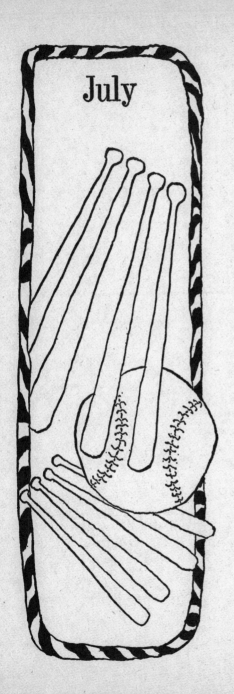

July

Arms and the Men

Jim Lonborg soaked his elbow in a bucket of ice, his skin turning blistered from its cold. The veteran Philadelphia pitcher, in his fourteenth major league season, seemed to welcome the familiar numbness, which others might call a frigid pain, gradually taking the place of the real pain that danced through his arm.

"There's nothing in particular wrong with my arm," said the thirty-five-year-old right-hander late in the 1978 season. "It just doesn't work anymore.

"I've had arm trouble since I broke into the minors. It's never entirely left me alone. There's just a general weakness now throughout the entire arm from the shoulder down.

"It feels fine. Let me make that clear," said Lonborg, who battled his recalcitrant body for years to stay in the starting rotation of a winning team at his advanced age.

"It likes the ice," said Lonborg, looking at his arm as though some malicious Martian had transplanted it onto him. "The cold helps it recover."

"I never sit on the right side of a bus or airplane where my arm might be in air-conditioning or a draft," says right-hander Tom Seaver of Cincinnati. "I can't sleep on my right side. If I accidentally roll over on it, I wake right up. I guess it's never out of your mind, even when you're asleep.

"Your arm is your best friend," said Seaver, grinning, "but you've got to treat it like it was your worst enemy. I swear, it'll get you if it can."

Even pitchers themselves hate to face the reality of how undependable, how changeable their arms actually are. All know the roller-coaster horror stories of hurlers like Pat Dobson who won 20 games, dropped to 3 wins in a year, struggled back to 19 victories, then plummeted suddenly back to 3 again. But they hate to face the fact that this syndrome is the hard rule, not the exception.

Of all baseball's active pitchers, how many have won 15 or more games for more than 5 seasons in a row?

Plenty, one would think, since the list of hitters who have

amassed 20 homers or 75 RBIs or .280 batting averages—or any comparable middle-echelon statistic—for 10 seasons in a row is as long as your arm.

The answer is four—Gaylord Perry (12 straight years), Don Sutton (8), Seaver (7), and Ferguson Jenkins (6).

"Any injury is worse for a pitcher," commiserates the frequently hospitalized slugger Johnny Bench. "A hitter can make adjustments, work around the pain, even develop a new swing. You can avoid aggravating the injury and still hit the ball. But any time a pitcher throws, it's a reminder. I caught Gary Nolan for ten years, and he was the worst I ever saw. He hurt all the time. Nobody can tell what he went through. But I watched his face for ten years, and I don't think he ever threw a pitch that didn't hurt."

"I try not to have too much sympathy for 'em," said Philadelphia catcher Bob Boone, torn by his position of being a helper of pitchers, and one of the hunted.

"But," Boone adds, "I'd sure hate to have all my eggs hanging on my cords."

Those cords—tendons, ligaments, muscles—in the shoulder, elbow, and even wrist and fingers, are constantly trying to go on the fritz. "Pitching is a totally unnatural motion," says Lonborg, who was a biology major at Stanford. "It's a hazard just to be throwing."

Most baseball fans have no conception of what their favorite pitcher looks like ten minutes after he walks off the mound. Bill Lee has his shoulder in a harness that looks as if he had been struck by mortar fire. Jim Palmer practically runs from the mound to the ice bucket, unless he wants a special shoulder massage or whirlpool treatment first. "There's only one cure for what's wrong with all of us pitchers," says Palmer, who has had or thought he had, almost every known pitching malady, "and that's to take a year off. Then, after you've gone a year without throwing, quit altogether."

The Pitchers' Union, the underground grapevine of counterintelligence on hitters, is well known. But the Pitchers' Medical Underground is just as complete and thorough. Special remedies, fad doctors, new training regimens, hypnosis, pitching coaches with mystic powers—all are discussed.

Word travels even faster about exotic or terrifying arm injuries.

The day Wayne Garland of Cleveland found out that he would miss the rest of the season because of the dread torn rotator cuff, Palmer was on the phone to him for details. By the next afternoon, Palmer was showing identical symptoms.

Before his next start, Palmer went to his personal physician in the afternoon. The moment the game ended, Palmer went to his doctor again for an after-midnight reexamination while the arm was still warm.

"Don't ask me anything about it," pleaded Baltimore Manager Earl Weaver. "All I know is Jimmy talked to Wayne and now he's worried about his rotar cuff."

Palmer immediately went on a streak in which he allowed 3 earned runs in 67 innings. "I guess," said Weaver, allowing himself a touch of whimsy, "that Jim's rotar cuff must not be totally torn."

Palmer, like many veterans, gets at least four levels of medical opinion on his arm—the team trainer, a team doctor, a local personal physician, and a nationally known specialist (in Palmer's case Dr. Robert Kerlan in Los Angeles).

Where medicine and the arm are concerned, there are only two types of pitchers—hypochondriacs and fools.

"A lot of us have learned the hard way that team doctors are seldom specialists," says Lonborg, who had bitter experiences in that area with Boston a decade ago. "As you get older, you learn to be patient with it," said Lonborg of his third-person neuter friend. "You learn to put the long-term interests of your career ahead of the short-term interests of your team.

"Time and proper treatment are the only remedy if you want to avoid corrective surgery. I tell the doctor, 'Get out the diagrams and the medical books. Don't leave me in the dark. I'm smart enough to understand this, and I want it explained.'"

However, even with his science background, it took Lonborg years, and a near-brush with a premature end to his career, before he would confront a doctor and ask, "What's going on here?"

"The way young pitchers are treated is brutal, practically a scandal," says Lonborg. "'Give him a little rest and get him back out there,' is the common theory.

"Some organizations like the Mets, who have always lived by pitching, never seem to have a sore arm. Other teams, like the

Reds, have always had young pitchers with sore arms. It doesn't seem coincidental."

The greatest debate within baseball for the last century has been how to care for and feed a pitching arm. No question approaches that one in importance to any team.

Seaver offers the classic theory on wind sprints and the art of Arm Maintenance.

"Let me make it as simple as I can," says Seaver like a kindly bishop explaining dogma to a doubter. "Here is your body and here is the baseball. You want to put 100 percent of the energy in your body into that ball. That creates velocity. But it's an impossibility to use all 100 percent. The unused energy of the windup and delivery has to dissipate somewhere. It's going to be absorbed by your body. How that energy, that shock at the end of every pitch, is absorbed, determines whether you have arm trouble. You want to finish your delivery so that the big muscles of the body— the thighs and buttocks—absorb the shock. That's why pitchers run all these damn wind sprints, to strengthen the large lower-body muscles. If your legs are weak, then you finish your delivery stiff-legged as you get tired rather than flexible and bouncy, and you end up with a ruined arm. In pitching," summarizes Seaver somberly, "the smallest muscles in your body—the ones in the wrist, elbow, and front of the shoulder—get the most abuse. You have to find a way to minimize that."

A nice, rational, irrefutable argument, right? Completely wrong, as far as super pitching coach Johnny Sain, 106-game reliever Mike Marshall, and Sain disciple Jim Kaat are concerned.

"There's nothing wrong with running," says Kaat, "but Sain teaches you that you strengthen the arm and become a better pitcher by throwing, not by running. The only way to strengthen the arm is to use it, not rest it while you run a million wind sprints.

"Sain and Marshall [whose ideas are similar] drive the old-timers crazy," says Kaat. "It's a completely new concept after a hundred years, and it's before its time."

"Nuts," says Seaver. "I wouldn't let Sain near me. All I can say about Marshall is that one year he pitched in 106 games and I saw him at the All-Star game, and three years later he was out of a job."

Arms, unfortunately, are not a subject of casual debate in locker rooms, like whether the manager should be fired. Arms are serious business.

"The essence of the pitching motion is to be aggressive, yet be relaxed and comfortable," says Lonborg. "But out on the mound, every pressure, every internal tension puts stress on your muscles and keeps you from being fluid.

"If we all had a million dollars in the bank, we'd pitch relaxed and there'd be a lot less arm trouble. Every once in a while, you see a guy like Mickey Lolich who goes on for years because he slings it up there like he doesn't have a care in the world.

"But you know, pitching is a greater thrill now," vows Lonborg. "Then you could get your kicks throwing it by guys.

"But they say no one can really call himself a pitcher until he has had arm trouble and had to learn to pitch all over again," said Lonborg. "I win now with my mind. Nothing matches the fun of seeing a guy break his bat on a mediocre fastball and cuss you all the way back to the dugout."

Tommy John of New York calls himself "the only right-hander southpaw" because a tendon from his right forearm has been transplanted to his left elbow by Dr. Frank Jobe to save his career.

Randy Jones of New York is semisuccessfully coming back from nerve surgery in his elbow. Two young fireballers—Frank Tanana and Dennis Eckersley—both claim that their best speed abandoned them before the age of twenty-five and that now they are learning to be total pitchers.

Fads come and go. Once, within a week, a shadowy operation called "shoulder manipulation" was performed on three million-dollar pitchers: Don Gullett, Catfish Hunter, and Mark Fidrych.

Gullett, after being put under anesthesia and having his shoulder moved into extreme position to tear down adhesions and free movement in the joint, won three straight games and claimed to be reborn.

Hunter and Fidrych were on their way to the same doctor's table within hours of Gullett's return from the land of the disabled. None were miraculously cured. But the search never ends.

After all, the dugouts of the major leagues have long been filled with men who understand what the public sometimes forgets— that the pennant race and the arms race are usually one and the same.

Salvation Through Salivation

> An all-out effort will be made in 1981 to eliminate the practice, which is becoming more widespread, of pitchers scuffing up the baseball. The following procedures will be strictly enforced . . .
>
> —Major League Directive to All Teams

Because he's young and healthy and doesn't need to cheat yet, Mike Flanagan had trouble finding a tool with which to deface the baseball. It took him at least five seconds to find a suitable implement in his locker.

"This coat hanger ought to do the trick," said the Baltimore Oriole 1979 Cy Young winner. Using the semisharp end of the hanger's hook, Flanagan scraped one side of the clean, fresh baseball three times, making inch-long scars. "That's much, much more than a real scuffleballer would need. God, Gaylord Perry or Tommy John could make this ball sing 'The Star Spangled Banner.'"

Flanagan grinned at pitcher Dennis Martinez. "Hey, Dennis, let's play a little catch.

"Any time I want four new pitches, I got 'em, because I can make a scuffed ball break in, out, up, or down. It's the same principle as one of those flat-sided whiffleballs. You hold the ball with the scuffed side opposite to the direction you want it to break. It takes no talent whatsoever. You just throw it like a mediocre fastball. The scuff gives the break.

"Here's my new slider," said Flanagan, throwing a three-quarter-speed pitch to Martinez that veered at least six inches at the last instant.

Martinez raised his eyebrows as if to say, "Nice. What was that?"

"Now, here's my screwball." Flanagan gripped the sinful sphere with the marks facing in rather than out. This pitch, again thrown effortlessly, dove down and away, sailing at the last second.

Martinez barely snagged the ball, then burst out laughing.

"That's a no-no," he said before even looking at the ball. It had taken him only two lazy pitches to spot the cheating.

By dropping down to sidearm, Flanagan then made the ball rise and sink, simply by changing grips and without any significant effort. "Finally, we take a look into the future, ten years from now," said Flanagan, imitating a radio announcer. "Here's thirty-nine-year-old Mike Flanagan coming in from the Red Sox bull pen. The old left-hander has had a remarkable come-back this year, just when everyone thought his career was washed up. How does he do it? His speed is gone and he doesn't even throw that big breaking ball anymore. But the old buzzard sure can get 'em out. Yes, fans, it's a mystery."

Flanagan does not deny that such a day may come. "I've also got a pretty decent bull pen spitter. Every pitcher needs an insurance policy." However, he is still in the stud stage of his career. His real stuff is much better than his phony stuff. He can afford to adopt a high moral tone.

"It makes me mad to pitch against cheaters, and the league is full of them. Whenever I pitched against Seattle or Oakland last year, for example, it galled me to watch their pitchers cutting the ball or using grease constantly and flagrantly. Guys like [Rick] Honeycutt and [Glenn] Abbott don't even try to hide what they're doing. The whole Oakland starting staff had one kind of spitball or another as soon as Billy Martin could have it taught to them. You see the bottom falling out of pitches from guys who never had a super sinker or a great screwball before.

"A good scuffballer can throw a third as hard and make the ball move twice as much as an honest pitcher. Every year I've been in the league [six], it's gotten worse. Last year, I think cheating was up 100 percent among guys under thirty.

"I can understand why they do it and I can't swear that I won't ever do it, but I still hate it. When I was hurt three years ago [bad ankles], I got to a point where I actually took the mound thinking I'd cheat that day. But I couldn't bring myself to do it. I thought, 'If you'll do this now, just to have a little better chance to win, what won't you do eventually?' I guess I just felt too conspicuous out there."

Conspicuous to whom?

"Myself, I guess," said Flanagan.

The number of pitchers who feel either conspicuous or guilt-ridden when cheating is diminishing every year. It has reached the point where a conservative estimate on the number of pitchers who sometimes use an illegal pitch would be about one third. Plenty of experts would place the figure higher.

"So many guys cheat," says New York Mets Manager George Bamberger, whose own best pitch was his Staten Island Sinker. "Who knows how many. About half of 'em, I guess.

"Right now, we're in the heyday of illegal pitches. Conditions have never been so good for it. Every conceivable rule is assbackward. It's as if some old spitballer like me wrote the rules. Any pitcher who doesn't seriously consider an 'extra' pitch, you got to wonder if he really wants to win. I used to be in favor of legalizing the spitter, but the way things are today, it's more fun cheating."

Says Baltimore pitching coach Ray Miller, a confessed spitballer himself, "Maybe a dozen guys in our league throw something illegal constantly, and about fifty others do it often enough to include it in your book on them. If a pitcher asked me to teach him the spitter and I thought it was the proper move for his career, I'd teach him."

The Johnny Appleseed of spitballers for the past fifteen years has been Gaylord Perry, who has sprayed his way through six teams. "Perry is the one who turned on Billy Martin," says Texas pitching instructor Paul Richards, as though he were talking about a drug connection. "Now, everywhere that Martin goes, he takes along [coach] Art Fowler, who was a pretty good spitballer himself. There's no doubt that the Oakland staff all had grease on 'em someplace last season."

Before a chautauqua of moral outrage sweeps the country, let it be said that cheating is baseball's oldest profession. No other game is so rich in skulduggery, so suited to it, or so proud of it. Stealing signs with binoculars, using corked bats, watering down the basepaths, freezing the baseballs when a slugging team comes to town, and sloping the infield foul lines to favor your own style of play are all time-honored forms of baseball rule-bending. The genuine fancier of "hardball" has always had to decide on a case-by-case basis the proper balance between idealism and pragmatism.

Bamberger, the most respected pitching coach of the past

fifteen years, states the code of the majors most succinctly: "We do not play baseball. We play professional baseball. Amateurs play games. We are paid to win games. There are rules, and there are consequences if you break them. If you're a pro, then you often don't decide whether to cheat based on if it's 'right or wrong.' You base it on whether or not you can get away with it, and what the penalty might be. A guy who cheats in a friendly game of cards is a cheater. A pro who throws a spitball to support his family is a competitor."

Ever since the spitball was outlawed in 1920, lawbreakers on the mound have been rampant. It's one of the sport's oldest and most colorful traditions. All-Star teams, and even the Hall of Fame, are loaded (pardon the expression) with all manner of admitted felons. Post-career confessions, or at least smirking non-denials, are on file from fellows like Schoolboy Rowe, Preacher "Bird Dog" Roe, Lew Burdette, Whitey "Slick" Ford, Don Drysdale, Dean Chance, Phil "The Vulture" Regan, Bob Friend, Joe Page, Bullet Bob Turley, Jim Brosnan, Ron Perranoski, and Mike Marshall. The list of insignificant suspects—like Bob Shaw, Tony Cloninger, Pedro Ramos, Ron Kline, Jack Hamilton, Orlando Pena, and a zillion others—would bore an actuary.

In fact, historians will tell you that the winning pitcher in the first professional league game ever played (1871, the Fort Wayne Kekiongas over the Cleveland Forest Citys, 2–0) was Bobby Mathews. Mathews' one flamboyant habit was wetting his fingers before he threw. Those who thought George Hildebrand invented the wet one in 1902 may, in fact, be off by a generation.

What causes the current predicament is the imbalance between crime and punishment. Everybody's doin' it and ain't nobody gettin' caught.

In addition to Minnesota reliever Doug Corbett and the Oakland starting staff of Mike Norris, Rick Langford, Steve McCatty, and Matt Keough—a quartet whose record went from 30-53 with 23 complete games to 71-48 with 83 complete games as soon as Fowler arrived—an all-star staff of gentlemen with dramatically suspicious stuff would include:

• Gaylord Perry, a nonentity at twenty-seven, discovered Vaseline, K-Y vaginal jelly, and hitter hydrophobia (spitter on the brain), and has won 296 games (so far). Perry periodically confesses (for an author's fee), recants, swears he's gone straight, then reappears in print after a seemly pause with subsequently profitable *mea culpas*. Says Baltimore's 25-game winner Steve Stone: "When Gaylord and I were teammates, he offered to teach me the whole course, but he said, 'It'll cost you $3,000.'" Perry's current lecture fee to teammates is not available. He has been frisked on the mound many times, but never arraigned. Since Perry smells like a pharmacopoeia, Billy Martin once brought a bloodhound to the park to sniff through the ball bag for evidence against Perry. What happened? "The dog died of a heart attack," says Martin. On another occasion, Martin asked umpire Bill Kunkel to "just smell the ball, please." Kunkel told him, "Billy, I have allergies and a deviated septum." "Jesus Christ," roared Martin, "I got an umpire who can't see or smell."

• Don Sutton (salary $900,000 per annum) has been accused of cutting, scuffing, sandpapering, and generally disfiguring balls in so many ways that he says, "I ought to get a Black & Decker commercial out of it. The only fun I get now is hiding dirty notes in my uniform pockets for the umpires to find when they search me. I have a bet with [PGA golfer] Gary McCord that if I'm searched on national TV, I'll strip to my undershirt and jock." Sutton vows that if he is ever disciplined, he will start by suing the umpire, then work his way up to bigger game. "Sutton has set such a fine example of defiance," says Baltimore's Miller, "that someday I expect to see a pitcher walk out to the mound with a utility belt on—you know, file, chisel, screwdriver, glue. He'll throw a ball to the plate with bolts attached to it."

• Tommy John is the elegant Rhett Butler of outlaws. In the fine Whitey Ford tradition of mudballers and scuffballers, the gentlemanly John can turn a tiny scratch into a double-play grounder. Asked how many pitches he has, John said, "Four basic ones—fastball, curve, slider, and change-up—plus eight illegal ones." Then he gave his best Sunday-school smile.

• Mike Caldwell, after beginning his career as a 40-58 pitcher, went 38-15 in his first two years under Bamberger. Then he developed arm trouble. Was it caused by throwing a spitter? "That's typical, one or two good years, then boom," says Richards. "The strain on a spitballer's arm is exceptional and you're endangering your career. You throw the spitter like a fastball but with a stiff wrist, squeezing the ball out of your fingers like a watermelon seed. Instead of a free-and-easy release, the shock goes back into your shoulder."

Says Miller, "Teaching a spitter to a young pitcher with a strong arm is the dumbest thing. How am I going to tell my GM, "Well, boss, Sammy Stewart blew his arm out while we were working on his spitter?'"

Adds Kunkel, a former big league pitcher who admits throwing a spitter (Boog Powell hit one in the upper deck), "Spitballers have enormous strength in their fingers and hands from that squirting type of release. They say you can identify them by their strong handshake. Of course, nobody can tell with Gaylord because his hand always slips out of your grip."

• Mike Torrez of Boston has always been a master of throwing, with the bases crowded, two-strike pitches that "Have the bottom fall out of them." Rumor has it that just such a pitch—a hanging spitter—was the one that Bucky Dent hit into the screen for a three-run homer in the 1978 Yankee-Red Sox play-off game.

• Ross "Scuzz" Grimsley, another Bamberger pupil, is said to have enough greasy kid stuff in his ultra-long curly hair to give A. J. Foyt a lube job and an oil change. "Grimsley can't throw hard enough to blacken my eye," Martin would scream. But umpires hated to run their fingers through his hair. Guuuunck.

• Bob Stanley of Boston was, until last year, thought simply to have an excellent sinker. Then waves of rumors spread that he was doctoring every pitch. "I think Stanley may have put out the rumors himself," laughs Miller. "When you're going bad, it's a good way to get an extra pitch. Just planting the idea in the hitter's mind is almost as good as having an illegal pitch. I was misquoted last year as saying that Dennis Leonard had a good spitter. He came up to me this spring to chew me out and I said, 'Dennis, you should thank me. Nobody can do a pitcher a bigger favor than saying they've got a hell of a spitter.'"

• Bill "Spaceman" Lee is the only active pitcher to say publicly that he has thrown spitters and has no intention of stopping. This is probably part of Lee's campaign of tweaking authority. He once said he sprinkled marijuana on his pancakes for breakfast. He was hit with a $250 fine from Bowie Kuhn for his "candor."

The most uncircumspect ballplayer in the American League in

1980 was Honeycutt (10-17) of Seattle. He was such a blunderer that he became only the second man since 1920 to be ejected from a game and suspended for throwing an illegal pitch. (He remained suspended for the first five games of the 1981 season, even though he is now a Ranger.) "Catching Honeycutt cutting the ball was about as difficult as spotting a whale in a bathtub," says Nestor Chylak, assistant supervisor of AL umpires. The only previous man to be caught red-handed was a St. Louis Brown in 1944. But what can you expect from a Brownie?

Actually, not much, which is about what you can expect from the accused when you broach the subject of illegal pitches. "I'm not putting anything on the ball," says Abbott. "But . . . I'm putting a whole lot of thoughts in hitters' minds."

Fowler is just amazed that anyone could think he teaches illegal pitches. "These pitchers don't throw spitballs," he says of his A's. "If they do, I don't know about it. You know, they always said Gaylord Perry threw a spitter, but he didn't when me and Billy [Martin] were with him in Texas."

Kunkel became the only umpire other than Hall of Famer Cal Hubbard in 1944 ever to call a spitter and thus invoke the automatic rule of ejection and a ten-day suspension. It happened during the last week of the 1980 season. "Seattle was playing Kansas City, and the Royals started asking before the first pitch of the game for me to check balls. By the time George Brett came up in the third, I'd asked the ball boy to hold two balls—each had three slashes—as evidence. Then the first pitch to Brett dives like crazy. George doesn't say a word, but he turns around and gives me this shit-eating grin. Now I've got three slashed balls. So as soon as [Hal] McRae comes up, I head to the mound.

"Honeycutt has a flesh-colored bandage on the index finger of his right hand which is sticking out the back of the glove. He turned his back and something fell on the ground before I ever got there. Then I said, 'That's a shame. How'd you cut your hand?' And I grabbed his hand while he was still fumbling with it.

"And there it was. He had a thumbtack sticking up through the bandage. I said, 'Son, take a hike.'

"[Manager] Maury Wills came running out, asking what I'd done. I said, 'Maury, look here.' Wills felt the thumbtack that was still on Honeycutt's finger, looked me right in the eye and said, 'I don't see a damn thing.' I told him, 'Well, you're a goddamn liar.'"

The next day, Wills apologized to Kunkel. "I was stunned," Wills said. "It hit me like a right cross. I just didn't know what I ought to do." And Kunkel, in turn, apologized to Wills for calling him a liar when he was instinctively protecting his player.

As Kunkel left the mound, McRae handed him a one-inch-square piece of machine sandpaper that Honeycutt had discarded, and said, "You might as well get the whole kit." Says Kunkel, "He was both cutting it and scuffing it, depending on what he wanted the ball to do."

In light of the Honeycutt incident, baseball has instituted its umpteenth campaign to clean up its public image on the illegal-pitch front. Discussion of these "reforms" has been delayed until now because their chances of success, if history is our teacher, are so close to nil.

Is a sport which has enforced its illegal-pitch rule exactly twice in sixty years suddenly going to find religion and clean up its act?

"We finally have a rule that will work," says Kunkel, enthusiastically. "In the past, we had to have physical evidence of what was being used to mark the ball, like Honeycutt's thumbtack, and that's very hard to come by. Now, the balls themselves are sufficient evidence."

The new procedure—and it may prove an excellent one—is simple. The umpire inspects the ball before each half inning to make sure it is flawless. From that moment on, the pitcher is responsible for the condition of any ball he throws. As soon as an umpire finds a marked or scuffed ball, he has authority to frisk the pitcher and, if nothing incriminating is found, warn him once and keep the ball as evidence. If another ball is found with similar markings, then the pitcher is to be ejected and suspended for ten days.

The key, obviously, is an umpire's ability to tell a deliberate defacement from an accidental scrape. "When a pitcher marks a ball, he does it the same way and on the same part of the ball every time," says Kunkel. "It's just like fingerprints. No umpire can tell me that he doesn't know the difference between a ball that's been cut on a belt buckle and one's that just hit a fence or landed on the cinder warning track.

"It was made clear at an umpires' meeting with the AL president that we'll get full support on this. Lee MacPhail said, 'We've got the rules. Let's use them.' Right now, the umpires are getting the best support on this we've ever gotten. It's in the rules that the pitcher is responsible for the ball. If you get three or four balls marked exactly the same, no court of law would uphold the pitcher."

Says Chylak, "It's a good rule. We got some Houdinis in this game. But once they've put the mark on the ball, how can they take it off? If they want to sue somebody, let them sue me. I have a car and a gerbil and my wife owns everything else."

Of course, this is an optimist's view. Umpires will still have to have the gumption to institute stiff penalties based on their own interpretations of rather minor marks and scuffs. "The problem," says Miller, "is that the penalty is so stiff. Who's going to walk out to the mound and eject a star relief pitcher for ten days in the middle of a pennant race? It'll never happen in this world. They need a less severe penalty. Give the umpire the discretion to call a balk anytime he considers a pitch illegal and you'll see shivers go through some cheaters."

Says Richards, "I'm in favor of this crackdown. But they're only touching the surface with scuffed balls. If they think that's the problem, they're crazy. It's the greaseball that's completely unfair. A scuffball is a decent pitch, but it's just a sailer, like a slider. It's not a mainstay. It's more a double-play pitch. The spitter is the great pitch because it breaks down so sharply. It's a strikeout pitch."

"They make all these rules and then they never do anything," scoffs Bamberger. "The last time they changed the rules [in 1968] to stop the cheating, they did the spitballers the greatest favor in history. The rule used to be that if you went to your mouth on the mound, you had to go to the rosin bag thereafter. That made it tough. When I played, I'd get a huge load of spit. Then the rosin bag would only wipe out half of it. But at least the rule worked a little. You could tell the umpire, 'He's getting the grease from behind his ear.' Then every time the guy went there, the umpire could yell, 'Go to the rosin,' and at least you had a chance of bothering the guy who was cheating.

"The new rule said you couldn't go to your mouth while you

were on the dirt portion of the mound. Well, big deal. Now all
you got to do is walk off the mound and you can do any damn
thing you want. You can set up a tool chest back there to work on
the ball. Guys like Mike Marshall would stand back there and just
blatantly grind on the ball until they had it just like they wanted
it. Nowadays, the umpires won't even make them go to the rosin
bag. It's a joke."

Even umpires admit that the spitball is now, *ipso facto*, legal.
Can the use of the spitball, greaseball, sweatball, and mudball be
diminished?

"I doubt it," says Kunkel. "The way the rules are now, about
the only way you could call a pitcher for a spitter would be to
jump in front of the catcher and grab the ball bare-handed yourself before anything except the pitcher's hand had touched it.
Once it hits the catcher's glove . . ."

Kunkel won't say it, but nobody wants to be sued and have only
his "umpire's judgment" to back him up before the judge. How
do you take a tiny dab of jelly or evaporating slippery-elm spit
into court?

Baseball may have found a way to deter its petty criminals, the
scuffers and scrapers. But its grand-theft felons roam free. "The
spitballers don't even tell their own teammates how they do it,"
says Chylak. "And they're so good at it that the other teams can't
spot it. They just guess. The few insiders who do know the tricks
have a code of secrecy. Mr. Bamberger may talk pretty big, but
I will paint your house if he will tell who does it and exactly how."

That's always the core of the issue. Spitballers must be the
Mandrakes of the mound. It was once said that no one suspected
Cincinnati's Bob Purkey of throwing a spitter until his catcher
went to the mound wearing a bib.

"The best way to hide the spitter is to fake all the tricky stuff—
Vaseline behind the knee or under the bill of your cap—then just
spit on your hand when they're looking at you," says Bamberger.
"I never did it any other way. Just get it from your mouth right in
front of them because that's when they don't think you'll do it."

This purloined-letter school of disguise probably applies best to
Perry. "Everybody thinks that all the places he touches are
decoys," says Bamberger. "I don't think any are decoys. I think
he's got that stuff everyplace."

Perhaps the pitcher who went furthest in subterfuge was the crafty Ford. He had a stainless-steel ring made with a rasp on the inside, and covered it with a flesh-colored Band-Aid. Ford's favorite technique, however, was a super-sticky compound that helped him grip his curveball better for extra break. He kept the contraband in a hollowed-out roll-on deodorant container. One day, Mickey Mantle, knowing that penny-pinching catcher Yogi Berra loved to mooch any kind of personal product, took Ford's magic goo and placed it on Whitey's locker shelf as though it were really deodorant. Berra took the bait. Minutes later, he came back from the shower room roaring, his arms stuck to his sides. The Yankee trainer tried alcohol under Berra's arms. When that didn't work, he cut all the hair under Berra's arms to release the straitjacketed catcher.

The blessing for baseball in this perennial litany of pitching rogueries is that, while throwing the spitter may be commonplace, it is by no means easy. Baseball is a game of skills more than one of raw athletic talent, and the spitball is clearly one of the game's most difficult and chancy skills. For every career it salvages, there is probably another that it helps to ruin. For every hanging curve that finds a bleacher grave, there is a spitter with too much spin that floats like a batting-practice meatball into the batter's power zone and disappears.

Perhaps the most just of all punishments for throwing a spitter is this: The surest gopherball is a bad spitter. The clubhouse axiom is: "Hit it on the dry side," meaning, "Wait for the one that doesn't break."

Baseball may or may not have luck in eradicating its latest cheap trick, the scuffball. But one thing is certain. Pitchers have not stopped searching—and never will—for ways to make a baseball do new things. And hang the cost to conscience.

"Guys are always trying to find new ways to grip the ball and release it," says Oriole coach Miller. "If you're a pitcher, you can't stop it. I was sitting in the dugout the other day thinking about Sutter's split-finger fastball. It's nothing but a legal spitball. I was looking at my hand, thinking of the ten years I was in the minors, never getting to the majors and, honest to God, the thought floated up, 'What if, fifteen years ago, I'd had my middle finger amputated? I bet I'd have had a hell of a split-finger fastball.'

"Then I came to my senses and laughed. For a minute. Then I realized that if somebody had proved it would work, I'd probably have been one of the guys in line for the operation."

Any man who would consider cutting off a finger to make the major leagues will certainly cheat to stay there. Always has, always will.

Baseball's Dark Lord

The pieces of Steve Carlton are not so much a puzzle as a mosaic. The person without a purpose, or a pattern, is the true mystery, no matter how much he talks. Silence is no barrier to understanding, if it is a silence, like Carlton's, that is surrounded by a lifetime of consistent and eloquent facts and acts.

To many, the Philadelphia Phillie pitcher seems to be baseball's richest enigma: The Southpaw Sphinx who, by his defiant silence and cultivated eccentricities, invites himself to be the subject of observation and deduction. Certainly, the man is unique, and, at first glance, inscrutable. Even Carlton's locker has no name or number above it, as though in the middle of a quasi-public place his space could be invisible, inviolate, and devoid of any traces of personality. A lair without scent.

"You have no right to look at my locker," Carlton said, his voice quivering with barely controlled emotion, a bat on his shoulder, as he sought out a reporter in the Philadelphia dugout. "I heard you looked at my locker."

And so, drawn up to full height as though looking down at a hitter, Carlton lectured for several minutes—in the slightly off-center, out-of-focus manner of a man who is a bit daffy on one subject—on the crime of looking at his possessions from a distance without his express permission. "You've made a big mistake," he said, over and over, with ominous mystery.

To those who don't know Carlton, the scene might have seemed irrational, sad, or comic. It actually was calculated, part of a deliberate pattern, and, from Carlton's perspective, totally justifiable. The 6-foot-5 pitcher is, and long has been, a student of force, mystique, and intimidation. He is in search of a solitary, self-contained superiority, and he has discovered a nearly perfect place for it: the mound. Carlton's energies—sometimes even those that appear unrelated to baseball—are dedicated to bringing more powerful tools of body and mind to his hilltop. For the sake of longevity and a trim waist in his baseball old age, the 219-pounder is a vegetarian. For greater strength and leverage, better understanding of torque and the body's potential for building muscular tension, then releasing it in one explosion, Carlton is a disciple of the martial arts, kung fu in particular. He has, for five years, worked with a Phils trainer, Gus Hoefling, who loves to talk about "positive and negative tension" and, generally, play the role of jock guru.

"Carlton does not pitch to the hitter, he pitches through him," explained former Phillie catcher Tim McCarver. "The batter hardly exists for Steve. He's playing an elevated game of catch."

Carlton is an introverted man of enormous intensity and pressure who is, while on the mound, seeking everything that is the opposite of his nature: peace, oblivious concentration, a trance in which he can reach deep and use all of his resources. So, he studies est and Eastern philosophies. He cultivates a private catcher with whom he has long discussions of every hitter so that their pitch-calling can be on the same wavelength with no distractions. Two minds as one, two ends of an exalted game of catch.

Because Carlton always has had a hair-trigger temper, a tendency as shortstop Larry Bowa puts it "to go crazy . . . but never in public, of course," the left-hander tries to categorically eliminate all factors that might disturb his work. Umpires' bad calls are ignored. Fielding errors receive a slight, disgusted shake of the head and then are forgotten. The cheers or boos of the crowd are not acknowledged. Eye contact with hitters, or even teammates, is avoided. In everything, Carlton cultivates the impression that he is above the petty forces that influence others, a sort of baseball Zoroaster wrestling apart with the forces of evil.

In the Phils' yearbook, seventeen players have homey portraits of themselves with their wives and children. Only Carlton and his bubbly wife Beverly ("she's the person I most admire"), and his two sons are conspicuous by their absence. In a survey of the tastes of the Phils, all twenty-four other players sought the regular-guy image by listing favorite songs such as "Blue Eyes Crying in the Rain." Carlton took every opportunity to isolate himself. Favorite musicians: Jascha Heifetz, Jean-Pierre Rampal. People you'd most like to meet: Socrates, Einstein, Thomas Jefferson, Napoleon, Jesus Christ, Gandhi. There is no ideological common thread among these big names, except that most folks wouldn't know quite what to say to them over the soup, and Carlton thinks he would.

One-upmanship, a fine knack of gaining a psychological advantage, is a strength of Carlton's pitching, but it also extends to hobbies such as his wine connoisseurship. Dine with Carlton and he's the guy who spent last winter touring the wineries in Burgundy. You may like the bouquet, but he knew the grape personally.

Those who one-up Carlton merit his special attention. Johnny Bench is one of the few hitters who "owns" Carlton. "I can read him. I can almost tell what's coming," Bench has said. "It's like I'm thinking along with him." Once, when Carlton was hunting with former teammate Joe Hoerner, Carlton missed a bird, then fired off a shot into the air. "There," Carlton said, out of left field. "That one's for Bench."

Few men have brought greater raw skills to pitching, or husbanded them more admirably. Carlton is pitching's rigorous, driven, art-for-art's sake master. "What distinguishes Carlton is his command of every pitch almost every time out," said Pittsburgh's Willie Stargell, who has faced him for seventeen seasons. "You can find a key to other pitchers: He can't get his curveball over tonight or he goes to his slider in a jam," Stargell said. "You find some thought that simplifies your job of getting a good pitch to attack. But Carlton won't discard a pitch or limit himself. He's always got the full arsenal going for him. Pitching is the art of destroying a hitter's timing," Stargell said. "Carlton understands that. He can take a little off, or put a little extra on all of his pitches."

"Just when you finally feel like you're screwed in on that damn curveball of his, along about your third or fourth at-bat against him, your eyes light up and you think, 'I've got you now, Lefty,'" veteran Phil Garner said. "Then, all of a sudden, it's a different curveball—he's pulled the string and you're out in front and on your way back to the dugout again. Carlton's got great stuff, especially that slider down and in to right-handed hitters. But he's not really uncomfortable to hit against. What makes him so great—the best, I think—is that he flat knows how to pitch. He's always got your mind messed up."

One Saturday night, the Phils released 2,883 balloons before the game—each the symbol of a strikeout conquest for the man who has more whiffs than any left-hander in baseball history. Those balloons were Carlton's cloud of glory.

"Carlton makes it look so easy 'cause he's worked so hard," Stargell said. "You can always tell an athlete who's reached a point where he's at peace with himself. You want your energy to flow, not to feel knotted. When you look at Carlton, that's how he is right now."

If only Veterans Stadium could be emptied before each game Carlton pitches, his athletic life would be perfect. From his promontory, Carlton looks down at a world of smaller men, hitters who are brought to their knees as they flail at his slider breaking into the dirt.

Talent and knowledge, study and endless regimen, have come together once more for Carlton, just as they did in 1972 when his record was 27-10 with a 1.98 ERA and 310 strikeouts for a Phils team that played in an anonymity merited by its 97 defeats. That season the only Philadelphia games that mattered were the ones Carlton pitched.

Then, Carlton, who meditates for an hour before he pitches, and jams cotton in his ears as he heads to the mound, had no need to seek solitude. Being a Phil sufficed. But, with the emergence of a Phillie powerhouse, with the doubling of attendance and the redoubling of media scrutiny, Carlton began to realize that, although he was standing on a mound, thousands of others were looking down at him, down from the cheap seats, down from the press box. The man who played for no one but himself and who accepted no judgment but his own found himself pilloried by nonathletes with beer bellies and cigars.

Why, in the play-offs of '76, '77, '78, did Carlton win only 1 of 4 starts with an ERA of 5.79? In a town that loves to castigate, Carlton was lumped with the rest of the Pholding Phillies. The Phils became a burned and gun-shy team, leery of their fans and press. Sometimes they ducked the limelight, hid from reporters in little anterooms. And sometimes, when things were rolling, they basked in the glory. Such vulnerability to glib public judgment was intolerable to Carlton. As early as 1975, the year the Phils became contenders, Carlton began closing his shell. And the silence deepened each year, until now it is complete.

"Baseball is a public game," Bowa tells Carlton. "We owe them something."

"It's our game," answers Carlton. "We only owe them our performance."

"Carlton is a thoroughbred," Stargell explained, "not one of the nags. He isn't bred for defeat or injury or anything that limits him. The horse lives to race and the thoroughbred athlete lives to perform. People don't understand when they talk to us, when they ask foolish little things, that a thoroughbred's mind is always on one thing: that game, that day, that ball park, that set of conditions. Sometimes I can go a whole game without knowing there's anybody in the stands."

Carlton and Stargell both have tried to tap the source of that force that allows athletes to perform at their thoroughbred best. Both will waltz into the Hall of Fame. Carlton, showing no signs of age (and with an as yet unrevealed knuckleball, years in the perfecting), may end his days as a 300 game winner and baseball's all-time strikeout king.

Stargell, however, has been blessed with that not too sharp, not too flat, but just natural tone off the field. His geniality, his compulsive camaraderie, feeds his performance as much as Carlton's pursuit of an intimidating superiority is necessary to his. Stargell has plugged into the bright side of his game's force, while Carlton willingly has opted to be baseball's haughty dark lord.

So, we see that there are no secrets, dark or otherwise, in Steve Carlton's locker. Neither money nor fame controls him. Neither victory nor defeat fazes him. With cotton in his ears, he stares down from his mound at his catcher. The hitter has been removed. The crowd has been removed. Those who praise or blame him have been removed. Carlton, in that moment of supreme intensity to which he subordinates all else, is a great thoroughbred—blinders in place—getting ready for a private game of catch.

August

Hustling to Tie Cobb

At two o'clock in the morning, Pete Rose was out on the town, trying to drown his sorrows.

Well, not exactly out on the town, and not exactly drowning his sorrows. Actually, Rose, just hours after having his 44-game hitting streak stopped, was sitting on a stool of an all-night lunch counter in Atlanta ordering a glass of milk. All around Rose on this historic baseball night in early August of 1978 were not the celebrities of this world, but whoever happened to be awake and wanted to find a clean, well-lighted place.

With a half-dozen "just plain folks" around him, Rose stood up and began showing anyone who cared to watch just how Braves pitcher Larry McWilliams had speared his line drive and just how reliever Gene Garber had fanned him to end the game with a wicked submarine changeup. As Rose strolled out of the restaurant and off to bed, shaking hands, winking to friends all the way, his new stool companions shook their heads.

"So that's Pete Rose," said a middle-aged man, trying to pick his jaw up off the floor. "Good Lord, he's just like he seems. Now that's a star."

Rose has never been the best player in baseball, but he may be the best thing his game has to offer. Defense, speed, power—Rose lacks those. Humor, character, generosity—Rose is always on a streak in those areas. Best of all, Rose truly is what he seems.

For most baseball fans, Rose captures the best of their game's traditional values. Perhaps no other player in the sport can bring the richness to a batting streak or World Series that Charlie Hustle can. Rose greets pressure with a serenity that other players find, in Tom Seaver's words, "almost saintly." Or, as Mike Schmidt put it, "Pete Rose makes me look in the mirror. If what he's giving is a hundred percent, then my hundred percent must be coming up short."

Rose would never accept such flowery tribute. "If you always give your best, then, hell, man, you deserve what you get," he says. "Go ahead and enjoy it." Noblesse oblige comes naturally to

Rose; he would rather talk baseball with the guy on the next lunch-counter stool than have dinner with Queen Elizabeth.

Extraordinary men often bring a fresh simplicity to the complexity of their chosen fields, carrying a sense of order and elemental sanity with them. Amid the subtleties of baseball, Rose is that man of fundamental qualities. Within his galaxy, he is the direction-setting lodestar. Other players—even the best—measure their performance, their attitude, their purity of purpose by Rose's.

In his youth, Rose seemed almost pathetically one dimensional. Even that nickname, Charlie Hustle, was meant sarcastically. However, in his athletic old age, he has become a hero with a joyful and unified sensibility, if a still fiercely focused one.

Rose likes to pretend he is the same person as the twenty-two-year-old rookie who broke in battling his own teammates, worshipping his bull-necked father ("My pap woulda whupped me for that"), and earning the scorn of veterans for sprinting out bases on balls. The mature Rose, however, is a hip fashion plate with tassled Gucci loafers, open-neck silk shirts, skin-tight rock-star slacks, gold medallions, and long, styled, collar-length hair (some of it gray).

What is most fascinating about Rose is his capacity for blending Rolls-Royce taste with an undeniable down-to-earth manner. He may be the only baseball star who works at not having charisma. Dirty jobs—collecting balls, fielding for the fungo hitter—appeal to Rose. Throwing a headlock on any stranger who begs him to stand still for a snapshot is a specialty. Other mediocre players resent an autograph; Rose shakes your hand, wrestles with you, and might autograph your forehead if you don't watch out. "Pete doesn't run with celebrities," says Sparky Anderson. "He can't stand phonies. His big buddy in L.A. ain't Sinatra. It's a funny old groundskeeper."

Rose's teammates like him because he won't allow them not to. Every rookie or newcomer gets the Rose treatment: saturation empathy. No favor too much. Among future Cooperstown residents, Rose is absolutely unique in one trait: He seems determined to prove the parable that the last shall be first and the first shall be last. No length is too great to go to prove his disdain for special treatment or star's privileges. Perhaps no incident could il-

lustrate that compulsion more clearly than Rose's first day as a
Philadelphia Phillie in spring '79.

Rose, fresh from signing the biggest free-agent contract in baseball history at that point ($3.2 million), arose long before the sun
on that first February day of spring training in Clearwater, Florida. By 6 A.M., he stood outside the Phils' training complex—proving a point and winning a bet. For years, Larry Bowa had always
been the first Phillie to report; the little insomniac shortstop often
appeared at the gates at 8 A.M. for the 10 A.M. workout. That was
his hustling, scrappy style, a *modus operandi* he admittedly borrowed from Rose.

"I'll be the first Phillie to report this year," Rose said casually a
couple of weeks before camp opened.

"Betcha won't," retorted the feisty Bowa as he, Rose, and a couple of other Phils headed for Las Vegas for a final off-season holiday.

Bowa returned from Vegas early as a precaution just to keep his
vow.

Rose called Bowa from the Strip at midnight, just hours before
the Clearwater gates were scheduled to open. "You can relax,"
said Rose to Bowa over the phone as the slot machines jangled as
background music. "You win. You'll be there before me."

"Like hell you will," thought Rose.

When Bowa wandered into the Phils' deserted clubhouse at
7:40 A.M.—twenty minutes earlier than ever just to make sure—
who was standing by Bowa's locker, in his new Phillie garb, but a
red-eyed, grinning Pete Rose.

"Geez, it ain't fair," bleated Bowa. "He musta been here for
hours."

Well, almost. Rose had grabbed an all-night nonstop flight
from Vegas to Tampa—landing as Rose put it, " 'bout two minutes late at 5:23 A.M. I went and changed clothes, then figured
I'd wander on out to the park . . . didn't have nothin' else to do."

Witnesses placed Rose at the Phillies gate by 6 A.M. "Nah,
nah," protested the deadpan Rose. "I just got here a minute or
two before that crazy Bowa."

Bowa, desperate to retaliate, incited the Phils' fitness wizard,
huge Gus Hoefling, to get Rose in a wrestler's throat hold.

"That's it," cheeped Bowa. "Put the sleeper hold on him. Turn the s.o.b. into an $800,000-a-year vegetable."

Minutes later, Rose was cackling, "Before I came here, the only way Bowa could get his name in lights was to autograph lampshades. Now I got him on the marquee of the Dunes."

All Rose's years of hard work and open-handedness toward any player who needed help—be it with cash or a batting tip—have come back to him, like bread on the water, in his baseball old age. Perhaps the turning point came in that '78 season when his 3,000th hit and his 44-game streak gave the baseball world a chance to say thanks. During that streak—the second longest in history—the players on each team who played the Reds made pilgrimages to congratulate Rose, tease him, or perhaps just touch him like a baseball talisman. After breaking Tommy Holmes' NL record (37), Rose's greatest pride was that every Mets player, down to the scrubs, sought him out to shake hands. Yes, he counted 'em. Many posed for snapshots with him. "Every one of 'em," said Rose, adding almost confusedly, "except Lee Mazzilli." The words almost seemed etched in Rose's face: "What have I done to Mazzilli?"

The marvel of Rose is that he arouses relatively little resentment or jealousy in a locker-room world that is constantly rife with those emotions. After all, it must be considered that this man has rarely done anything for which he did not get full acclaim. Few men have mined the ore of their talent so completely, but it is equally true that few have had their skills so totally appreciated in dollars and cheers. Yet, in recent years, the baseball fraternity has taken pleasure in watching Rose collect almost limitless fame and wealth. The reason, of course, is that Pete—the only Rose that ever wanted to smell like a man—has perfumed his accomplishments with sweat, not toilet water.

The key to Rose's universal acceptance within baseball is the entirely correct perception that Rose does not have a phony, deceitful, or malicious bone in his body. His simple, no-frills conscience always seems to allow him to come out smelling something like a Rose. Since Rose's off-field tastes have always been quintessentially those of the typical old-time ballplayer—gambling, hijinks, and pretty women—he has never been shy of problems. "The Reds have covered up scrapes for Pete his whole career," Baltimore general manager Hank Peters once said. "He's always been in some little jam . . . but people never seem to hold it against him."

Honesty, it seems, can make up for a world of faults, especially in a man who knows his appetites and never apologizes for them. When Rose loses at the dog track—and he's an expert at it—he admits he's a lousy bettor. "The best thing about Pete's big contract," said Sparky Anderson, "is that now I know he'll never go broke. You can't lose three million dollars at the two-dollar window. And Pete would never feel comfortable moving up to the hundred-dollar window. When Rose's wife, Karolyn, filed for divorce in '80, and ended up with a $1-million-plus settlement, Rose never denied her contention that there had been girlfriends. How could he, when he once gave a Tampa beauty a piece of jewelry inscribed, "To my Rookie of the Year."

No ballplayer ever took less care to hide his indiscretions. To Rose, that million dollars was small change next to the deeper cost of playing the role of deceiver. Have a girlfriend, sure. Lie about it, never.

Similarly, Rose is forgiven his periodic faux pas in the social or financial arena because his motives always seem so hearteningly innocent, based on a grinning see-no-evil common sense. The day he visited the White House to be feted by President Carter for his hitting streak, he looked at the Oval Office visitors' list for that date—Dr. Brzezinski, Ambassador Young, Vice-President Mondale, Senator Kennedy, and Mr. Rose—and muttered, "Man, that's a tough lineup to bat cleanup in." Hardly daunted by the batting order, Rose brought gifts for the most powerful man in the world: a $9.95 Pete Rose watch for daughter Amy; "Hustle Makes It Happen" T-shirts for the President's softball team, and a bottle of "Pete!" chocolate drink for the President himself. Before President Carter could utter two sentences, Rose had handed him the watch for his daughter. "We thought we'd frisked Pete at the door," laughed an aide to Representative Thomas Luken (D-Ohio) who arranged the meeting. "We dissuaded him from the chocolate drink and the T-shirts, but he had the watch in his side pocket."

Rose also showed his blend of candor and business craftiness in the crude coast-to-coast auction at which he sold himself to the

Phillies. Rose and his lawyer made themselves the most endearing city-to-city robbers since Bonnie and Clyde as they played all ends against the middle and wrung the financial arms of a half-dozen owners until they nearly fell off.

Again, Rose's air of naïveté served him well. When he met with the Phillies, he looked like Sad Sack telling them how miserable it made him feel to tell them that their $1.8 million offer was about half what he would consider. At the Phils' disconsolate "we-lost-Pete" news conference, Rose dragged out all the reasons why he really wanted to play in Philadelphia, making it clear that cash was the only obstacle. No one ever put on a multimillion-dollar squeeze play with greater finesse or a more insouciant smile. When Phil president Bill Giles asked Rose if he'd listen to one more offer, Rose stammered, "Golly, I'll be home Sunday."

After his baseball Brinks Job, was Rose shy or apologetic? "I got so much money," he said, "that if you stacked up all the cash, a show horse couldn't jump over it." Somehow, he made it seem like a victory for the working man.

Perhaps the greatest piece of good fortune in Rose's whole blessed career, however, was that 44-game streak which moved him from the sports pages and "Game of the Week" to Walter Cronkite and the "Evening News" for a solid fortnight. Rose went from a baseball name to a household name.

That amazing skein from June 14 to August 1, coming on the heels of his 3,000th hit early in the season, did a perfect job of placing both his personality and his feats in their ideal long-range perspective. "I can remember when nobody cheered for me but little old ladies," says Rose, who for a decade was a bête noire in every visiting city. "They were the only ones who could remember the old-timers who played like me." Those days are now behind Rose forever.

Fans could want no more symbolic pairing than Rose and Di-Maggio as the hitting-streak record holders for their respective leagues. What richer contrast could be concocted than the stubble-chinned Aqua Velva man and icy Mr. Coffee. Rose and Di-Maggio are the ultraviolet and the infrared of the spectrum of baseball temperaments. DiMaggio, the thoroughbred of ball-players, meant style, adoration, and inaccessibility. Rose, the dogged donkey, brought dignity to lack of grace and scorned adoration in favor of learning his fans by their first names. DiMaggio was natural; Rose self-made. Even in marriage, DiMaggio meant flowers on Marilyn Monroe's grave, while Rose had a stormy family like the tempestuous one down the block. For DiMaggio, the aloof deity, there was always awe. For Rose, Everyman's bowling partner, there began a growing rooting interest.

That '78 season also situated Rose in proper relationship to Ty Cobb, the Hall of Famer to whom he is both most similar and most blessedly dissimilar.

"I been readin' Cobb's life story at night," said Rose as he passed Cobb's longest streak—40. "We're both a lot alike . . . a couple of rotten guys . . . When Cobb was a kid, he was like me . . . always the smallest; liked to fight." It is true that like Cobb before him, Rose wears his statistics on his sleeve. He has always performed with the pertinacity and directness of a man consciously carving his place in history. Where else in baseball history can we find such conspicuous, unashamed frenzy? Yet as Rose has gotten older, the vicious edge of his drive—the indifference to dealing out injury—has been ground down a bit. The hard slide remains; the spikes are lower. With age, Cobb showed more and more clearly the neurotic track on which he ran—one fueled by cruelty and obsession. With each season, Rose has shown an increasing capacity for gentleness and quick ball park wit.

A hitting streak proved to be an unsurpassed stage for that sharp bantering mind. No modern ballplayer has so relished being interviewed, nor been so good at it. "I don't give interviews. I have conversations," says Rose in the same tone in which he says, "I was raised, but I never did grow up."

In an age when rich athletes have shied from their own double-edged gift of speech, Rose looks out at notepads and microphones and says, "These people can't do anything to me but make me money."

Fifteen big league seasons prepared Rose for his daily Meet the Press; and he won every round unanimously.

—"I got a fake phone call after the game from somebody pretending to be President Carter. It was a pretty good imitation, but I could tell right away it wasn't Carter. He didn't sound worn out enough."

—"We got people on this team who'll tell you where to go and how fast to get there."

—"I hate off days, 'cause I might get hit by a train."

—"Get out a clean ball, Jerry (to umpire Jerry Dale), 'cause I'm about to put this one in the Hall of Fame."

—"They say the odds are 91 to 1 on me catchin' DiMag. Anybody know how I can get a bet down on me?"

—"I'm glad it didn't rain in the sixth (which would have killed the streak). I didn't want the folks to tear down the stadium. They would have, and I don't think Cincinnati could have built us a new one by Friday."

—"After I catch Wee Willie Keeler, I gotta pass Sidney Stonestreet. You know, he hit in 48 straight. Betcha never heard of Sidney Stonestreet. That's 'cause I just made him up. He played for the Rhode Island Reds in the Chicken Coop League. With a name like that, I figure he musta been an old-timer. I gotta have something between Keeler and DiMaggio to shoot for, and I think Ol' Sidney's gonna be a lotta help."

For the last ten days of his streak, the world tried to sit on Pete Rose's shoulders.

And he never even noticed. In circumstances that would have tortured others, Rose knew that he had the chance-of-a-lifetime for fun. When, in the forty-fifth game, third baseman Bob Horner robbed him twice, Rose strolled past the rookie and said, "Kid, will you go some place? I can't hit it over, under, or through you, and I ain't figured out yet how to make 'em curve around you." Finally, when the streak was over, Rose snapped, "Hell, no, I don't feel 'relieved.' I wanted to see what it would have been like to get up in the fifties. Why? No, not so much to break DiMaggio's record but just for the experience, just to know the feeling."

Rose could not hide his true colors at the last. His final at bat galled him deeply, but in such a subtle way that millions of fans could never appreciate it. Garber threw him changeups with 2 outs in the ninth and a 12-run Atlanta lead.

Only a ballplayer would know that such a tactic, under *normal* circumstances, would amount to treachery. You don't get cute in that spot; you "challenge the hitter." Rose's final at-bat was, of course, not in any sense normal. When the crowd in a visiting town is standing and chanting, "Pete, Pete, Pete," it's not normal.

Garber was in the spotlight of history, and he had every right to throw any pitch he wanted.

But Rose's mind was tangled by a special consideration. For two weeks, he had been reining himself in, playing in almost every situation as though no streak existed. In close games, he refused to try for selfish bunt hits when the game situation dictated against it, and, more important, he repeatedly refused to swing at "cripple" pitches because he knew that under "normal" circumstances he would take such pitches in the interest of drawing a walk.

Rose, you see, has a code: the ballplayer's code. It is unwritten, and some articles of the code are moot. But Rose, being all ballplayer, believes in every clause.

Because Rose was willing to act as though his streak did not exist, he thought it a minimum professional courtesy that his fellow ballplayers acquiesce. After weeks of having the "code" work against him, Rose finally thought he would get a break—a cripple pitch to hit when he really needed one. So, when he saw submarine changeups, he cursed Garber. The outside world did not, and does not, understand; Rose, of course, refuses to relent in a position that only he could understand.

"Oh, well," said Rose finally, as he dressed and prepared to find some all-night lunch counter where he could get a glass of milk, "I'm glad I went down hittin' the ball hard. Makes me feel better. Aw, hell, it's not what I was aiming for, but forty-four ain't bad."

Sparky Anderson, overhearing his old friend, looked down at his shoes and chuckled. "Pete don't know it," he said, "but that crummy forty-four will probably stand forever in this league."

Certainly, Rose's career monument will last as long as his sport. No living man could enjoy a game, or embody it more than Rose-in-bloom did baseball.

But how will a fading Rose react to a life without 162 baseball games a year. Rose may set goals for breakfast, lunch on records, and eat pressure for dinner. Even Cobb's incredible 4,192 career hits may not prove to be beyond Rose's will and endurance. Yet, sooner or later, the man who, in a sense, *is* baseball will have to forsake his vocation. "I'm a fan. I'll still be in the ball park every night," Rose protests, as though that would be the same thing to him. To be sure, Rose may even be a manager. Nevertheless, the game which has been his whole soul for a quarter century must finally leave him behind.

Rose knows it, of course. Perhaps the scene that should last longest in memory is the 1980 World Series when Rose fulfilled yet another of his grinning, boasting vows: "If I can get the Philadelphia Phillies to win the World Series after a hundred years, then I can do anything."

Few athletes have savored anything as Rose did that Series. "You know, the older you get . . . well, the days are coming to an end, so you want to enjoy them. You can't bear to give one away . . . not even one . . . Everything's real vivid these days. I kinda look at things from the inside and the outside at the same time."

The hundred million eyes that watched that Series, watched Rose save it in the last inning of the last game—with a reflex grab of a foul pop as it bounced out of the catcher's glove with the bases loaded—could see no difference in Charlie Hustle. Perhaps you would have to live the game to the bone—live *for* the game, as he does—to know the tiny telltale differences that speak only to him. It isn't the gray streaking into his hair more each year, or the way his upper trunk seems slightly less imposing with time, or even the wrinkles in his weather-beaten skin that makes the sweat, when it is pouring down his face, look like rain running down the bark of a tree.

It isn't the mirror that concerns Rose. He has never been handsome, neither as Joe Crewcut nor Prince Valiant. The best that can be said is that, with age, he has become powerfully ugly, along the lines of Lincoln, and that, when his mug lights up, the true innocent, infectious enthusiasm and confident simplicity of the man bursts through.

Often in that Series, Rose sat alone on the bench, leaning forward with his bat, handle up between his knees so that his chin could rest lightly on it. In repose, the face looked almost sad. Pete Rose could never pass for The Thinker, but he seemed to be taking an interminable time-lapse photograph of the scene before him, one that would be etched into his memory for life.

That only seemed fair, since we have been taking the same long, lingering, appreciative look at him for years.

Captain Bad Body

Chavez Ravine at sunset after a World Series game, with the crowds gone home and the San Gabriel Mountains aflame behind the outfield fence, is the most beautiful, transcendent setting in baseball. As Thurman Munson walked slowly around the upper deck of empty Dodger Stadium one such October evening, he shuffled along like an old man with sore feet, stretching the minutes before he reached the gate marked "Exit" and had to leave the place he loved best.

Because the game was over, the deadlines past and only an all-night flight from Los Angeles to New York was ahead of us, Munson was in no hurry—just talking softly about the sundown and the silence and about how the park was at its best when empty. This was how the New York Yankees usually saw their captain, their almost ideal leader and perfect teammate. Gruff in public, acerbic on the bench, maniacally intense on the field, Munson suddenly became calm and unpretentiously puckish in private. Munson's mouth played tricks under his walrus moustache as he walked, showing hidden glimpses of the mischievous, prankish nature buried deep under a layer of protective pride as bristly and thick as any animal hide.

"You've changed since you won the MVP award last year," Munson was teased. "You've gotta work to stay grumpy. Pretty soon you'll be a nice guy and a lousy ballplayer."

Munson liked that, since it flirted with bad taste, hinted at the truth, and dared him to make a denial. If humor holds a kernel of truth, then the adroit insult holds more—it was Munson's metier. "Now the guys can call me Captain Bad Body or anything they want," Munson said. "The Fat Kid's doing okay."

Thurman Munson, who died at thirty-two in a crash while piloting his private airplane, cultivated a misunderstanding with the world at large, just as he nurtured a powerful camaraderie with those he loved—his teammates and his family.

Small talk, which might only bore others, infuriated Munson. Good manners he disdained as weakness or fraud. Intransigence—

take me or leave me—he had raised to a standard of personal integrity. Introduced to a stranger, he might begin, "Where'd you get that ugly shirt?" It was his method for finding his social bearings quickly. "The same place you got that ugly face," was always a proper answer.

A creature of the locker room, Munson was comfortable with conversation only when it was dangerous—balanced on the edge between humor and hostility. In the dugout world where a fistfight may be seen as only a minor incident that often clears the air, Munson's sharp-sighted straight-for-the-jugular salvos did not need to be muffled. In fact, they made him a sage among his peers. Being worthy of Munson's needle was a badge of honor. "It's unbelievable to other players that Munson is thought of as silent and surly," Baltimore captain Mark Belanger once said. "I'd say that he is the most talkative player in baseball, and maybe the funniest, too."

It may be Munson's unfortunate legacy that he is remembered as a caricature—almost the reverse—of himself, because he happened to disdain the sports media. Often the feeling was mutual.

"For the people who never knew him, didn't like him, I feel sorry for them," said Billy Martin.

"When I played against him, I hated him for years," Munson's Yankee friend, Graig Nettles, always said. "He was an absolute competitor. He wanted to be liked, but he was too proud to politic for it."

Many will be amused at perhaps the soundest of Munson's eulogies, that of Bowie Kuhn, who called him, "a wonderful, enormously likeable guy."

Since Munson's public manner did no public harm except to himself, it is only fair to judge him by his private face, which did much good, and by his style on the ball field, which ennobled his game.

"Nice guys are a dime a dozen," said the great Army football coach, Red Blaik, "but leaders are the rarest of breeds."

It was a nice irony that Munson found it incomprehensible that he was the first Yankee captain since Lou Gehrig. "If I'm supposed to be a captain by example, I'll be terrible," said Munson, who was the heart of perhaps the most appealing of Bronx champions, those of '78.

"I seem to attract dirt," Munson once said with pride. "The

game was only ten pitches old tonight and I was filthier than anybody else was all night." To those who appreciated him, Munson was a sweat hog, who, beneath the tools of ignorance, was the essense of pride and rude wit.

Great catchers bear a different dignity than other players, since what they do in their game is in every sense work and only in the highest sense play. He approved of that tradition which labeled a broken finger a sign of virtue. Although his statistics may one day squeeze his squatty body into the Hall of Fame, Munson's most indelible contribution to the game was his manner—a ring of roustabout power that seemed to encircle him and protect him in those moments of crisis that he relished.

At the plate, where he was a .300 hitter five times, batted .339 in three play-offs and .373 in three Series, Munson took his sweet time, digging in his back foot defiantly, adjusting his batting glove interminably, twisting the last kink out of his fidgety neck, then pawing, yanking, and nodding until he was absolutely ready. His message to the pitcher was evident to the entire stadium: "When I get all this finished, you're in trouble."

"You'd jam him with every pitch, the way you know you ought to," Jim Palmer said once, "but he'd actually move into the pitch and let it hit him."

On the bases, Munson revealed the all-sport athlete who was concealed under shin guards and chest protectors as he dashed first to third as though his britches were on fire, ending his digging, stumbling dashes with a variety of wildly improvisational slides that left him deliciously filthy. If Pete Rose epitomized conspicuous hustle in his era—flavored with a taste for self-promotion —then Munson was the greatest of hidden hustlers who disguised his injuries, never curried the crowd's favor, and was best appreciated by players who universally saw him as their model.

As a receiver, Munson had a jerry-rigged three-quarter-arm throw that made him seem comic, plus a scrambling style on low pitches that was weak. Yet on key plays, key steals, he usually seemed to win. And his secret strength was his studious knack for calling pitches and needling hitters. Munson spent countless hours gabbing around other teams' batting cages, pretending to chitchat but really studying stances. Everybody knew his motive, but was helpless.

"Munson always said, 'How's it going, kid?' to rookies, and 'How's the family?' to the veterans when we come to the plate," Belanger said. "One day, I got furious and said, 'Thurman, we all know what you're doing. You're trying to distract me and I'm hitting .190. Just leave me the hell alone. Just shut up when I'm up here or I'll hit you with the bat.'

"He got this terrible hurt expression and said, 'Jeez, Blade, I didn't know you felt that strongly. I swear I'll never say another word to you.'"

On his next at-bat, Belanger was all ready to swing when the high-pitched penetrating voice behind him said, "How's the family, Blade?"

If Munson had an instinct for victory on the field with his indestructible will, he had a penchant for feeling bitterly slighted at other times. For years, he felt he played in the shadow of glamorous Carlton Fisk of Boston. He almost had apoplexy when Cincinnati Manager Sparky Anderson said of Munson, "Don't embarrass him by comparing him to Johnny Bench." When the Yankees paid Reggie Jackson, a slugger of few all-around baseball skills, more than Munson, the catcher was permanently galled. The list of indignities, real and imagined, was long.

Yet Munson, contrary to his image, often laughed about his annoyances, saying, "I'm just happy to be here," or, "The Fat Kid was not consulted." Those who thought Munson obnoxiously serious in all his grumbling about money were unaware of Munson's guileful and lusty ability to acquire capital—and real estate. The dugout scuttlebutt on Munson was that he would eventually own Ohio as Ty Cobb wished to acquire Georgia. Munson flew airplanes for two reasons central to his misunderstood personality: 1) because he disliked big-city bluster and loved his family in Canton, Ohio, and 2) because he planned on owning not just one airplane but eventually an entire commuter airline.

Ballplayers do not leave epitaphs, only memories and friends. Munson, the man who may have been baseball's ideal teammate, was rich in both.

Though some may wonder why, the mourning for Munson will be just as genuine and deeply felt within baseball as it was for the last Yankee captain who died too young. The Fat Kid left memories of a style of play as indelible as those of any man of his time.

The Barnum of the Bushes

Engel Stadium on its fiftieth anniversary is a symbol of everything that minor league baseball once was and is no more. This home of the Chattanooga Lookouts of the Southern League is both a monument to its decade-dead angel, Joe Engel, "The Barnum of the Bushes," and a tombstone for a marvelous era in baseball legend.

The grand ancient ball park—gone to ruin and slated for the wrecking ball just seven years ago—is also, however, a freshly painted emblem of what the refurbished bushes may be again. Both the rich history of the minors and its problematic future are captured in this huge concrete ballyard by the railroad tracks where every star from Babe Ruth to Henry Aaron has played and paid his respects. One man has the right to tell the tale of this stadium—Jim Crittendon, president of the new Class AA Lookouts, who calls himself "old Joe Engel's son in spirit." The year Crittendon was born—1936—Engel and his carnival ball park, with its "world's largest scoreboard" and forty-foot-high outfield walls, were in their heyday.

On a May night that season, a minor league record crowd of 24,839—twice the park's capacity—jammed the joint, covering most of the outfield with humanity. Engel, the father of almost every baseball attendance gimmick from Bat Day to giving away a wheelbarrow of silver dollars, drew the throng by giving away a fully furnished house with a new car in the garage. Engel even figured out how to play a game with 12,000 people standing in the outfield. For a man brash enough to trade a troublesome shortstop for a turkey, or challenge Dizzy Dean to a $10,000 fistfight at home plate, it was a small challenge.

Engel simply froze the baseballs for a week so no one could hit them much past the infield.

Crittendon, in his first year as president, also gave away a furnished house—his own. "Maybe I'm a fool," said Crittendon, who personally chopped down trees in the Engel Stadium outfield after the park lay dormant for a decade, "but I say you've gotta do something in this life. I've been in love with this park since I was a child. And I'm going to save it."

In Crittendon's boyhood, Engel Stadium was the heart of Chattanooga community life; it had been ever since Clark Griffith, the Old Fox, built it in 1929 and handed it over to his buddy Engel to operate as the Washington Senators' top farm club. Just as Engel the master scout had discovered and signed almost every Senator star of the '24 and '25 World Series teams, so Engel the drumbeater developed almost every decent Washington player of the '30s, '40s, and '50s at his Chattanooga fiefdom. "The Lookouts were the main attraction in town. People dressed for the occasion like it was church," recalls Crittendon. "School let out for Opening Day and there were usually 10,000 to 14,000 fans in the park." Crittendon's Knothole Gang memories were of feuds between Engel and Bobo Newsom, who would retreat to Chattanooga during his numerous exiles from the majors. "Bobo claims we had a gentleman's agreement on his contract," Engel once stormed. "Couldn't be. No gentlemen were involved."

As Crittendon grew up, so did a generation of Senator sluggers —Jim Lemon, Harmon Killebrew, and Bob Allison. None made so much as a home run ripple at Chattanooga. Engel, the son of a Washington saloonkeeper and a Nat pitcher on the same staff with Walter Johnson, made sure of that. He vowed that *his* park would make hitters cry. Engel Stadium's legendary left-field wall is 368 feet away and 40 feet high—*down the line*. In center, the wall is more than 420 feet away and is 25 feet high. Nevertheless, Chattanoogans claim Babe Ruth hit the world's longest homer here: the ball cleared the right-field wall, landed in a moving coal car, and was found in St. Louis.

For decades, Lookout baseball flourished, occasionally outdrawing a major league team. As minor league baseball began to shrivel in the late '50s and '60s, so did Engel. Elephants in the outfield, treasure hunts in the stand, pigeon races starting at home plate. All seemed bush league in the most depressing sense in the sophisticated age of TV. Engel fell so far from grace with the Griffiths (attendance down to 900 a game), that in 1959 the Nats told Engel to pay off the players and close up shop. Instead, Engel bought the club himself. By 1965, the Lookouts had expired. Four years later, mercifully, so did Engel.

Once, the baseball world laughed when the skinflint Old Fox sent Engel to Minneapolis and told him, "You pick two players off that team who will help us, and trade them for yourself." By the '70s, it was merely a footnote that almost all Bill Veeck's promotional genius was a direct borrowing of Engel antics that were decades old. Peaceful Chattanooga learned, after fostering minor league baseball since 1910, that it could live without the sport. In so idyllic a setting, it was easy. This railhead of the Confederacy, burned by U. S. Grant in retribution for Chickamauga, lies in an emerald valley surrounded by Missionary Ridge and Lookout Mountain. This town of 157,000, hugging the Tennessee River with its old black iron bridges, fancies itself as rich in lore as its Indian name and as defiantly romantic as its staunchly maintained drawl.

When Chattanooga threatened to demolish the fallow Engel Stadium, a group of investors, including Crittendon, could not stand the thought and picked up the fallen banner. They resurrected the Lookouts for the 1976 season. "About twenty of us volunteers worked on the park every weekend," said Crittendon. "The place was a total wreck. Trees as big around as your arm were growing in the outfield. The wood seats had rotted. The place was a haven for pigeons—a flyway. The entire grandstand was under two to four inches of pigeon shit. It took high-powered fire-department hoses to wash it off." For its efforts, all the group succeeded in doing was driving itself $200,000 in debt as attendance dropped each year from 135,000 to 90,000 to 45,000 in '78. Surely, this was the end of the line.

Instead, it was the beginning for Crittendon, who combined with the vice-president Don McKeel to buy controlling interest in the club. "We're turning back the clock," said Crittendon, who owns a chain of optical stores. "We're doing everything Joe Engel did. Every night's a promotion, a giveaway, or a happening." The Lookouts gave away three [used] cars and an Engel-style pot of gold. "We had both change and dollar bills in our pot," said Crittendon. "One fan was a scooper; the other was a picker, who only picked out the bills. The scooper got twice as much [$1,500] to carry home." Willing to try anything, Crittendon had five sky divers bombard the stadium on opening day. "Four of 'em made it," said Larry Fleming of the Chattanooga *Times*. "The other 'un landed over in those trees." Once the parachutes had settled, the county's highest political executive, Dalton Roberts, sang the national anthem. It helped that Roberts was the author of that country-and-western hit, "Don't Pay the Ransom, Honey, I've Escaped."

Crittendon also added two missing elements to Lookout life: home runs and beer. The previous Lookout boss forbade beer because his wife opposed it on religious grounds. "What would Engel have thought of that?" said Crittendon. "It was against his religion to lose money."

Amidst the blizzard of promotions, the Lookouts could not have foreseen one of their happenings. A bridge stands just above and beyond the center-field fence. A spectacular car crash took place on the bridge, almost as though staged for the crowd. "The boys in one car had been drinking," said McKeel. "Before the smoke cleared, all four doors flew open and they were throwing beer cans off the bridge—destroyin' evidence. Trouble was, a coupla thousand people were watchin' 'em."

"I honestly think we're going to make it," said Crittendon. "It's been a month since I tended to my businesses. I have employees who probably think I've gone to South America with the funds. We're here until 2 A.M. every night, doing a million little things. I'm out on the tractor working on the field, or painting the stands. I dream about this work. I live it and breathe it." Hard labor is the easiest part of the task.

"I haven't really been able to grasp the role of club president yet. I came from a white-collar business, and this is roll-up-the-sleeves-back-slapping. I'm not as much a natural at this promoting as Joe Engel was."

Crittendon and friends are just at the beginning of a long road. They may never match the tall tales of Engel Stadium's past. Will Crittendon ever hire and fire the same player ten times over the years as Engel did to Charlie Letchas? What will the reborn Lookouts do to match the time that the Old Fox sent his son to manage Chattanooga? The full-of-beans young Calvin Griffith followed the umpires into their dressing room to complain—only to get punched in the nose by an ump and be carried out.

Crittendon will do his best to join the tradition this summer when he gives away his own second home, a rental property in the handsome Riverview section of town. Joe Engel may have traded himself, but it's doubtful that he ever gave away his own house, even if it was No. 2.

The Engel Stadium press room could tell many tales: of Babe Didrikson fanning Babe Ruth as a gag, or of Satchel Paige barnstorming with the Chattanooga Black Lookouts. The walls of that room are covered with fading mural cartoons that Engel loved. One cartoon says, "I was living the life of Reilly . . . until Reilly came home."

Now it is Crittendon who is living the life of Engel. If the Barnum of the Bushes suddenly came back home, he wouldn't mind at all.

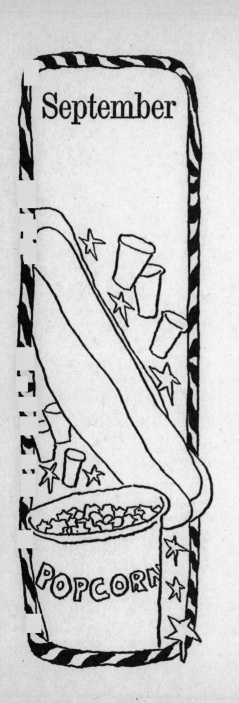

September

POPCORN

How Life Imitates the World Series

> Pressure? Well, it ain't hittin' in forty-four straight games
> 'cause I done that and it was fun. The play-offs are pressure.
> —Pete Rose, Philadelphia Phillies

Baseball is often praised as the sport with a relaxed, sane pace. It supposedly serves as an antidote to modern life, a free pass back to the tempo of an earlier time. Perhaps that is why we are reluctant to acknowledge that it is the inner tension of the game that really attracts us so strongly. On the outside, the game appears tranquil, a green chess board with human pieces and a 20-second clock. Yet, baseball's mainspring is a daily winding up of tension that is never fully unwound before the next game. Inning to inning, week to week, the pressure builds. We become hooked on the delicious suppressed anxiety of an emaciating pennant race, a chilly, klieglighted World Series, and best of all, that brutally truncated distortion of the game called the play-offs.

Only occasionally do our other major professional sports slow down time, isolate performers, and turn the screws of tension. The basketball foul shooter, standing alone on the court after time has expired and the score is tied, feels it. So does the last-second field-goal kicker when his opponent calls time twice to let him think. Such instances are the norm, not the exception, in baseball, the sport that transformed those turn-of-the-century automotive terms, "clutch" and "choke," into "clutch player" and "choked on the pressure."

Our other team sports are hot-blooded, sweaty, and continuous. Once immersed, a player loses himself, leaving pressure behind and relying on years of conditioned reflex and practice. Only baseball is cold-blooded and discontinuous. The game explodes at unpredictable instants: You start to sweat *after* the play is over. Between those bursts of action, the sport offers hundreds of fecund pauses.

The worst pressures are not within one game, but between games. Success seems as ephemeral as the next day's game, while failure is cumulative. The glow of victory often lasts only as long as it takes to fall asleep, then wake again.

In addition, baseball is played at two wildly different paces—regular-season and postseason, the six months of April through September, and then October. They present different strains and require almost antithetical responses. The regular season rewards a phlegmatic stability, a capacity to endure long aggravation and ignore many losses and embarrassments. The postseason asks the opposite—a knack for instant resiliency and an intolerance of even one defeat.

Since no one baseball game is proof of anything, the sport does its basic testing over a 162-game season. Then, after establishing those ground rules—actually ingraining them in the texture of a player's life—it reverses them in October. The last days of a hair-breadth pennant race, the three to five games of a play-off and the fortnight of a Series are such a drastically new and powerful experience that Hall of Famers, like Ernie Banks, who never tasted them are pitied as though they had spent their careers in foreplay.

Something in every sport must be of unquestioned value. In baseball that *sine qua non* is the divisional flag. Probably the reason for this is simple. Only in the last days of a pennant race do we see a combination of the long-range endurance required in a whole season, as well as the ability to rise to the occasion in a crisis. Even as great a player as Ted Williams had trouble amassing a statistical brief to back the claim that he was as good in a pennant race, play-off, or Series as he was at all other times. And the prickly flip side of Reggie Jackson's nickname, "Mr. October," is a natural curiosity about why Jackson is not so spectacular in other months.

The faces of players who have lived long with baseball's special late-season demands tend to have a cured-and-aged quality. Carl Yastrzemski's mug looks as if it had been chiseled accidentally by nature out of some pleasantly weathered New England rock. "At this time of year," said Yastrzemski, sitting in the guts of Yankee Stadium in autumn '78, "I think about baseball when I wake up in the morning. I think about it all day. And I dream about it at night. The only time I don't think about it is when I'm playing it."

In that race, as in others, Yastrzemski simplified the mental anguish of wondering when he should rest, when he should let injuries heal, when he should take it easy by never resting, never healing, and never taking it easy. He exchanged physical pain, which he could stand, for mental doubt, which he feared more. At age thirty-nine, he played with ankles taped so tightly because of weak Achilles' heels that he had to look down to see where his numb feet were in the batter's box. He played with a thumb so sore that he experimented with taping the bat to his hand until he realized he couldn't run the bases that way. "I've gone beyond good sense many times," he said. "Durability is part luck." In other words, rather than face the self-doubts that confront any player, Yastrzemski preferred to risk a career-ending injury, and oceans of pain.

That response to pressure, with courage obliterating judgment, is common among fine players. High-paid Dave Parker endured a mediocre year in 1980 in large part because he played through every sort of injury. "The show must go on. Ain't but one right way to play this game," said Parker. "When I'm finished, I want them to say about me, 'He played every game like it was his last.' I'd like to be like Frank Robinson was in the clutch . . . spontaneous . . . into the game . . . a leader . . . whatever it takes. Some guys won't go into the wall, you know? They got numbers on their minds. You either play for the stats, or you play for the wins."

That is a reassuring simplification. Few men can function if their minds are full of "Will I do this?" or "Maybe I shouldn't do that." Pressure does not create cowards. Far more often, it creates foolhardy heroes. Every pennant race is full of them. In '78, Butch Hobson rearranged the bone chips in his elbow between hitters, but it didn't stop him from making 43 errors (five of them on consecutive grounders) and earning the cruelly unfair name, "Butcher." In August of 1980 in Baltimore, Reggie Jackson tried to run through a fence while making a catch. The wall should have been taken to the hospital for X rays.

"When somebody on your team does that," said Oriole coach Ray Miller, "you say, 'What guts! What a gamer!' When a guy on the other team does it, you say, 'What a dummy! There's no percentage in that.' When it's the other guy, you become a cynic. The only way Reggie could have made a better play on that ball was if he'd jumped over the fence and landed on Gossage."

Of all the manifestations of pressure, the most common isn't striking out with the bases loaded, but trying to play beyond your abilities. In recent years, almost every team that has been said to have choked has done so because its response to pressure was to try too hard, be too brave, and play too hurt—day after day, until something irreparable happened. This syndrome is most common among teams that feel growing humiliation at seeing huge leads dwindle. The '78 Red Sox were a perfect death-march example, while the '80 Yankees tried hard to fit the mold. Yankee center fielder Ruppert Jones, chagrined when several balls fell in front of him during a particularly important series, atoned by leaping into fences. In Baltimore, he went above the center-field wall twice to steal homers and crashed head on into the barrier on another futile try. When Jackson was shown a dramatic picture of Jones' theft catch, he told Jones, "Man, that picture's going all around the world. That'll be in Khomeini's newspaper for breakfast."

One week later, in Oakland, Jones tried the same kind of catch for a fourth time. Different wall, different photo: severe concussion, separated shoulder, carried off unconscious and out for the season. Such casualties should be tagged "victims of pressure." Other results of pressure are more subtle.

The most important part of the word, "pressure," is the first part. Press. The first natural response to crisis or increased tension in baseball is to press. It is such a constant, predictable factor that wise teams even build strategy around it. A fine example came in August of '80 when the Orioles won 6 of 8 games against New York in an 11-day period because they elected to use a pitching style that would exacerbate the pressure on several key Yankee hitters. The linchpin that had to be broken was Jackson. To do so, the Orioles pitched around him, giving him only bad or borderline pitches. The Birds' hole card was the knowledge that, even if Jackson walked often, the five, six, and seven hitters behind him would face greater than normal pressure and expectations because Graig Nettles was sick and absent. In those eight games, Jackson hit .120. More incredibly, the Yankees' five, six, and seven hitters came to the plate 91 times with a total of 53 runners on base during those at-bats and drove home none. Zero. By the seventh of those eight games, Jackson was so frustrated that, in the words of one Baltimore player, "He was swinging hard enough to hit it off the planet." In that game, he finally got some pitches to hit—fast-balls down the middle—yet fanned three times. "Right in my wheelhouse," fumed Jackson. "I don't understand. If I'd hit one, it would have gone nine miles." (When last measured, the deepest fence in Memorial Stadium was 410 feet from home plate.)

In baseball, a hard swing is called a long swing because it takes longer to start, has a longer loop and arc, and takes longer to get to the impact zone after the hitter pulls the trigger. Not much longer, just the imperceptible fraction of an instant necessary to ruin a batter's timing. That is to say, ruin everything. Because he is using more effort and trying harder, the hitter thinks he is being quicker, when, in fact, he is slower. This is universal in baseball. It is a reason that the desperate slumper's decision to revert to "just hitting singles" often leads instantly to home runs. And, of course, it is the most basic reason that batting averages almost always go down in postseason. Taken as a group, hitters will usually press and get themselves out in the biggest games. That's why the cliche, "good pitching beats good hitting," is particularly true in October. Consider that the 61 games played in the 10 World Series of the 1970s produced 469 runs, an average of only 7.68 per game, while an average of 8.30 runs were scored per regular-season games during the same period.

Golfers face the same demon and chant the mantra, "tempo," to exorcise it. Ballplayers only recognize the source of their affliction half-consciously, telling each other to stay loose. Almost all excellent teams have some ritual release of pressure. So do the bad ones, but nobody cares.

The old Big Red Machine teams in Cincinnati instituted the mock fight. Either Tony Perez or Lee May would pretend, each day, to be in a venomous argument with a teammate, thus letting the mate say to them what he wanted to say to his manager or mother-in-law.

The champion Yankees of 1977–78 took the needle and barb a step farther, making the blatant insult a dugout staple. Thurman Munson took the lead in dealing abuse. This role-playing psycho-drama has been refined by many Montreal Expos who delight in terrifying visitors to their clubhouse. One season pitcher Rudy May was the team's designated murderer. Grabbing a long knife, he would stalk Gary Carter, recalling the entire history of why he was going to kill his useless receiver. The Expos would plead with May and even pretend to be making risky plans to stop him at the last second. The performance was good enough to make Sherlock Holmes bite the stem off his briar pipe.

Ballplayers often heap their cathartic wrath on symbols, like innocent gifts sent by fans. Sparky Lyle made a Yankee tradition out of dropping his pants and squatting on the cakes sent to the Bomber clubhouse. As his teammates chant, "Lo . . . Lo . . . Lo," Baltimore sub John Lowenstein will take a bat and, with a samurai yell, demolish a huge cake that has been placed in the center of the clubhouse. Perhaps cakes have such a tough life in the big leagues because they are excellent emblems of fawning yet fickle fandom, which will bake pies for you one day, then throw them in your face the next.

Of baseball's contenders, only two are conspicuously sober-sided —Boston and Philadelphia. These are also the two teams that seem most burned and burdened by the myopic scrutiny of the sports media. Other clubs maintain their own locker-room atmosphere and, naturally, force interlopers to blend with its tone. But the Bosox and Phils sometimes go so far as to abandon their central clubhouse. The result is the odd scene of large athletes cramped in smallish off-limit anterooms playing Skittle Pool so they can avoid questions from frumpy folk with cigars, elbow patches, and pencils. It is hard to avoid the notion that the team that hides together also feels pressure together. The painful late-season records of the Phils and Red Sox for the past half-century or so are probably coincidence. Ironically, 1980 was the season when both finally exhausted the enthusiasm of their long-frustrated fans and were largely written off early, even in their own towns. So, free of high expectations, both have played better than anticipated.

Team mood can only go so far in helping stabilize the individual's mood. Often, the clubhouse clown, like Don "Stan the Man Unusual" Stanhouse, who lets out a bathroom death scream ten minutes before game time, is far less important than the quiet man who follows Shakespeare's dictum: "He who would be calm must first put on the appearance of calm." One dominant personality, by giving the appearance of carrying disproportionate weight with ease, can make all other loads lighter. No one is better at this than Stargell, who sits silently amid the Pittsburgh Pirate party of disco, ribs, and card games. Late in September '79, Stargell broke up an extra-inning pennant-race filibuster in Montreal with a home run at 1:40 A.M. As the aged Stargell dressed with creaky slowness in his gunfighter's rig of plumed cowboy hat, snakeskin boots, and all-white suit with black-and-white vest, he drawled, "Why don't you kids let ol' Pops go to bed?"

It is Stargell's gift—the genuinely rare one—that he deals with disappointment even better than he does heroism. On the next-to-last day of the '79 season, the Bucs lost to the lowly Cubs to fall into a tie in the loss column with the Expos. The goat of the day was Stargell, who made the game-losing error in the thirteenth, then fanned with two men on to end the game. Afterward, the Buc bravado was gone. The only player at the communal Pirate table was Stargell, munching at his ease and playing cards with the clubhouse man. "Lay it on me," he said. "Don't make excuses for me. I was as bad as you can be."

Among those who seek truth between the white lines, this is called "being the horse." It is the most difficult, pressure-laden of all leadership roles. Few want it. Baltimore, for instance, has no player who would touch the task with a long stick. Rose pulled it off in Cincinnati and in Philadelphia. In Kansas City, George Brett gradually has proved to be a natural, emulating the hard-nosed style of Hal McRae, who learned his gritty panache from Rose. Jackson has gone from mere superstar to bearer of pressure as well. "I can't afford to lose my edge," he says. "And I can't be on edge. What I do causes ripples."

Nothing beats a great horse, but the next best thing may be a hot-tempered gadfly. They come in all sizes, from 6-5 Dave Parker to 5-8 Earl Weaver. But when they explode, they serve the same purpose: A mounting mood of tension breaks along with their rage, whether real or feigned.

Before a vital series in Philadelphia in 1980, Parker strode into the Buc dugout, diamond in ear, and began bellowing blue insults at the Phils, with whom the Pirates had had a beanball brawl in their previous meeting in Pittsburgh. "First year in the big leagues and the busher's got something to say," roared Parker at a Philadelphia rookie who had done some brave talking in the press after the fight. "Ain't even got a bubble-gum card with his picture on it, but the pig-faced sucker is already running his mouth. I don't hear Mr. Pig-Face talking to me, do I?"

My, my, how eloquent silence can be.

While Parker's fury caused a hush, Weaver's tantrums bring laughter. The motive, however, is the same—to create a simpler mood in which it is easier to perform, whether it be Parker's clowning anger, or, in Weaver's case, mock hysteria. Weaver's best tirade to date—one that was worth a three-day suspension—came at what might well have been the emotional fulcrum of his team's 1980 season. His Birds, after cutting New York's lead in the loss column from 11 to 2, lost back-to-back games at home with the Yanks. In the second beating, Weaver erupted in a medley of old favorites: the flying-equipment, the cap-kick-and-stomp, the poke-'em-in-the-eye, and the cover-home-plate-with-dirt. He even perched on top of second base, prompting umpire Steve Palermo to quip, "Earl figured that was the only way he could be as tall as we are, but they don't make bags that tall."

Weaver, not his team, came in for scrutiny and criticism. Even the Yanks talked about Weaver, not their victory. "That's a 'ten,' no doubt about it. I'd pay to see that," said Goose Gossage. "Loved it," said Jackson. "Just loved it to death."

So, in their way, did the Orioles. Nary a reporter grilled them on a night when their comeback bubble seemed to have burst. "Maybe Earl is a very good actor," ventured the eminently relaxed Mark Belanger. "This is a tense and intense time. He helps us relax. Let's see . . . tomorrow's Sunday . . . got a game at 2:05. John, will you be here?" he asked the player on his left.

"Yeah, I'll make it."

"Dan, how about you?" Belanger asked the mate on his right.

"Okay, okay, I'll come."

"Well, that's three of us," he said. "I think we'll be able to round up a few more."

The Orioles won their next eight games.

Quite often, the level of pressure that players feel, and their ability to deal with it, seems altogether outside the parameters of such things as team mood, team leaders, or managers, and even the composure under stress of any one player. Year after year, we see players and teams that seem to be caught, almost helplessly, in the strong riptide of the entire flow of a season. The whole evolution and theme of pennant races sometimes seem to have their own interior driving force.

One manager this year described how it felt to take the lead in an important game, lose that lead, fall behind, then catch up and finally win. Unwittingly, he seemed to touch on something that might be called the emotional equivalent of the law of averages for team sports.

"When we were building that lead, we were excited," he said. "But once you build a lead, you get nervous. I get scared to death and start smoking those damn cigarettes and thinking about all the things that can go wrong. You keep imagining how one thing can lead to another and wipe out your lead. You can't help it. Even when they tie it up, you're still thinking about how you screwed up. But when you're behind, you're not nervous. You know nothing. As soon as they're back in front, you're totally calm. All you're thinking is, 'Let's go get them. They can't do this to us.'"

Ballplayers, as a group, firmly believe that over the course of 162 games the better team almost always wins. Even in the postseason, they think that justice is usually done. So, it is of considerable concern to them, as they fly all over North America and sit in hotel coffee shops, dugouts, and locker rooms for seven months chewing the baseball fat, to decide in their heart of hearts which team actually is better. In the end, perhaps the best way to know who will win a pennant race is to listen to the tone of voice. The team that is convinced it ought to win, whether for bona fide reasons or not, has a huge advantage.

That club will be more likely to play within itself and resist the urge to press beyond its controllable skills. The foe with doubts will double its real task by running into walls, playing hurt, and trying too hard. Though hindsight is always clear, the greatest comeback in American League history followed exactly this pattern in 1978. Anyone who saw every Red Sox-Yankee game that season knew which team had few doubts, even when it was far behind, and which would press as soon as the defending champion Yankees appeared on the horizon.

The bottom of the ninth of the Red Sox-Yankee play-off game was probably the finest single baseball pressure moment of a generation, as significant as Bobby Thompson's home run in the '51 Giant-Dodger play-off.

As Gossage stood on the Fenway Park mound facing his last hitter—Yastrzemski—he says that he thought to himself, "The worst thing that can happen if we lose is that, at this time tomorrow, I'll be skiing in the Rockies."

Such mental and emotional gymnastics are the norm in baseball. The proof of the magnitude of the game's pressure is the length to which players will go either to deflate it or deny that it exists. In baseball, almost every act has an accountability. The box score must add up with each run, hit, and error charged to someone. For this reason, many ballplayers believe in luck, charms, magic, locker-room religion, and every form of depressurizing fatalism that can break the grip of responsibility.

For years, Luis Tiant came to the park on pitching days dressed in white from head to toe—shirt, pants, belt, boots, wallet, socks, and underwear. He also carried a small can of spray paint to touch up the regalia once he had neatly hung it in his locker. For his first fourteen years as a pro, he wore a religious belt of many-colored scarves under his uniform instead of a plastic protective cup. In 1973, a line drive convinced him of the limits of faith.

"Man is not big enough to handle these intense pressure situations by himself," said Jackson before a '78 Series game. "In a no-deposit, no-return game like this, you have to find some way to find an inner peace."

"I have little tricks," said Steve Garvey in that same Series. "Once I get to the park, I keep as busy as I can. If I sit in one place too long, I start to get too tightly wound. I'm not a heavily religious person, but I've found it really helps to say to yourself, 'Lord, I put my life in your hands.'"

Such seemingly unwarranted seriousness—the resignation of will by the most strong-willed of people—is generally associated with experiences much more traumatic than any "game." However, it would be naïve to think of October baseball as a game.

In this cauldron of pressure, nothing is more tonic to a team than an astringent dose of reality. In the 1979 World Series, the Pirates played tightly and nervously for the first four games. Before the fifth game, Manager Chuck Tanner's mother, who had been very sick, mercifully died. That news hit the Pirates like a sobering, but also relaxing, wash of cold water. Long thoughts put other thoughts into perspective.

It struck them as ugly that Tanner, who had never before reached a World Series, would have to tolerate defeat on that particular day. So they won, their worst pitcher, Jim Rooker (4-7), beating Baltimore's best, Mike Flanagan (23-9). That victory changed the internal chemistry of team pressures.

In the final Series game, one player gave a nerveless performance—Stargell, whose four hits were as many as the whole Baltimore team's. All his nerves were gone, long ago. "I've been going through this every fall for years," Stargell had said exactly thirty days earlier after that 1:40 A.M. game-winning homer in Montreal.

"I've got three A.M. shadow," he muttered, stroking the stubble of his beard as he shouldered his travel bag and trudged into the crisp Canadian night to catch a plane to another town. "In just a few hours, we got a damned doubleheader. You can't ever stop pushing this time of year. It's a game of survival. I'm not crying. I asked to be a ballplayer.

"But there's nothing in the world like this pressure. You wind up and wind up. Then you have to wind down fast so there'll be something left of you when it's time to wind back up again."

Baseball is really two sports—the Summer Game and the Autumn Game. One is the leisurely pastime of our national mythology. The other is not so gentle.

How Can You Tell the Dancer From the Dance?

The cleanup crews come at midnight, creeping into the ghostly quarter-light of empty ball parks with their slow-sweeping brooms and languorous, sluicing hoses. All season, they remove the inanimate refuse of a game. Now, in the dwindling days of September and October, they come to collect baseball souls.

Age is the sweeper, injury his broom.

Mixed among the burst beer cups and the mustard-smeared wrappers headed for the trash heap, we find old friends who are being consigned to the dust bin of baseball's history. If a night breeze blows a back page of the *Sporting News* down the stadium aisle, pick it up and squint at the one-time headline names now just fine print at the very bottom of a column of averages.

Each year, the names change of those who have "lost it," and probably won't find it again. This year's list for 1980 of those who are past thirty and into that inexorable stat slide includes Sal Bando, Lee May, Ed Figueroa, Gene Tenace, Fred Patek, Manny Sanguillen, Willie Horton, Bernie Carbo, Bud Harrelson, Bobby Bonds, Randy Jones, Dave Cash, Mike Torrez, and Ross Grimsley. Not a bad season's haul, once you consider that, when the seine is finally culled clean, it may also hold Willie Stargell, Bill Lee, and Joe Morgan.

"I like a look of Agony," wrote Emily Dickinson, "because I know it's true." For those with a taste for a true look, a glimpse beneath the mask, even if it be a glimpse of agony, then this is the proper time of year. Spring training is for hope; autumn is for reality. At every stop on the late-season baseball trail, we see that look of agony, although it hides behind many expressions.

In Pittsburgh, "Pops" Stargell rides a stationary bicycle. A depressed giant sitting on a ridiculous toy, he pedals to rehabilitate an arthritic knee that has deteriorated for a decade. "Everything gets better slower each year," he says. "And, finally, it doesn't get better at all."

In Houston, Morgan helps the Astros with the sad bits and pieces of those skills that are left to him. The back-to-back MVP, a .240-ish hitter for the past three years, says of his last career stage, "I'm still a ballplayer, but you couldn't really call me Joe Morgan . . . I'm used to laughing at other players. Now they're laughing at me."

In Montreal, "Spaceman" Bill Lee, in bull pen exile, spends these pennant-race days exorcising the nervous energy that consumes him. Lee spends half the game jogging just beyond the outfield fence, his cap and prematurely grizzled hair bouncing at the edge of view like a bobber on the water's surface being jerked about by a hooked fish. "I'm not through. They can't get rid of me," he says. "I pitched hurt for 'em for months. That explains the [bad] stats. But they don't appreciate it. Just wait. You'll see next year." It's an old litany. Lee's ERA is 5.47. Even Spacemen get jettisoned.

Finally, the towns become a swirl. The player's face is familiar with its look of wounded dignity, but the uniforms change. Jim Kaat, forty-one, has won 270 games, but his uniform gets harder to remember as he bounces from league to league, hanging on. "It's tough to love the game," says Kaat, now a Cardinal, "after she's stopped loving you."

To a ballplayer, the game is a seed he planted as a child, a kind of beautiful creeping ivy that he was delighted to have entwine him. As an adult, he felt supported in every sense—financial, emotional, psychic—by his green, rich, growing game, just as ivy can strengthen a brick wall. But ivy, given time, can overpower and tear down a house.

So, in a way, the aging player, whose life seems to be a mansion, knows that he is in a strong and even dangerous grip. In the end, he may not know how much of his strength, how much of his ability to stand alone, comes from the brick and mortar of his own identity and how much is borrowed from the vine that engulfs him more each year, even as it props him up. No wonder he is so fearful when the time arrives to hew through the root and pull free.

Mickey Mantle, retired a dozen years, still has a recurring dream that makes him awake in a sweat. In the nightmare, he is trying to crawl under the center-field fence in Yankee Stadium, but something is snagged and he can't move. The PA system intones, "Batting fourth . . . No. 7 . . ." In the dugout, Whitey

Ford, Billy Martin, and Casey Stengel ask each other, "Where's Mickey?"

"And then," says Mantle, "I wake up."

This dream needs no interpretation. It epitomizes the nub of raw, disoriented fear, and the sense of nameless loss, that many fine athletes must feel if they were ever good enough to mesh their characters with their skills. How can we tell the dancer from the dance?

Even the most dignified and self-possessed of former stars occasionally shows a twinge of what haunts Mantle. Returning from a USO tour of Korea, Marilyn Monroe told her husband, Joe DiMaggio, then retired, "Oh, Joe, it was wonderful. You never heard such cheers."

"Yes, I have," was DiMaggio's clipped reply.

The desire for applause, for camaraderie, for the hard coin of indisputable accomplishment is a powerful pull. The green of the field has many rich connotations that it even makes the green of a dollar bill seem faded by comparison.

In all baseball history, there is perhaps only one case of a great player who cut the vine, stepped free, and tested his legs long before he lost it. When Sandy Koufax was thirty, he won 27 games. And after the World Series, he retired.

"I was looking for time," he now says for explanation.

Only after thirteen years of casual wandering—neither a recluse nor a public figure—did his nest egg run low. He returned to baseball, as a Dodger coach, because it was a painless way to make a buck as a pitching professor emeritus.

Koufax is simply the exception that proves the rule. Far more typical are Hank Aaron and Warren Spahn, the top home-run hitter and winner in modern, lively-ball times. The former Brave teammates never faced each other in their careers, but they did this spring in San Diego when the forty-six-year-old Aaron came to bat against the fifty-nine-year-old Spahn. They weren't kidding.

Not since Babe Ruth faced Walter Johnson for charity when both were in their fifties have such legends met. The pretext for this time-warp freeze frame was a Padre vs. Pirate home-run-hitting contest. But the real curiosity was watching Aaron and Spahn face each other from opposite ends of the tunnel of middle age. Aaron looked like he had spent his four retirement years locked in a bakery. Spahn might have spent fifteen years prospecting in a desert, his skin weathered to rawhide, his bandy limbs and barrel chest shrunken.

The scene was elegantly set. Warming up, Aaron missed half-speed pitches. The crowd murmured its collective embarrassment and empathy as though an innocent prank had turned ugly. Meanwhile, thanks to aluminum bats and Japanese rabbit balls, Dave Parker, Dave Winfield, and Stargell were having a tape-measure orgy. Aaron was mercifully forgotten.

Once the contest started, Aaron whiffed meekly twice against the Padre batting-practice pitcher. Then, on the third of six allotted swings in the round, Aaron conked a homer. The crowd cheered with relief. Then, while their pitying applause was still in the air, the next pitch had already been dispatched even farther into the left-field bleachers. The crowd was rising and roaring. Reporters scrambled back into the press box just as players popped back out of runways into the dugouts to watch. The next pitch also went over the wall, delivered there by a sweet slash of the wrists. And, on his fourth consecutive swing—all this in thirty seconds or so, as emotions had gone from depression to glee—Aaron smashed his last pitch off the top of the center-field wall 430 feet away, missing a fourth homer by a yard.

For the final round of the contest, Spahn pitched, lobbing in mushballs for the monsters to mash. Aaron hit last, needing just one homer to beat all the active stars. Spahn peered in, grinned, and threw. Aaron swung and missed. He smiled back at Spahn. Spahn repeated the ritual and threw again. Aaron looked at the pitch as though it were a rotten mackerel. Although he was due five more swings, Aaron gently laid down his bat, turned his back on Spahn, and walked away, ending the contest by fiat.

Back in the dugout, Aaron was asked, "Why'd you quit? Hurt yourself swinging?"

"No," said Aaron brusquely. "Spahn was throwing screwballs."

And they say Walter Johnson threw sliders to Ruth.

In baseball, you see, no one ever believes he's really lost it. No American team sport is half so fascinated with the process of aging as baseball, perhaps because none of our games is based on skill and timing rather than brute force. Nor does any sport offer prospects for an athletic old age that is so rich in possibilities for either humiliation or the greatest fame.

Every athlete in every sport deteriorates. But in baseball that battle against time—where a standoff means temporary victory—can be extended for as much as a decade by a dogged will and an analytical mind. Perhaps no sport encourages its men to rage so nobly against the erosion of their youth.

The ultimate cases in point are Aaron and Spahn, statistically the greatest old hitter and the best old pitcher ever. They alone among Hall of Famers actually got better after they turned thirty-five. Aaron hit 245 homers and had his two best slugging-percentage years after that supposed watershed as he actually became a better pull hitter with age. After Spahn turned thirty-five, and concurrently mastered the scroogie, he won 20 games seven times and won 180 games. No one is close to either mark.

Baseball, it seems, rewards stubbornness and indomitability, as long as those qualities are mixed with a basic humility, self-knowledge, and willingness to adapt. Baseball's highest and most appealing type may be the veteran. No sport is so full of 10-, 15-, and even 20-year pros, or is so defined by them.

"I disagree," John Keats once wrote in a letter, about the world as a "vale of tears . . . Call the world, if you please, 'the vale of soul-making.' Then you will find out the use of the world."

Only with age do athletes discover that their playing fields have become vales of soul-making. Only as they become vulnerable, flawed, and afraid do they seem truly human to us and most worthy of our attention. Nothing can stop the slow bleeding away of talent and confidence, but character is the best tourniquet.

"The player who ages poorly is the one who lets his vanity get in the way of his judgment," says Yankee Coach Charlie Lau. "Making 'adjustments' is another word for having the good sense to know you're getting older."

As an example, Lau cites those good friends, George Scott and Reggie Jackson. Each, with age, showed a hitting flaw. Scott, proud of his strength, could no longer manage his huge 38-ounce bat. Jackson had trouble with high and outside fastballs, popping them harmlessly to center. Scott, for three years, refused to use a lighter bat. Despite humiliating reverse shifts—with defenses playing him as though he were a weak lefty hitter—he persisted in his persona as "The Boomer." Now, he's out of baseball and doesn't understand. Jackson, on the other hand, worked with his stance and weight shift until that troublesome pitch suddenly became his bleacher meat.

"Even after everybody else told Scott he needed to change, he wouldn't," summarized Lau. "But before anybody said anything to Reggie, he already had."

No better text could be asked to illustrate baseball's capacity for allowing age-with-dignity than the performance in the closing months of the 1980 season by the New York Yankees. Of all champions, they may well be the oldest, the most infirm and the most emblematic of what we mean by veteran fortitude.

If ever a team ought not to have borne inspection, it was these Yankees with a pitching rotation at that time of Gaylord Perry (42), Luis Tiant (40), Tommy John (37), and Rudy May (37). Yet they began that September 20-3. Autumn must be their proper season. More than half this team had, at one time or another, heard the words, "You've lost it." Names like Piniella, Nettles, Jackson, Watson, Murcer, Spencer, Rodriguez, and Stanley had among them an average age of thirty-five.

Look below the Yankee dollar signs and New York headlines. That was a team familiar with the look of Agony. Its players had been forced to look in the mirror. For most, their baseball world long ago became a vale of soul-making. So, demands for September character were within their reach.

Age, with his broom of injury, will sweep them all out someday. Nonetheless, those Yankees remain a standing lesson of how old men, who are really young, can staunchly refuse to go gentle into that good night.

October

Mr. October

Mark Twain said that politicians, old buildings, and prostitutes become respectable with age. Reggie Jackson would like to make it a foursome.

It isn't easy for a hurricane to become its own calm eye, but the former Buck Tater Man is trying. After years of straining to be the straw that stirs the drink, it has dawned on Jackson that, perhaps, he is the drink that is getting stirred.

When you go to the movies and get sued, when you walk to your car and get accused of battering a child, when you sit in your car and somebody walks up and points a revolver at your nose from six-inch range, it makes you wonder who's getting stirred. When your house burns down, it makes you wonder who's in control. When you foul off a sacrifice bunt and get suspended for insubordination, when you jog in from the outfield and your manager is waiting in the dugout to punch you, or when you step in a hole and disable yourself for a month, it makes you wonder about your luck, about your approach to things.

All this, and much more, has happened since Jackson came to the New York Yankees in 1977. From clubhouse fights, to an IRS-audit brouhaha, to banner headlines screaming, GUNMAN FIRES AT REGGIE ON MANHATTAN STREET, Jackson has never lacked for somber subjects to mull in his idle, thoughtful hours. Slowly, he has changed. And is still changing. Like any fine protagonist in fiction, Jackson alters, grows, learns, regresses, doubles back, stakes out new ground before our eyes.

Jackson has not outlined his new position—his new image, as he perhaps unwisely chooses to call it—in any single way, but rather in a dozen ways. "I must take off my black hat . . . I have to control my tongue . . . I have to substantiate my thoughts rather than just raise hell . . . You have to sell yourself and politic a little in this life . . . I have to stop getting into things too deep . . . I don't want to offend . . . It's good to feel wanted and respected . . . Part of the trouble with Billy [Martin] was that I misunderstood his wants."

These snippets of conciliation, these bon mots of a once-burned, twice-shy man, are extracts from Jackson's conversation—all said within fifteen minutes. If the New York Yankee slugger suddenly has to go on the disabled list, no one should have to ask why. It'll be a slipped disc; this is a man spending a lot of time bending over backward. Jackson seems to be a man in the midst of a long, gradual, yet uneasy personal transition. His locker in the New York clubhouse is in the corner, almost hidden, as though he were an animal gone to earth. If Jackson now feels most comfortable with his back protected by a wall, he has good reason.

From his first day in pinstripes, Jackson was baseball's King Midas of fame, its Hester Prynne of sluggers with a dollar sign on his chest. Everything he touched turned to instant celebrity. Since Aesop, men have been warned to be careful when they make a wish. It just might come true. Jackson asked the free-agent genie for millions of dollars, a candy bar named after him, and a Yankee uniform.

And, brother, did he get it!

A passion for fame, for a lasting place in folklore, is perhaps the most easily comprehended, and the most easily excused, of vanities. Yet Jackson, who hit more homers than any man in baseball during the first fourteen full years of his career (424 from 1968 through 1981), is seldom judged generously. Few exceptional athletes have had to hear the words "fraud" and "phony" applied to themselves so often, even by teammates.

"Reggie is an average player," said Baltimore's average pitcher Jim Palmer after Jackson left Baltimore.

"Reggie Jackson has never done anything in his life that was not for effect. He's a total phony," said pitcher Bill Lee, perhaps proving the adage that we say of others those things that apply best to ourselves.

"Reggie is a charlatan, but a charlatan with credentials," said pitcher Don Sutton. "He cons people and sells himself, but he produces."

After the greatest slugging World Series in history in '77, what was Jackson's reward? His manager, Martin, platooned him against southpaws, batted him seventh, and put a slew-footed catcher in his right-field position. What other star was ever treated so preposterously, yet remained so relatively silent? "I never pay any attention to anything Reggie says anyway," said Martin, while still Yankee skipper. "Why should I? His teammates don't."

Jackson's basic difficulty, one that may take him years to solve, is that, like politicians and poets on a grander scale, Jackson does not live a life in the conventional, everyday sense. He manufactures a legend, a personal history, with himself and his exploits at the center. Jackson's sin is that he has always been uniquely bad at hiding this conscious myth-making process. Baseball elects its heroes for life by bleacher plebiscite, not by self-appointment. The old game has never forgiven Jackson for proclaiming himself a "superstar"—the one-word title of his autobiography—before his public and peers had time to come to the same conclusion.

The irony, of course, is that with each year, with each new accomplishment, it becomes more obvious that Jackson is, and always has been, everything he claimed. The most elementary Jackson statistic—his glory in a nutshell—is that in those mere fourteen seasons he has been the cleanup hitter and offensive leader on nine division champions and five world champions. That alone, without a single personal stat, ought to be enough for Cooperstown.

Even when Jackson knows that his feats should speak for themselves, even when he knows that humility is the right card to play, he has always tipped his hand. He can mix hokum and genuine insight, subtle phrasing and pathetic bombast like no other star. Few men match his knack for having a good idea, then mopping the floor with it. If Jackson discussed the Bill of Rights long enough, he'd make you want to repeal it.

Yet this marathon philosophizer is the soul of pith. Who else in baseball says, "It was an insurance homer; that's why I hit it half-way to the Prudential Building," or "I hit it so far my eyes weren't good enough to see it land. That one had some voltage." Of all the athletes in all American sports, perhaps none has so much fun making phrases, or gets himself in so much trouble doing it. Jackson's epigrams—"hitting against Nolan Ryan is like eating soup with a fork"—are a mixture of image-laden Baptist preaching and a college-educated mind. The cruelest epithet that trails Jackson through the years is Mickey Rivers' taunt: "Reginald Martinez Jackson—white man's first name, Spanish middle name, and a black man's last name. No wonder you don't know who the hell you are." The truth is that, consciously or not, Jackson has chosen to meld and blend all the strains in his background, all the cultural lineages that he can draw upon from ghetto to campus to Park Avenue, and contain them in one personality. The result is often a brilliant blend of streetwise cynicism, tangy language, and the genuine worldliness of a man who has read some good books and seen a lot of great places.

It is impossible for such a man not to put a high value on his own opinions. No one ever mastered the tricks of the limelight game better than Jackson—the places to be, the times to be there, the expression to have on your face, if you want the microphones, the notepads, and the cameras to gather.

"I know how to answer questions," says Jackson. "I know how to tell the truth, but not hurt too many feelings . . . I can recognize a colorful quote . . . I don't think ballplayers understand the trouble they could save themselves if they paid attention to how to give an interview . . . I am aware that I sell myself and promote myself. Sometimes you do or say something for effect. But the real reason I have a good press is that I treat interviewers like people. In other words, I treat them the way I am not treated."

Of all Jackson's traits, the one which is most resented is his off-hand ability to steal headlines. In a prosaic locker room, he stands out like a walking poem. The most difficult task for Jackson as he matures will probably be the need to muzzle himself, renouncing the great pleasure he takes in ruminating. Already, it seems, he no longer seeks attention in the little ways that rankle other players. When he is not sedulously avoiding the media line of fire, he is driving the wordsmiths away with kindness, channeling the conversation to dull baseball labor topics or the like.

It may be Jackson's misfortune that the new Reggie, when he is eventually noticed, will be mistaken for a Madison Avenue concoction by a man who, after selling candy bars, jeans, VW's, and cologne, can certainly take care of repackaging and selling himself. It is probably more accurate that Jackson is simply showing the flip side of himself that has always been there, that has always been the best side of him, but also the least noticed.

"I didn't really know what I was getting into when I came to New York. I never guessed how tough this town was," he says.

"It's a city that loves visiting celebrities and treats them great. Makes you want to come here. If they see you two days a year, you're royalty. If they see you every day, you're a bum."

How dramatically tunes change. When Jackson came to New York, former teammate Ken Holtzman predicted, "He'll love it. Reggie just soaks up attention. His desire for fame may be insatiable." Even Jackson, the spring after his three-homer Series game in '77, said, "You can't get too much of a good thing; I don't understand that idea. I wanted to come to the Yankees. I wanted to hit five home runs in a World Series. I've earned everything I've got. It's been hectic, sure. It's been hard. But it's been a pleasure."

However, like Midas, Jackson has had second thoughts about his good New York fortune. It is bitterly ironic that Jackson should have found Apple fans so hard to satisfy. Within big league dugouts, Jackson is categorized as a player best appreciated by those who see him every day. But it takes an eye.

"Reggie's not a difficult player to manage, 'cause he's what you call a 'hard' player," says Baltimore's Earl Weaver. "He hustles, runs everything out, hates to embarrass himself. He'll take a guy out on the double play, or run into a wall, make a sliding catch. His whole career he's missed games because of 'hustle' injuries.

"Most important, he can reach a special level of concentration in the key situations that win games—just like Frank Robinson. And, kinda like Frank, when the score's 9–2 either way, his concentration lapses and he gives away at-bats or makes a meaningless error. That may hurt his batting average or his fielding average, but it don't hurt his team none," said Weaver.

"Reggie's a curious person and he's a person who likes to be shown the respect he's earned. He'll ask you why you made a certain move that involved him, which is unusual, 'cause most players don't give a damn. You explain it. You teach him somethin' maybe he didn't know. He nods. He appreciates it."

Jackson is delighted with this synopsis of The Care and Feeding of Reggie as seen by The Certified Genius. "I loved playing for Earl Weaver [in '76]," said Jackson. "Now I could play for the little Weave. That man will chew you out, read you the riot act down to the ground, and then forget all about it."

Jackson's most endearing trait, but one that few people see, is that he respects anyone who will challenge him, force him to defend his position cogently, cut through the bluster. "Earl's right, he's right," says Jackson. "I give away at-bats, I'm careless. Last night, I wasn't 'in' the game until the sixth inning. The cold weather distracted me . . . took my mind off business. Maybe that's an area where I can improve as I get older."

Like anyone with a true talent, Jackson searches for people who can spot his genuine flaws. Changing, improving as he ages, achieving a middle ground where all sides of his nature are put in perspective are now priorities for Jackson. One step in that direction was the short tenure of Dick Howser as Yankee manager. "Dick shows a lot of respect for me, makes me feel wanted," said Jackson, who, at thirty-four under Howser, had his best season since he was twenty-three. "He knows people, tries to understand them," adds Jackson, who, like the gifted child in class, is a devil when he must demand attention, but an angel when he gets it. "I'd go out of my way not to offend Howser because I think he's a fair man."

About the unfairnesses of the past, Jackson has learned to remain mute: Every time he has talked, he has lost. "I don't think Billy is gone for good. I think he'll be back as manager of the Yankees. I can't explain why. I just think so," says Jackson with the same reverse-English assurance as the golfer who roots for his putts by yelling, "Don't go in the hole . . . don't you dare go in the hole!"

Of the other fellow in the old Yankee vicious triangle, Jackson says, "I have to realize that Steinbrenner's never been late with a paycheck. A professional athlete has to accept responsibilities. I've always understood that, but I thought it applied to staying in shape, bearing down every game. I understand now that it also means controlling your tongue, not being too disparagingly critical of the owner.

"Maybe I'm just seeing the other side—the side of the people who run things. I represent companies [in commercials] and accept their money, so I have a responsibility to project an image, to come across as a person who substantiates his thoughts, not as some guy who's blowing off again."

No project could be more difficult or against-the-grain for Jackson than this reining-in process. Just look at him. He wears his uniform like a star—tight, muscles bulging, top button of shirt open. He runs distinctively, bent forward, a picture of barely controlled power. He seems to carry a stage with him everywhere. It is as difficult for him not to mention his alleged 160 IQ as it is hard for him to remember not to flash his wallet full of $100 bills. And, everywhere, he runs into those who want to prick his balloon, like Rivers the day he cackled, "Reggie says he's got an IQ of 160. Out of what? A thousand?"

Even if Jackson's intelligence quotient doesn't test out a little above Mozart and a tad below Voltaire, Jackson has always wanted to run in the intellectual fast lane, or at least, somewhere near it. He loves the big words and the complicated issues, wants very much—perhaps too much—to have an opinion on all the topics he thinks a smart man should have one on. He can't resist a pretentious subject any more than he can lay off the fastball in his wheelhouse—even if it's a ball. So he'll always strike out plenty.

Most ballplayers, most people probably, would be inflamed if anyone wrote such things about them. Jackson once walked up to me with a story I had written. He pointed to the paragraph just above this one—word-for-word the same—and, shaking his head, said, "So true," then walked away.

It's not easy being a man who is embarrassed by short home runs.

For Jackson, the struggle continues to be all things. He wants to be compassionate, simple, religious. But he wears gold chains and owns a fleet of kingly cars. He loves being his team's player representative. No star warms more genuinely to the "noblesse oblige" of losing money in a strike since it benefits other marginal players who really need a union. The anomaly of being a millionaire labor spokesman is just his style.

It is not a rare psychological bent to want to be both the cop and the robber, the oppressed and the oppressor, the hero and the villain, the object of love as well as hate, the loner who is also the leader. But it is wearisome, this always swinging for the parking lot, always changing costumes and masks so that every role in the play can be yours. It is so much easier to be undisciplined, to fly in all directions at once, to satisfy all the different appetites and personalities in one half-forged mind. But even for such a man, the time comes when he must choose among all the characters in the cast of his soul.

The campaign for quiet respectability and the calm affection shown aging future Hall of Famers has already begun. "I want very much to be in the Hall of Fame. I'd kind of like to wait until the room is empty at night and go in once to look at the plaque. I worry some that I've made enemies, that I have a reputation that might hurt my chances. I think 500 homers and 1,500 RBIs would prevent that."

What distinguishes the great player, the man in the Hall?

"The pride," says Jackson, "that makes a player believe that he's better than the rest."

Reggie Jackson says these words like a boy bringing home a drawing from school, one that has "A-plus" written in the corner. Perhaps he really doesn't mean to boast. What he wants, and still so seldom gets, is a measured, unhysterical response. Neither the rabid cheers nor boos that are supposed to be his fuel, but rather a friendly, honest appraisal that indeed his hard work has been found worthy.

1980: *It Wasn't Pretty But It Sure Was Fun*

What if the attack dogs had been brought into play just one out sooner? Then what would Pete Rose have done?

After all, before the final inning of the 1980 World Series, umpires gave the most bizarre ground rule in baseball history: "Animals are in play."

What if that menacing menagerie of dogs and horses had made its massed entrance with two outs left to go, instead of only one? When Frank White's foul popped out of the hands of Bob Boone, his gold glove turned alchemically to lead by the black magic of Phillies' history, would Rose's lizard tongue of a mitt have flicked out so quickly to gobble the fly?

Or would that baseball have been appropriated by the fangs of a devil-dog sent to insure that the Phillies remained destiny's doormats?

That, you see, is how our winter mind recalls a baseball season, not with chalk-dry statistics or records, but with a few vivid, richly associative moments of truth. Of all those moments, perhaps the most lustrous is Rose's reflex catch. It may not have been the best or most important play of 1980—or even of that sixth and last game of the Series—but it was the most symbolic. That tenth-of-a-second grab earned Rose all of his $2.98 million contract, for with it he absolved the Phillies of being themselves. Washed them clean of a century of baseball sins, he did, all in a tingling instant. "Not this time," his innermost synapses said.

This was the ultimate game when the Phillies' life passed before their eyes—all ninety-seven years of it. This was a team that not only had to defeat the best-hitting club in thirty years—the Kansas City Royals—but had to renounce its own anti-tradition as well. Born to failure in 1883 and entrenched as the sport's ninety-seven-year weaklings ever since, the Phillies survived an October in which they had a dozen chances to drown.

Their last two chances to gasp for breath, swallow deep, and die came in the sixth game of the World Series as the Royals loaded the bases in the eighth and ninth with the Phils ahead by a 4–1 margin that felt like half a run. What Phillie fan could help but think back on fifty-one seasons in the Baker Bowl, thirty-two years in Shibe Park (later Connie Mack Stadium), and finally another decade in the antiseptic Vet, and still nothing in the way of diamond-centered rings? That is how you measure real failure— not in seasons, but in buildings crumbled under the weight of defeat, parks that lasted longer than the lives of men and now are gone.

In the eighth, that ancient premonition machine began to chug. If Macbeth's first witch had commandeered the PA system and said, "Here I have a pilot's thumb, wrack'd as homeward he did come," no one would have doubted Dallas Green was the pilot and the thumb in question was the one he had used to send Steve Carlton to the showers. Why, in the name of Gavvy Cravath, Wild Bill Donovan, Kaiser Wilhelm, and Danny Ozark, had Green yanked Lefty, the Sphinx of the Schuylkill, the man Rose proclaimed, "the best pitcher in the world, unless the Russians have got one I haven't seen"?

On came the only relief pitcher with a tugboat named after him: Tug McGraw. He was beyond the help of Tylenol. This was a frazzled man on a solitary mound with only his savvy and guts to preserve him. "I'm mentally exhausted," McGraw had said. "It's a good thing I don't pitch with my brain, or I'd have to soak my head in a bucket of ice."

McGraw had a right to his sore brain. In Montreal, he pounded the dirt with his open palms when he won the division clincher in the next-to-last game of the season. In Houston, he embraced his mates after he saved the fourth and series-tying game. And he would, in a few minutes, lead the Phillie cotillion as it danced off the diamond amid hooves, helmets, and truncheons after he had saved the World Series.

But first all the threads of the Phillies' championship skein had to tangle themselves into one ball, and that ball had to plop itself squarely into Rose's hand. In that split second when White's foul ball squirted from Boone's glove to Rose's, everything went from fast-forward to stop-action. "Cut . . . that's a take . . . print it," said the director. "Bring on the animals. Unsheathe the billy clubs. Anybody wants to kiss these guys, they got to get maced and beaten. Oh, Tug, one last thing. Yeah, I know you're tired.

Just strike out Willie Wilson, will you? Sure, just like the other eleven times."

Thus, so tired that "if I hadn't gotten Wilson, I'd have called Dallas out to get me," McGraw finally saved the Phillies. Just as Rose had saved McGraw, and they both had saved Green. That was the proper triumvirate: Green, plus his left- and right-hand men. When baseball comes to its last turn of the screw, it is still aggressive leadership that is of primary importance. That's when ballplayers revert to atavistic tribal habits, particularly leaning on a few old chieftains. For the Phils, that meant Green setting a policy of close-order drill and blunt home truths, with Rose and McGraw testifying loudly that such a system could work. Rose demonstrated what it meant to hustle and play hurt. "Jeez," he said, "we got guys who think they're toughin' it out if they play with a headache." While Rose talked attitude, McGraw talked tactics, calling Green the best handler of a pitching staff since Gil Hodges. And Green himself . . . well . . . he just talked: "Players don't like to look in the mirror. Well, I'm their mirror. I told this team in spring training that I was going to give them one more chance to live up to their talent. A lot of guys are on their last hurrah here, but somebody had to remind them."

And how long did it take this doctrine to sink in among the Phillies? "We had a meeting in August after we lost four in a row to Pittsburgh and looked like dead meat," said Green. "I aired 'em out as good as I know how to chew. Maybe that helped a little. But I can't honestly say we sniffed it, really got after it, until the last week of the season."

Huhhhh?

That heretical statement gives a clue to not only the Phils but the whole 1980 season. If this baseball year opened as a Broadway play, it would get an ambivalent review: aesthetically and technically erratic, sometimes even abominable, yet dramatically wonderful, almost unsurpassed. For such a theme, the Phils were perfect protagonists.

This was a season when our baseball characters seemed particularly vivid, because they seemed especially isolated and vulnerable. That's why, when the curtain dropped, we felt an unexpected sadness that the long, weird season—with its odd juxtaposition of tense individual virtuosity against a backdrop of slapstick—was finally done.

This was the year when all twenty-six major league teams showed up without a destiny. How dull are those seasons when we realize that one team has swaddled itself in a cocoon of protective myth-making, calling itself a "team of destiny," or the like. A club can shield itself with its own fabulous tale-telling, a sort of group hypnosis. In 1980, nobody could hide within the camouflage of a Family, least of all the Astros, Royals, and Phils, whose histories were laminated in failure. After six months of assuming they were dukes and princes of their sport—but probably not kings—these clubs, which ranked third, fourth, and sixth in victories, suddenly found themselves in water over their heads. And they sensed it.

Under such conditions, baseball is a brutally difficult and solitary game. Under pressure, each man stood alone, pinned in a limelight radiance. At times, these sound, but self-doubting teams played as though they were standing in a mine field.

Appropriately, the most memorable Series play was a ball clanking from one glove to another. This was a Series of snafus as much as game-winning RBIs, a championship that, truly, was Left on Base. Never have two October foes hit so well when it didn't matter, or so atrociously when it did. These teams with the highest combined batting average for a six-game Series (.292) put 168 runners on base but only scored 50 of them. With no one on base, they batted .300. With runners in scoring position, .236. That trend worsened as pressure grew. In the last four games, the Phils batted .356 with none on; .175 with men in scoring position. Let's not hear too much about The Team that Wouldn't Die. For the last five Series games, this Kansas City club with the highest team average since '50 (.286) batted .340 with the sacks empty; .191 with runners in scoring position. Said one Kansas City official, "We're so tight we squeak."

The regular-season trademark of both these swift teams was their explosiveness. Yet, in the Series, they become implosive, collapsing into themselves like dying stars turning into black holes. As the Series progressed, both emitted less and less light.

The progression of the Series conspired to tie K.C. into knots. In the opener, 20-game winner Dennis Leonard blew a 4–0 lead and lost 7–6 to Whirlybird Walk, a rookie who, in his short career, had gone to bat without a bat and taken the mound without a glove Perhaps Walk's true calling was to be one of the young Red Sox pitchers of 1980 who got Don Zimmer fired. Like Wilhelmus ("Last Call for . . .") Remmerswaal, who, after establishing precedent at Pawtucket by missing three of the team's first four flights, was called up and immediately missed the Bosox bus to Yankee Stadium. Asked why he was late, Remmerswaal said, "I took a taxi." Unfortunately, the taxi took Last Call to Shea Stadium. Remmerswaal's first victory of 1980 came in a game when Zimmer called the bull pen, barked "Get Win up," and was told, "He's out in the bleachers buying peanuts."

The Royals then put 19 men on base in Game Two, 18 of them against Carlton, but scored only 4 runs and lost 6–4 when the Phils filibustered for 4 runs in the eighth against quippy reliever Dan Quisenberry.

After these two days in Philly, the Royals were ready for every sort of self-flagellation. Catcher Darrell Porter tiptoeing into home plate to avoid a collision with Boone was just the outward symbol of a suddenly meek and disoriented team. "We seem intimidated by the crowds, intimidated by being in the Series," said K.C. rookie manager Jim Frey. His solution was to call a pep-talk team meeting, then invite a Howard Cosell imitator into the clubhouse to insult and ridicule every Royal in sight.

You could say it helped. That is, if you didn't happen to see the next game. The Royals won (4–3) in 10 innings only because the Phils lost in 9. In a kind of reverse classic, the Phils put 20 men on base in their 200-minute agony of clutch failure. Thirty Phils stepped up with runners on. Only 2 could drive home a run. A single in any of 12 different spots would have meant a win. The perfect Phillie emblem was Mike Schmidt, the eventual Series MVP. Schmidt hit .381 for this 77th "Classic" with 7 RBIs, but he also stranded 11 runners in the Series, including 9 in this game. By contrast, Brett came to bat with only 14 men on in the whole Series, compared to Schmidt's 23. Sometimes, luck is fate.

That humble victory loosened up the Royals—for exactly 1⅔ innings. Of the first 14 Royals to bat in Game Four, 1 walked, 2 singled, 3 doubled, 1 tripled, and Willie Mays Aikens—who had already hit 2 homers in the opener and won Game Three the night before with a sudden-death single off McGraw—crushed two

450-foot home runs. In that nightmare, the Phils saw the Royals take five extra bases on them. Philadelphia starter Larry Christenson left with an ERA of 108.00. The Royals hit the ball between outfielders, into three-cushion pin-ball corners, into water fountains, and over the car parked in the Kansas City bull pen.

Then, suddenly, the Royals abated like a Kansas twister blowing itself out. The Phils helped. They waited until Brett's next at-bat, then had Dickie Noles throw a 90-miles-per-hour fastball that missed Brett's temple by inches as he cartwheeled, foot-to-the-sky. It was the perfect tactical message to a team that charges the plate and defies opponents to retaliate.

"I believe in Hammurabi's Code," said Brett. "An eye for an eye and a tooth for a tooth." However, Frey doesn't. It's annoyed his traditionally pugnacious team all year. Frey is from the Earl Weaver School and never orders a knockdown pitch because he doesn't want it on his conscience. So when Brett pinwheeled, Frey put his best face on matters, charging onto the field to point at Noles and scream with Rose. Nevertheless, the Royals came out looking like genial slow-pitch softball noncombatants. From the moment Brett went down, then fanned, the Royals hit .083 with men in scoring position for the rest of the Series, and Brett, after starting 6 for 12, went 1 for his next 10.

All the tension, insecurity, and worry pent up within this Series came to a head in the pivotal ninth inning of the fifth game. A season without destiny resolved itself into an inning constructed of coincidence and dumb luck. Of all the minimal art rallies in this Series, the Phils' 2-run ninth for a 4–3 win was the pip. Philadelphia hit 6 consecutive grounders or line drives, all of which could or should have been caught—and this turned the Series for the Phillies.

In one lone Series game, everything is luck. Or nothing is luck. You can watch for decades and never quite decide. That's how it was with Schmidt's lead-off grounder that smacked Brett's glove as he dove left, then bounced away. And with Del Unser's one-hop bullet that Aikens should have blocked at first had he not committed the cardinal sin of bad fielders: He tried to make a good play instead of a safe one and got nothing but air. And, finally, Manny Trillo, the dependable Phillie MVP of the play-offs, cracked a liner that Quisenberry got both hands on at his navel, but couldn't grasp as it trickled away.

The fans of Kansas City, who join with the PA tape deck in an unselfconscious seventh-inning rendition of "Take Me Out to the Ball Game," may say, "Shucks, just a little bad luck." But don't try that bunk on Philadelphia folk. They know baseball. The box score has to add up. You must lose for a reason. If there isn't one, you gotta start inventing. Those with sharp eyes and hard hearts will convict the Royals of terminal jitters and use that final inning of the fifth game as Exhibit A. Ill fortune attendeth the team that thinks it's going bad. And just how bad were the Royals going?

You know you're going bad when your wife takes you aside and tries to change your batting stance. And you take her advice. Ask superstar Wilson (230 hits, 79 steals), who hit .111 before his wife told him, "Stand up straighter, dear," and .176 thereafter.

You know you're going bad when an usherette calls you to the box-seat railing, hands you a bat, and says, "You gave this to me on June 2 when you were hitting .333. Now, you need it more than I do." And you use the bat in the game. Ask Porter, 1 for 20 in postseason before getting two hits with the new-old bat.

Plenty of Royals were going bad and couldn't forget it. So, when Game Five reached its apex—Phils ahead by a run, bases loaded with Royals, 2 outs in the ninth—K.C. needed the perfect star-crossed character.

That's right. Jose Cardenal.

This Series spotlighted two quintessential journeymen—Cardenal (37, vet of 10 teams, glad-hand bon vivant in cowboy regalia) and the Phillies' Unser (35, vet of 5 teams, shy gent in corduroy and patches). Both, in repose, have the hound-faced look of too-frequent defeat. Both came to their current roles as last resorts before retirement. And each finally had the feast of fame set before him. Four times Unser delivered in the postseason pinch, once with the season-saving, game-tying single and three times with doubles that were the nub of game-winning rallies. After thirteen years, you're entitled. But, after eighteen years, wasn't Cardenal entitled, too? Unser got the candy. Cardenal just got the fuzzy end of the lollipop.

Many managers have pet reclamation projects. Cardenal is Frey's. So Jose materialized in right field in Game Two, went o for 4, and let Schmidt's eminently catchable game-winning liner land on the warning rack while he pulled up short so as not to be too near the scene of the crime. And, in the final crisis of Game Five, Frey stuck with Cardenal, instead of .305 hitter Duke Wathan.

One reason that men like Unser and Cardenal have lengthy, unspectacular careers is The Book. The Book on Cardenal is all in capital letters: JAM THE LITTLE FELLOW. So McGraw did. Every pitch. Cardenal's rebuttal was a weak foul as his bat flew to the mound. McGraw and Cardenal met at the foot of the hill. Until that instant, Cardenal had been thinking, "One hit and you will be everywhere, even on the 'Good Morning' talk shows." As Cardenal reached McGraw, the southpaw said, "Here's your bat," then, holding the bat handle forward, jabbed Cardenal in the stomach. Had that bat been a lance, the rally could not have been slain more effectively. After the game, after his final strikeout, Cardenal still came back, again and again, to McGraw. "Everybody knows McGraw is crazy," he said. "Jab me in the stomach with my own bat."

If this Series seemed blessed in scenes from a Theater of the Absurd, and if the Phillies seemed more at home in such surroundings, there was a reason. During October and the Five Games War against Houston, the Phillies had stepped through the Looking Glass and into a baseball world inhabited by mad hatters, dormice, and Cheshire cats. Game after game, the line score should have read: winning pitcher—Alice; loser—sanity. These Phils make a science of finding diamonds in the garbage.

The night when the Phillies began to arise from a century's sleep was a miserable, dank evening in Canada. The Phillies slunk into town dead-tied with Montreal with 3 games left. They were still burdened by the ignominy of losing 2 of 3 to the Expos in the Vet the previous weekend. That series had ended with the Philadelphia fans in their customary autumn pall, growling in disgust as they bent, folded, and mutilated their programs into paper airplanes which they used to pepper the beloved Phils from the upper deck. Between innings, it took six hustling grounds crewmen just to clean up the debris. With that as prologue, plus a week of warfare between Green and veteran players, the Phils were expected to perform a patented Philadelphia dive. "We just have a different form of exercise," said McGraw. "We flush our minds in public."

All that Friday night in Montreal, the Phils played like men of stone. All except Schmidt, the Phil heretofore most petrified by late-season adrenaline overdoses. This was a game that the Phils could have lost 1-0, and quietly died. But Schmidt, who has spent his life ardently pursuing relaxation—through meditation, feigned coolness, religion—had discovered the ultimate relaxant. Germs. "Probably just what I need. I'm so miserable I'm limp as a rag doll," he said after a sacrifice fly and a sixth-inning homer had created a 2–1 win. "You know me," he said, clenching his fist and biceps into a knot. "Can't get loose [cough, cough]. Whenever I feel blah, I always make out like a bandit [hack, wheeze]. I figure my temperature is about 111½."

Schmidt, who set a major league record for homers by a third baseman (48), had gotten the Phils to the hump, but the Expos helped them over. On the final regular-season Saturday, in a seven-hour, rain-delayed game that tasted like swill, the Phillies ended up drinking champagne. The Phils made 5 errors, had 4 men trapped between bases in rundowns, and had another thrown out at the plate. The coup came when Greg Luzinski got a 2-run, bases-loaded single that ended up as an inning-ending double play (DP 8–6–5–4–5–3–2).

The Expos were worse. Don't ask particulars. After all, the Montrealers, playing without injured Ron LeFlore (broken wrist) and Ellis Valentine (sprained ego), were shorthanded. Suffice it to say that one normal-speed ground ball somehow rolled directly between the legs of both the Expo third baseman and left fielder on the same play. Finally, Schmidt's 2-run homer in the eleventh clinched the pennant and began a celebration that was equal parts wine and spleen. The Phils smashed champagne bottles into garbage cans so violently that players were ducking flying glass. The team split in three parts. Some, filled with vindication and fury, screamed and led obscene chants. Some were numb and perplexed, looking at a side of their mates that they had known about, but perhaps wished had stayed hidden. And a few sequestered themselves in a small room. "If we don't get to the Series," said a subdued Schmidt, "then all of this doesn't mean shit. We'll still be the same old fucked-up Phillies."

Eight days later, the Phillies would have their cathartic evening for the washing away of bad dreams and bad blood in a bath of sweeter champagne. Some said the Phils would never in this world reach the Series. They were right. By the time the Phils had escaped the Astros, they had discovered that the land of their dreams was on the other side of normal baseball reality. When the final Astro flyball came down out of the dungeon grayness of the Dome roof, Bowa had the right idea. He jumped up and down in one spot as though touched by some Pentecostal gift of tongues.

The final two NL play-off games—both breathless extra-inning Phillie wins—were something out of a hookah dream. For those two days, it seemed that baseball was playing the men, not the men playing the game. The sport itself seemed to be showing off for the 100 million watching eyes, as though saying, "Now that I've got these silly humans totally in my control, watch what I can do." Would you believe three double plays in one game, all started on balls hit to the outfield? What about Maddox's soft liner back to the feet of Houston pitcher Vern Ruhle with men on first and second. For fifteen minutes, as umpires, managers, and the NL president had a sequence of terrified meetings, no one in America was certain if he had just seen a triple play, double play, or just one solitary out.

But Game Four was just the stage-setter. Game Five was the goose-bump champ. The Phils had many escapes, but none nearly so improbable as their 5-run eighth inning against Nolan Ryan in the last game. Few things in baseball are more certain than The Ryan Express with a 3-run late-inning lead, especially when he is gusting up to 99 m.p.h. Since the 1972 season, Ryan has protected 97 percent of the leads that his teams have given him from the eighth inning forward. It is a statistic no one can fathom, a sort of natural phenomenon. Like Ryan's fastball.

The Phillies' great uprising was classic because it happened primarily in the mind. The Phils may be fatalistic, but Ryan is a walking snake pit. Bowa bit him first with a single. Next, Boone rapped a one-hopper back to Ryan that should have been a double play. But Ryan has as many Achilles' heels as a spider, fielding being one. His tragic flaw is that he refuses to master any aspect of the game not directly related to throwing unhittable pitches.

The ball clanked off his glove for a scratch hit. Sensing Ryan's ruffled state of mind, Greg Gross laid down a bunt. Ryan never budged. Stage set: bases loaded, Rose at bat.

The Phils could have asked for no better man. "It was Rose who led us in the play-offs," said Schmidt. "I was just a spectator." That October may have been the last vast chunk of baseball fun that Rose could gobble like a greedy child. For the first time, he talked about his fortieth birthday and the need to start taking days off in 1981. "The older you get," said Rose, "well, the days are coming to an end, so you want to enjoy them all. You can't bear to give one away."

Rose savored his showcase, redeeming his .282 season by hitting .388 from the final Expo series to the end. Here we thought that no living man could enjoy a game, or embody it, more than Rose-in-bloom did baseball. And now we discover that a fading Rose loves it even more.

In his previous at-bat, Rose had smoked a liner to Ryan's glove, then got into a needling match with one pitcher few hitters would dare annoy. "Aw, we were havin' fun," explained Rose. "I just told him if he was so fuckin' proud of the fuckin' curveball, why don't he throw it to me the next time up and we'll see if he catches that one."

Perhaps only Rose could figure out how to get a man with a 100 m.p.h. fastball to throw him 80 m.p.h. curves with the pennant at stake. Insult him, challenge him, and smile the whole time like it's just a picnic and you're too dumb to have an alterior motive. And believe it or not, with the bases loaded, Ryan threw curveballs. Rose gratefully took them, putting Ryan in a hole. Finally, after a full-count foul tip, Rose walked to first and a run walked home. Ryan walked to the shower. Against mere mortals from the Astro bull pen, the Phils finished the great comeback. Nolan Ryan, so proud—so proud of his no-hitters, and strikeouts, and his lead-protecting stats. Take your base, Pete. Take your pennant. Take everything.

But not easily. Not against the Astros. Twice, Houston was 6 outs away from the Series—leading by 2 runs in Game Four and 3 in Game Five. Twice the Phillies rallied against the team with the best ERA in baseball (3.10) to go ahead, with 3 in the eighth on Saturday and 5 in the eighth on Sunday. And twice the Astros came back to force extra innings, with a run in the bottom of the ninth Saturday and with 2 runs in the eighth Sunday, the latter time against McGraw, whose ERA had been 0.59 for six weeks.

What else would you expect from a team that, after losing three consecutive pitchers' duels by 1 run on the last three days of the regular season in Los Angeles, could come back to Chavez Ravine to swamp the Dodgers 7–1 in a play-off game when every smart guy expected them to pull the all-time eleventh-hour fold? If anything toughened the Astros for a play-off that ended with four consecutive extra-inning games, it was J. R. Richard's midseason ordeal with a blood clot in the neck and a stroke. Next to his fight for life, the Astros' baseball difficulties seemed mild.

Richard's tragedy was more than personal. His stroke sent a wave of nausea through the game that had, for almost two months, turned his mysterious malady into a subject for jokes and innuendo. "J.R. almost had to die before anyone would believe him," said Houston coach Deacon Jones. "It seems like the big contracts have taken away our humanity. Sign a million-dollar deal and you're no longer a person. They boo Schmidt in Philly. They throw rocks and batteries at Dave Parker in Pittsburgh. We've become commodities. And that's why players are saying, 'To hell with the fans and the press. They don't care about me as a person, so why should I care about them.'"

Perhaps this year's extreme example of dollar-dehumanization was the 103-win New York Yankee team, a romantic underdog team of marginal veterans who, outside New York, got little but the most grudging praise. To the casual fan, the Yankees seemed a self-evident proposition. Weren't they the supremely rich and arrogant team that had spent $17 million on free agents? Weren't their injuries a mere balancing of the scales of baseball justice?

Perhaps such cynicism was partially merited toward previous Yankee champions, but not toward the aging veteran team that battled Baltimore for two glorious nose-to-nose months, refusing every invitation to pity themselves, until, finally, they prevailed, 103 wins to 100.

The Yankees had been forced to look in the mirror far back in August when the Orioles beat them 6 of 8 games, then finally cut what had been an 11-game margin in the loss column to zero.

That night, late in August, when the Yankee margin in defeats had finally fallen to nothing, the club dragged into the Oakland Hyatt like so many lost souls. The Yankee faces, short of sleep, irritable, looked like those of a beaten team. Perhaps they were. After all, the Orioles had just checked out of the same hotel hours before, freshened by 8 straight wins. No group of Birds ever preened more. "If we don't win this thing going away," said Oriole 25-game winner Steve Stone, "then call me a liar."

Stone wasn't a liar. He simply fell for that Scylla and Charybdis of every pennant race, a double lure that every hot team feels—natural pride in themselves and equally natural prejudice toward undervaluing an opponent.

The Orioles, who played .692 over the last 104 games, had made up ground so gleefully and for so long that they mistook riding the whirlwind for their normal baseball state. Their bad April (7-11) they explained as simply an aberration due to rust from the eight-day preseason players' strike, plus general worry on this strong pro-union club over the April 22 deadline for the strike, which was averted at the eleventh hour. The real Orioles, the 102-win club of 1979, simply showed up a bit late. But in late August, all was thought to be well in Birdland. They waltzed out of that Oakland Hyatt and on to Seattle, flying directly over Mount St. Helens' gaping maw, with a classic case of overconfidence. Still in second place by half a game, they carelessly thought that first place was a matter merely of time, not a matter of deeds.

The Orioles met Seattle—the worst team in baseball before and after they hired Maury Wills as manager—at a point when the Mariners had not won 2 games back-to-back in more than 9 weeks. But they won 2 in a row from the Orioles, who played as if covered by volcanic ash. Compounding the impact, the Yankees lost twice in Oakland to manager of the year Billy Martin and his gang of guerrillas. The A's two best pitchers—Mike Norris (22 wins) and Rick Langford (28 complete games on a staff with a league-leading 94)—both won. And 100-base thief Rickey Henderson ran wild.

Who could miss the meaning? Two irretrievable Oriole opportunities lost. New York and Baltimore stayed locked in the loss column for three more days. Then, slowly, the Yankees evaluated their good fortune, regained their wind and forgot how to lose for almost a month. Their lead inched out to 5 games—and thoroughbreds held on to the wire.

But how much did that long Yankee push take out of them, especially compared to Kansas City's cakewalk in a Western Division that played 74 games under .500 and had only one other winning team (Oakland, 83-79)? Anyone who saw the Yankees the night they finally clinched a tie for their division crown had reason to fear for them in the play-offs. They celebrated not a whit. Instead, the Yanks knotted in a small room to watch Muhammad Ali on closed circuit as "The Greatest" officially lost his youth and his magic. For a team trying to ignore its own athletic mortality, it was not a comforting sight.

Meanwhile, back at the ranch the Royals were feeling their oats, growing in fame and confidence. The world came to George Brett's doorstep to see if he could hit .400, and, by accident, discovered the Royals. While the Royals got some of the morsels of notoriety that they have coveted since they won division titles, but not renown, in 1976, 1977, 1978, Brett's chase brought him, in his words, "more attention than I wanted, needed, or deserved."

In the AL, 1980 was the Year of George Brett. Therefore, it was altogether meet and right that the play-offs should be his private stage. With signs reading "Bretter Than Ever" bedecking Royals Stadium, the Hemorrhoid Hero announced himself in the opener with a walk, double, and homer as the Royals romped 7-2. To the public, it meant little; to the teams, it was harbinger. In the regular season, Kansas City had beaten the Yankees (8 of 12) by 33 runs—more margin than might be expected if the 1927 Yankees played the Blue Jays. "They've hammered our starting pitching all year," said Reggie Jackson, whose best season since he was twenty-three was dampened only by the fact that the vast majority of his 41 homers and 111 RBIs came before the Ides of August. "They're clearly the best Kansas City team we've faced."

The Royals, their whole franchise and city smarting from three play-off defeats, as well as an ancient abject history as a Yankee farm town, could smell a sweep and wanted it. However, had it not been for the most aesthetically pleasing play of 1980, the Yankees might yet have found a way to insinuate themselves into the Series again. There has seldom been a more exciting 10-second

masterpiece of full-field baseball than the 3-man relay on which
K.C. cut down swift Willie Randolph at the plate in the eighth
inning of Game Two to save a 3–2 victory. This was baseball at its
wealthiest, with the eyes darting a dozen times on one play, measuring time and distance, guessing at the limits of luck and skill, a
whole season teetering in the balance. The game exists for such
moments. And, of course, it was Brett, the man who can't take
enough homely infield practice, who made the impromptu play of
his life without the slightest hesitation.

Randolph on first. Two outs. K.C. ahead 3–2. Bob Watson
ripped a liner into the left-field corner, fair by 10 yards. Suddenly,
the Royals, so unlucky for so long against the Yankees, became
thrice blessed. First, Randolph was given the "must steal" sign,
but he never saw it. Instead, he faked a false start, and got only a
hesitant break toward second. Next, Watson's rocket, instead of
hitting the six feet of padding on the wall, struck the one foot of
bare concrete at its base. Had the ricochet been muted, Randolph
would have scored standing. Instead, the carom came to Wilson
so hard it almost handcuffed him. A mural in motion was unfolding: Randolph, turning the bases, trying to cut milliseconds as he
dug into each bag and came out faster, like a swimmer doing tum-
ble turns; Wilson, perhaps the most gifted left fielder the Lord
ever made, fleeing to the ideal retrieval point, then letting go a
too-mighty heave over the head of the normal relay man, U. L.
Washington. Ten years ago, that would have killed the play. But
in 1973, Bobby Winkles brought a new wrinkle to the hoary
cutoff play when he came to the majors from Arizona State. He
stationed the third baseman 50 feet beyond the shortstop as a
"trailer." Guess who? "I've trailed a thousand times," said Brett,
"and it's never come to me before . . . until tonight." Brett threw
a strike to Porter. Umpire Joe Brinkman peered into the chaos of
dust and limbs, then threw up his thumb. "I saw disbelief in the
Yankee's eyes," said Brett.

All that remained was a closing crescendo, a curtain call for
Brett. The scene was grandly set as Brett stepped up in the seventh with New York ahead 2–1. Rich Gossage stood on the
mound like a glowering condor. Royals danced off the corners.
Yankee Stadium might have been one great stained-glass window

with its blue seats, white facade, blazing light towers, roaring fans, and the black haze of chill evening.

Actually, the Yankees assumed this strategic juncture was meant for them. Seventy-nine times during the season they had taken a lead into the seventh inning, and 77 times they won. Such a belated entrance by Gossage, whose 33 saves were the heart of the Yankee stretch drive, was like keeping Darth Vadar off the screen until the third reel. But now that the man Coach Stan Williams called "prehistoric" had finally arrived, the Yankees expected him to establish that the late innings of this, and all future games, would be their exclusive property. So confident was George Steinbrenner upon seeing this Gossage person, who had once thrown a curveball into the opposing team's dugout, that he had one of the worst perches in his own palace, tucked in an aisle of the mezzanine deck. But then Steinbrenner had had a bad week, doing his one-man production of Bonzo Goes To The Play-offs. The owner had capped one of his better seasons of bully bluster by turning his third-base coach into a scapegoat after Game Two.

The confrontation between Gossage and Brett lasted only one pitch. Gossage's best murderball came in at light speed and Brett sent it out at Warp Factor 1. Make the jump to hyperspace, Wookie.

Everyone knew. As Brett said, "How many rows up in the upper deck did it land? Do I hear six? How about ten?" Everyone except Steinbrenner. The ball disappeared from his view. He bent to glimpse the ball as it climbed as high as the highest light tower. When it landed, only one part of his body moved. His throat clenched, every muscle, as though someone had stabbed him in the back.

Baseball's cruelest practical joke is that twenty-five of the game's twenty-six teams end their seasons with this same sensation of having been stabbed in the back. The former world champion Pirates, for example, felt it one early September day when a doctor told them that Willie Stargell would probably spend the rest of the pennant race peddling a stationary bicycle in a subterranean trainer's room while the rest of the Family went nowhere without him.

Few players, not even the best, are allowed to spend their winters with only pleasant thoughts. Kansas City All-Star Frank

White, who won the AL play-off MVP award for hitting .545 against New York, batted .080 in the Series, making the perverse metamorphosis from butterfly to worm in only a week. That final championship victory is the only moment that washes everything clean in sport. But why shouldn't the absolution be more general? Why must our triumphs lack generosity?

In other years, that often seems unfair. But this year the fluke of victory, the bizarre happenstance of a championship, seems very proper. For ninety-seven consecutive years, it was always the Phillies who slept the winter on the cold floor of hard reality. Never were they permitted illusions or heroes or the occasional benediction of harmless exaggeration. For a century, Philly had to face the facts. For one short winter, the thought of baseball can be pure pleasure. Now that the season has ended, all fans can glance back with a slow appraising eye over a vast blurred exhibition.

The City of Brotherly Love will remember only masterpieces.

Always Leave 'Em Laughing

You may notice his wooden leg first, but it's his face that you remember. It's a wreck, as in Veeck. Here is a man with the gift of radiant homeliness.

"How can you be a sage if you're pretty?" rumbles Bill Veeck, with a rhinocerine laugh. "You can't get your wizard papers without wrinkles."

For thirty-five years, with various hiatuses for exile or illness, Veeck has been both baseball's most intellectual sage and its most gleefully vulgar wizard.

Though he has retired now—at sixty-seven, he no longer has the health of wealth to compete as he would wish—Veeck is still looked upon by baseball people with affectionate perplexity. The game would like to trundle him off to a safe corner as a sort of gadfly Long John Silver who built exploding scoreboards and sent a midget to bat.

Veeck has always been beyond the ken of his kin. "Whatever I've said over the years," says the roistering son of Bill, Sr., the starchy president of the Cubs (1919–33), "the owners have looked at me as though I were a little boy trying to run fast so the propeller on my beanie would spin."

In a lifetime saturated with appetite and anecdote, Veeck has incorporated too many natures into one personality for most folks to grasp and reconcile. Veeck says of his lifelong friend, William Shakespeare, "He writes as though he were ten different men." We often say of others what best applies to ourselves. Veeck, too, is a man of double-digit personae.

He is a renegade who at nineteen, when his father was dying and could only keep wine in his stomach, hunted up Al Capone and made the gangster a proposition: season tickets for the finest prohibition champagne.

He is the millionaire businessman who, when he bought the Indians in 1946, did so by inventing a financial scam called a debenture-stock deal which was such a sweet loophole that the IRS fought him for eleven years—then gave up. Brilliant? Says Veeck, perversely, "I've always been singularly disinterested in business."

He is a literateur who says of Anthony Trollope, "just a small-town Dickens"; of Herman Melville, "I liked *Omoo* and *Typee* better than *Moby Dick*"; and of Robert Frost, "He was a man who convinced others to accept his own evaluation of himself. I'll take Poe."

He is the handyman extraordinaire who, because he "loved a beautiful line in a building," studied blueprint design in night school. When an engineer ran out on a project, Veeck gathered a desperation crew and in one night directed the building of the Wrigley Field scoreboard, which still stands.

He is a student of politics and history who says that he is basically apolitical because, "I have customers and my country has a secret ballot. It's nobody's business." But he will add that he has voted for Socialist presidential candidate Norman Thomas many times. "In fact, I even kept on voting for him after he died because I'd rather vote for a dead man with class than two live bums." When Veeck got 20,000 hate letters after he signed the first black player in American League history (Larry Doby), he answered them all by hand.

He is an unabashed hedonist who, for much of his adult life, has smoked four packs of cigarettes and drunk a case of beer a day. He seems to live by Oscar Wilde's dictum: "The only way to get rid of a temptation is to yield to it."

And yet he is also the doting husband and father who is almost totally dependent for emotional solvency on his wife of thirty-one years, Mary Frances, and on his nine children from two marriages —five boys and four girls, aged eighteen to forty-four.

Perhaps most remarkably, and most revealingly, Veeck has, for more than half his life, been a sufferer of Jobian curses that would have killed other men several times over. Yet he defiantly describes himself as "a cripple, but never handicapped."

Veeck gives an impression of indomitable vigor. He swings his wooden leg from the hip so that it thuds on the floor like a man tolling on a door with a baseball bat. You might not guess that ever since a recoiling artillery piece smashed his foot and led to its amputation when he was a Marine in World War II, Veeck has soaked his stump in a warm bath each morning for two hours to be able to tolerate his artificial leg.

Veeck, you see, does not like wheelchairs. Or crutches. He has always known the cost of his refusal to pamper his leg. The wear, tear, and inevitable infection from his relentlessly active life have led, over the decades, to more and more surgery and less and less leg, until now Veeck's limb attaches near the groin. Beer and courage have always been his painkillers. In a sense, Veeck has measured out his life by what was left of his right leg.

The hair on Veeck's chest seems to be trying to climb up and out of the open-necked shirts he always wears. Even on the coldest Chicago days, he refuses, as he has all his life, to wear an overcoat or hat. He loves the feeling of zero at the bone. Yet this is a man who has a permanent case of walking pneumonia that requires periodic hospitalization to drain his lungs.

"Last September, it got so bad that I couldn't breathe. I got in a cab to the hospital and told the driver, 'Go as fast as you can.' I stuck my head out the window to force more air down my throat. Until that day, I had smoked four packs a day for fifty years. Since then, I haven't touched a cigarette. The moral is that courage is usually abject cowardice, at least in my case. You get so scared that you're going to die that you do whatever you have to do."

Veeck's whole body seems hypersensitized, almost overloaded with stimuli. He seems larger than his six feet because his gestures are so expansive. His short, frizzy hair seems like a million raw nerve ends trying to make their great escape from his scalp. His fingers are always doodling, touching, examining—when they're not drumming painfully hard against the gristle of his large floppy ears, as if to awaken them.

He is deaf in his left ear—the one that gets the hardest thumping, as though being punished for malfeasance in office—and half deaf in the other. Veeck long ago stopped going to movies or watching much television because it enraged and saddened him to lose track of dialogue.

Veeck's laughter, his rubber-mugged smile, and his temper are all close to the surface. He's impatient, direct, uninterested in manners or small talk beyond what civility requires. Cut to the nub, or cut bait.

As suits the pattern of this man who seems to have lived out not only his own life but that of his anti-self as well, Veeck has spent a huge portion of his adult life in the most silent and boring place on earth—a bare hospital room. Hemingway by nature, Proust by necessity.

Veeck has had so many major operations, including six on his "good" leg, that he has developed a unique hobby. "I count sodium pentothal shots. I'm up to thirty-two. I don't know the record. You get conditioned to it. To me, being operated on is like someone else taking a half-dozen pills. Suffering is overrated. It doesn't teach you anything."

All Veeck's recoveries are the same. The prescription is rest, silence, no excitement, no people, no vices. Everything, in other words, that Veeck detests. He obeys orders until he feels well enough to start killing himself again. His tombstone should read, "Cause of Death: Life."

Years ago, for instance, Veeck had a chronic concussion so bad that if he started coughing he would continue uncontrollably until he blacked out. That illness almost snuffed him and forced him to retire from baseball temporarily in 1961. For many years, Veeck ate hard candy constantly to suppress his cough, until the candy itself became a problem. Now, when Veeck coughs once, he stops everything and pays attention to nothing else, as though an old enemy were knocking on his door. So many parts of Veeck's body are trying to slip him the black spot that a lesser man could spend his whole day waiting to collapse.

Instead, Veeck pulls a silly plastic gizmo out of his desk. It has three cylinders, three golf-ball-sized spheres, and a tube. "This is my lung machine. The day I couldn't breathe, I didn't have enough lung capacity to hold the balls up for one second. Now I can hold them up for seven seconds." And taking a deep breath, he does.

Perhaps no man in baseball has had his life despaired of—by others—as often as Veeck. He has proved an unreliable corpse for twenty years. "Some of us are afraid that, after all the things he's survived, Bill has finally decided that he's going to die this year," says Ray Grebey, the owners' chief labor negotiator and a good friend of Veeck's for thirty years. "Bill has things wrong with him that only he knows. He has a growth in his throat that he won't talk about. I think that's why he's sold his interest in the White Sox and retired as team president."

"That's wishful thinking," erupts Veeck good-naturedly when

told this affectionate but sorrowful diagnosis. "Ray's a fine fellow, but he's been around those owners too long. They thought they were rid of me in 1961, too. All the owners presented me with a huge embossed, illuminated book listing all my contributions to baseball. It was the sort of ode to a widow that you send out when somebody in the front office dies. Well, nine years later, I testified in Federal Court in favor of Curt Flood and against the reserve clause. My fellow owners challenged my competence as an expert witness. So I said, 'Your Honor, may I submit this lovely book in evidence. It's a souvenir of the last time I died.'"

In other moods, Veeck can hint at darker thoughts. "There have been days when I thought, 'If lightning struck me today, I wouldn't care.' I don't believe that any man is immune to that," says Veeck.

"I remember a book by Ernest Seton Thompson, the great nature writer, called *Waab, a Bear*. It was about grizzlies. You never see their carcasses left to rot in the wild. I lived in the Southwest and it's true. When their time comes to die, they go off to places where they know they won't be found. They just disappear, start the exodus to some remote canyon. You never know what happened to them.

"I feel like Waab. The time has come to depart the premises.

"The career operators, the lifelong baseball men, are like dinosaurs. Our time is past. Calvin [Griffith] and I are the last. There won't be any more."

The Bard's Room in Comiskey Park has dark wood paneling, soft lights and walls covered with a montage of black-and-white photographs of Chicago's famous and infamous sons, like Mayor Richard Daley, Clarence Darrow, and Carl Sandburg. All this, including the steer horns on the wall, was rescued from the Sirloin Room of the Stockyards Inn when it was torn down. The Bard's Room, with its mahogany furniture, looks like an intimate, unpretentious restaurant. For the last six years, Veeck has made this combination saloon and salon his office.

To be sure, Veeck had a proper president's office. But he hated it, just as he has always hated ties, coats, and the words "sir" and "mister." Veeck gave his office a fair chance, just as he had his others during his terms with the Indians (1946–49), Browns (1951–53), and White Sox (1959–61). Then, as always, he had the office door torn off its hinges and all locks removed. "I find the idea repugnant that I would consider doing anything in running a baseball team for which I should feel ashamed enough to lock myself behind a door."

Nevertheless, the Bard's Room beckoned. Would any other sports executive have considered setting up shop in the team's press room? Veeck loved the idea. His father, after all, had done time as a sportswriter. So he had a telephone installed at a corner table and that became his office. Now any fan who wanted to drop in off the Southside streets had a chance to tell the boss what he was doing wrong. Or they could just phone him. The number was listed.

Veeck at work is much like other men at play. A beer stands always before him. He is the center of a constant relaxed flux. Everyone talks to him—or he talks to them. A bit like Dr. Samuel Johnson, he has made a name for himself from a public life whose staple seems to be casual, vastly enjoyable conversation. In fact, looking back on a life in which he has read nearly a book a day since childhood—his father bought him fifty volumes every Christmas, then had to replenish the supply before Easter—Veeck admits there are few men he resembles more in style than Johnson.

The immodest comparison here is, of course, not of talents, but merely of traits. The similarities are interesting: physical strength matched by constant and various physical sufferings; an ugliness transformed into compelling personal presence with energy and enthusiasm; great bouts of work; a passion for collecting people and their anecdotal histories; insomnia and spectacularly irregular hours; a wanderlust love of vast cities; a devotion to words and a respect for their precise meanings; a taste for renegade friends.

Chisox Manager Tony LaRussa, a bright young Veeck favorite who may be the game's first true clubhouse lawyer, since he has passed the Florida bars, sits at the next table, jotting notes for an off-season speech that evening in Joliet. "The key word is caution, right?" says LaRussa. "Keep the old foot out of the mouth."

"Caution is always the easy way out," says Veeck, a veteran of nearly 10,000 rubber-chicken speeches in his peripatetic promoting career. "A man who is cautious never sleeps with a girl, quite. He's so timid that he never savors anything completely. Even an after-dinner speaker should be a little like a drunk on a tightrope.

It keeps everyone's attention. Don't be cautious, Tony. Just don't be injudicious. If you write out your remarks, it's an insult to an audience. It shows that your first priority is to protect yourself against them. They sense it. If you just have a few notes on a scrap of paper, you'll walk away with more friends. They'll think, 'Hey, he's honest.'

"I have never liked those who are cautious. My first wife was an equestrienne in the Ringling Brothers Circus who jumped a horse through a ring of fire sidesaddle. She also was an elephant trainer, lying under their feet. It's not true that elephants never forget. Years later, we went back to the circus and she went up to her favorite, Modock the Elephant. He swung his trunk and knocked her flat. There's a lesson in there, I suspect.

"She was a very interesting woman. The divorce was my fault. I couldn't leave baseball alone. In the end, we parted on very good terms, which, of course, is the saddest way, since it means that everything we had had slithered away and been denigrated. Politeness is the end of passion."

Veeck's unique quality, as Dr. Johnson said of Shakespeare, is that he always carries with him a vivid sense of first-hand "acquaintances with life and manners" and that "all his ideas are caught from the living world."

"I've never graduated from anywhere," says Veeck, who was "invited not to return" to several preparatory schools and whose stay at Kenyon College was shortened when, while standing in a fourth-story window with one hand grasping a beer and the other gripping the window sill, he saw a friend and, not wanting to spill the beer, waved with the free hand. Veeck fell and, luckily, was so drunk and limp that he only broke both legs. Today that same dorm room is occupied by the son of Ray Grebey. "It concerns me somewhat," says Grebey. "I'm sure it's a room with a rich tradition. I'm not sure I want my son to continue it."

Veeck's scholarship is spontaneous, voracious, and eclectic. He reads everything, especially while he is soaking his leg in the morning and when he can't sleep at night. During the past two weeks he has finished books on the Horn of Africa, thirteenth-century Manchuria, and Aztec culture, new novels by Iris Murdoch and Anthony Burgess, a history of Catherine the Great's Russia and a comparative study of Spanish-speaking countries in the western hemisphere. "I must be terribly undiscriminating, because I find everything interesting," he says.

What we have here is a man who, when he reads an author, whether it's Mark Twain or one of his favorite detective pulp writers, doesn't buy one book but the collected works. He seldom watches TV except for news and sports. "With television, you are at the mercy of the mentality that created the program. You have lost your power of determination."

For Veeck, watching classic literature replaced by faddish film is saddening. "It isn't just the feeling for something remote, like Shakespeare's comedies, that we've lost. We're even beginning to lose the feel for the Marx Brothers.

"We're losing our natural instincts and tastes. They're either watered down or dulled by cynicism. The only way a movie remake of a wonderful adventure like *The Three Musketeers* could be done was to turn it into phony camp. We're jaundiced, sated. We can't even, or won't even, accept the excitement of Jules Verne. We've got submarines, so how can Captain Nemo interest us?

"This is a confused and confusing society in which we are in danger of feeling that we only semi-exist. We can't afford to lose basic emotions. When I speak on campuses, I still sense that it's declasse to be enthusiastic or, heaven forbid, inspired. It's a carry-over from Vietnam. I felt terrible back then. I spoke at Berkeley, Harvard, Kent State. I didn't get picketed once. It was a terrible blow to realize I had no social significance. The watchwords were speed, violence, cynicism. I felt hopelessly out of step. The sports that fitted the times were football, hockey, and mugging.

"In the last few years, things have gotten better. In 1975, when I got back into baseball, I felt that it was a sport whose time had come again. This is a game to be savored, not gulped. There's time to discuss everything between pitches or between innings. Baseball is a game that encourages our natural gregariousness. The sixties was a time for grunts or screams. Football passed baseball. Now maybe we've reached a point where we have a desire to talk again. I hope so. I think conversation is our natural state."

Baseball's time may have come, but Veeck wonders whether his fellow owners will ever truly get in touch with their sport. With the years, it has given him less and less pleasure that so many of his grumpy predictions have come true, and that, so often, his suggested solutions have been adopted grudgingly or too late. Some twenty years ago, at a league meeting in Phoenix, Veeck proposed that baseball increase its sharing of gate receipts and also pool its TV revenues for the common good. Now those notions are in vogue. But then, the only people who wanted to listen to him were in the NFL.

"My own baseball people laughed at me, called me a communist. I didn't get one vote. The only person who contacted me was [NFL commissioner] Bert Bell. He said, 'Let's talk about this TV-money-sharing idea.' I spent a weekend at a retreat of his in New England discussing it. I didn't create the NFL system [which is now the cornerstone of the league's financial health], but I was a part of it."

At the time of the Flood decision, Veeck was equally prescient in predicting the free-agent era to come, and even in outlining its pitfalls. "I warned them about almost everything that would happen," he says without trying to hide his career-long bitterness at the way his advice has traditionally been dismissed as all show and no substance. "I am on record since 1941 as saying that the reserve clause was legally and morally indefensible. I knew its death was coming.

"But I also told them there was a way out. Years ago, the U. S. Government sued the vast DuPont holding company and won some antitrust rulings. However, the Supreme Court decided that it was unfair to DuPont stockholders to drastically change the company's framework at one stroke. They authorized 'an orderly transition to be done under a ten-year period under the aegis of the courts.' That's what baseball should have tried to get—an orderly transition period from the reserve clause to free agentry under the aegis of the courts. They wouldn't have been given ten years, but they also wouldn't have had the disaster of every player in baseball being thrown on the open market in such a short space of time. And we would have a permanent structure for the game now, instead of facing a labor crisis every spring."

Part of the reason Veeck has so seldom held sway in baseball's meeting rooms is his manner (brash) and posture (unyielding). He rubs his lonewolf methods in the faces of his foes and delights in making stuffed shirts squirm. Often he has taken too much pleasure in being right and not enough in compromising to achieve his ends. "I've got a helluva temper," Veeck says.

Nature abhors a vacuum and so does Veeck. If he sees a viable position that no one else has staked out, he'll go for it on the dead run, even if he has to dope out some of the ramifications as he goes. A typical example came the day of the release of American hostages from Iran. Commissioner Bowie Kuhn, a Veeck nemesis because he led the owners who defeated Edward DeBartolo's attempt to buy the Chisox, unilaterally issued lifetime major league passes to all fifty-two hostages.

"Don't get me started," growled Veeck as soon as he saw the Telex notification to teams from Kuhn. Within minutes he was on the phone to the commissioner's office, leaving a long hot message for Kuhn.

"This is the first time since the Barbary pirates that we've paid ransom," said Veeck. "And then we sent a fireship and blew them up. Are these hostages supposedly heroes? Did they do something wonderful? I thought they were professionals doing a job. And the job went badly. I have sympathy for them. But I don't think we should, as a country, congratulate ourselves for losing or celebrate our defeats as though they were victories. Did we give lifetime passes to the POWs of World War II?

"This is just a grandstand play by baseball, and it disgusts me. We've lost our heroes, and these are pretty poor substitutes. When my Browns finished last, we didn't give them World Series rings. Well, I have registered my complaint. Doubtless, you will get no others."

After Veeck was off the phone, he added, "Bowie is always jumping into some highfalutin thing, trying to set a grand moral tone. Bowie's problem is that he's not really sure whether or not he was named after a racetrack."

Since Veeck adores a dangerous idea, it is a measure of his self-knowledge that he has chosen to love a person that is yin to his yang. Veeck's wife, Mary Frances, who was billed as "the world's most beautiful press agent" when she pitched the Ice Capades in the late forties, has made a career, Veeck claims, "of getting me out of trouble after I get myself into it." Where Veeck sometimes is a roiling sea under heavy weather, Mary Frances Ackerman has the placidity of a sequestered pool. Veeck, for all his charm and generosity, is essentially a self-absorbed personality—one concerned about his own thoughts, his own opinions, his own projects, and his own legacy. His wife is one of those rare people who are so self-assured and at peace that they can concern themselves with others.

Whenever he mentions his wife—and mother of six of his nine children—Veeck gets a look in his eye usually associated with pathetically love-struck kids. "She's brighter than I am," he confides to those about to meet her. Then, later, he says confidently, "See, I told you."

Veeck's radio show in Chicago was called "Mary Frances and Friend." That probably comes closest to his own view of the matter. They seem different. He is the free-thinker, the "very casual Catholic," who says, "I believe in God, but I'm not too clear on the other details. Sometimes, when I look at the world, I don't quite know why it wasn't created a little better." She is the daily communicant. He makes friends and enemies, she makes only friends.

However, as in many strong marriages, their faces assume almost identical expressions when they hear a story—some parable from the living world—that moves them both in the same way. Veeck, talking about his boyhood friend John Lardner, recalls how that son of Ring Lardner "supported four families at one time. He was working day and night, free-lancing stories for magazines in Australia, to help keep relatives afloat."

"I think it was five families," Mary Frances says, and quietly names them.

Talk turns to another gifted reporter who has been blackballed nationally ever since he got into money trouble and took a kickback from a fight promoter about whom he was writing. "I wish, just once in my life, I could write five hundred words as well as that man," says Veeck, who has co-authored four autobiographical books. "Journalism prefers a Simon-pure mediocrity to a touch of tarnished genius."

"Isn't that the way of the whole world?" observes Mary Frances.

The man in Chicago who danced with his wife was probably Bill Veeck.

The quality in Veeck that most sets him apart is not his success as a baseball executive. Plenty of others have taken two teams to the World Series as he has the 1948 Indians and the 1959 White Sox. Nor does his promotional skill make him unique, although he has consistently done more at the gate with less product than any baseball hustler in history. Even Veeck's breadth of serious interests would simply make him the norm in a university faculty lounge.

No, if Veeck were to walk through *Pilgrim's Progress*, his name would be Courage. It has been said that courage is man's chief virtue because it makes all the other virtues possible. Veeck has always had the courage to follow his instincts unquestioningly.

"I was the only one-legged guy in line at the Rotunda at five A.M. to see John Kennedy lying in state," says Veeck, who thinks nothing of flying 1,000 miles when his emotions demand.

When Veeck was told three years ago that he could not get a visa to visit Cuba, he simply chartered a plane and landed in Havana. He wanted to see the then-and-now of Batista and Castro. So he did.

"If you got off the main street in Cuba twenty-five years ago, you were in abject poverty. Men would sell their sisters. People were living ten to a room. Now, nobody has a great deal, but everybody has something. They can all remember 'how it used to be,' so everyone is happy. No one wants too much. But that purity of purpose will change before long. You're looking at a slice of the revolutionary process that is so fleeting. In time, the human animal will emerge for what it is—just that, a voracious animal."

Sam Johnson, asked by a woman once if he thought mankind was "naturally good," replied, "No, madam, no more than a wolf."

That appreciation of the wolfishness in man has served Veeck well. He learned as a child that the paragons of his father's National League champion Cubs "were mostly drunks off the field and craftsmen on it." By the time he was twelve, he had, literally, tried on the shoes of his idol—the bandy-legged 5-6 Hack Wilson, who once drove in 190 runs—and discovered that they were too small for him.

The Veeck creed is a savvy locker-room mix of calculated wariness and instinctive magnanimity. "Most people will act better than you'd expect, if you'll give them a chance to," says Veeck, probably knowing that Faulkner said it first. Veeck's method is to greet all comers with open arms, but with a hand on his wallet. He is fascinated with the particulars of personality. "Nothing beats a well-told tale," he says. To that end, he has made an avocation of exploring and examining every out-of-the-ordinary fellow who crosses his path. "I'd rather give a speech at the federal pen than on the Gold Coast," he says. "And I seem to go over better there, too."

Is Bill Veeck the guy who holds hands—that's right—with Mary Frances? And who discusses Salvador Dali with his daughter Marya, a painter? ("I love him better now that I'm grown," Marya says. "When I was a child, it seemed he gave so much of himself to everybody he met, when he could have been giving it to me.")

Or is he the guy who recently walked into a predominantly black Southside saloon full of boisterous gusto? Four Africans at the bar erupted in delight. "Bill, you ugly son-of-a-bitch, come here," roared one who was wearing a three-piece suit and $50,000 worth of jewelry. Veeck answered with a cannonade of laughter and a salute—he raised his leg with a flip of the hip until his peg was head high.

Holding Veeck in a hug-hammer-lock, the big man poured out his troubles, just as folks always have to Veeck. "My ex-wife is after me again. I pay her $45,000 a month. I give her $400,000 for a New Year's gift. And now she has tried to get an injunction to keep me from leaving the country. You are a wise man, Bill. What am I going to do?"

"Why would you want to leave our country, Cawlee? Isn't it a little hot for you back home?" chided Veeck. "By the way, what is the name of your father's country this week?"

"From no other American would I take such abuse. The best families in America invite me into their homes, but I will not go. I spit on them. They are oppressors. I am a revolutionary," said the African, son of a Third World dictator, as the bar lights danced off his gold watch with his initials inlaid in diamonds. "What are you drinking? Michelob? Waitress, bring Mr. Veeck six more beers on my tab."

After Cawlee had moved on like a squall line following the twists of the Ganges, Veeck said quietly, "He is not entirely the fool he seems. I sort of like him. He left his father's principality for, shall we say, everyone's mutual benefit. But he'll return some day. Maybe to be a ruler. I am curious about my new friend Cawlee. There are things I have yet to learn about him."

Soon, six beers arrived in the hands of an embarrassed waitress. "Miss," said Veeck, "send six beers to each member of Cawlee's party."

The beer-buying war was on. Five minutes later, Veeck's table and the one next to it were so covered with Michelobs, courtesy of Cawlee, there was barely room for the ash trays and nuts.

"This is Af-ri-can hospitality," intoned Cawlee, with his elegant English prep-school accent. "You will not leave until you have drunk them all."

Two hours later, Cawlee's army of Michelobs had turned into a staggering body count of dead soldiers by Veeck and his small party. As he left the watering hole, Veeck veered toward Cawlee's company to inform them that the challenge of African largesse had been met. For several minutes, Veeck stood at the center of a laughing, whispering, hugging confab of jewelled princes. They bellowed their farewells and he headed for the door like a sailor in heavy weather. As soon as Veeck was out of sight, his eye was clear, his walk almost steady. "I found out," he said proudly. "Cawlee is siphoning $10 million of his country's money into Swiss banks and American real estate."

A full day, a day to exhaust even a healthy man with two legs and two ears, let alone one leg and half an ear. But he is not finished. He will take Mary Frances to dinner, then make another speech to promote a White Sox team that, in a few days, he would no longer own any part of. Even then, he would end his day just as he began it—with hours of reading.

"I always hate to go to sleep," he says. "I'm afraid that something fascinating is going to happen and I'll miss it."

The walls of Comiskey Park, so dreary and forlorn when Veeck arrived six years ago, are a sparkling white now. When the taxi arrives at the front gate, the cab driver, Donnell Rawlings, is in a good mood. "I've been a White Sox fan since the forties," he says. "I lost faith in them for a while, but when Mr. Bill took over the team, I started coming again.

"You know, my radio doesn't work too well. They went to this new seven volt, and mine is just a five volt—but I always listen sharp for Mr. Veeck's call. I've gotten him twice. Just like I figured, he sat up front. Only white man who ever sat up front with me.

"Right away, he found out that I'd visited the same part of Jamaica he had. He seemed to want to know all about me. I don't tell many people that I write poetry, but I told him. He sat there with a big smile on his face and made me recite everything I could remember."

Why doesn't he call Veeck by his last name—you know, Veeck, as in wreck?

"He told me to call him 'Bill.' So, I did. But when I talk about him, I call him 'Mr. Bill.' You know, out of respect."